Politics for a Rational Left

Politics for a Rational Left

Political Writing 1977–1988

ERIC HOBSBAWM

VERSO

London · New York

(In association with *Marxism Today*)

First published by Verso, in association with *Marxism Today*, 1989
© Eric Hobsbawm 1989
All rights reserved

Verso
UK: 6 Meard Street, London W1V 3HR
USA: 29 West 35th Street, New York, NY 10001-2291

Verso is the imprint of New Left Books

British Library Cataloguing in Publication Data
Hobsbawm, E.J. (Eric John), 1917–
    Politics for a rational left : political
    writings 1977–88
    1. Great Britain. Labour movements, to 1988
    I. Title
    335′.1′0941
ISBN 0-86091-246-9
ISBN 0-86091-958-7 pbk

Library of Congress Cataloging-in-Publication Data
Hobsbawm, E.J. (Eric J.), *1917–*
    Politics for a rational left : political writing, 1977–88 / Eric Hobsbawm.
        p.   cm.
    ISBN 0-86091-246-9 — ISBN 0-86091-958-7 (pbk.)
    1. Labour Party (Great Britain)   2. Socialism—Great Britain.
3. Great Britain—Politics and government—1979–   I. Title.
JN1 129.L32H63   1989
324.24107—dc19

Typeset by Leaper & Gard Ltd, Bristol, England
Printed in Great Britain by Bookcraft (Bath) Ltd

Contents

Preface   1

PART I
Exploring the Problem

1 The Forward March of Labour Halted?   9

2 The Verdict of the 1979 Election   23

3 The Debate on 'The Forward March of Labour Halted?'   29

4 Looking Towards 2000: the Politics of Decline   43

5 Falklands Fallout   51

6 Labour's Lost Millions   63

7 Labour: Rump or Rebirth?   77

8 The Retreat into Extremism   87

PART II
The Intelligence of History

9 Fifty Years of Peoples' Fronts   103

10 Socialism and Nationalism: Some Reflections on
     'The Break-up of Britain'   119

11 Labour in the Great City   143

12 Farewell to the Classic Labour Movement?   159

PART III
Making a New Start

13 Past Imperfect, Future Tense   169

14 Snatching Victory from Defeat   181

15 The Emancipation of Mankind   187

16 Out of the Wilderness   203

17 Offering a Good Society   215

18 No Sense of Mission   221

19 The Signs of a Recovery   233

Postscript   239

Index   242

Acknowledgements   250

Preface

This book has grown out of a Marx Memorial Lecture which, as a historian of labour and labour movements, I was asked to give in 1978 on 'The British Working Class One Hundred Years after Marx'. It was not intended to start a debate, although labour historians, and especially Marxist ones, are naturally aware that their analyses have political implications. However, when the lecture was published some months later under the provocative but not inaccurate title 'The Forward March of Labour Halted?', it led to a lively, not to say impassioned, discussion in the pages of *Marxism Today*. This was continued in a book with the same title published by Verso in association with *Marxism Today* in 1981. In retrospect this seems less surprising than it did to the author at the time. While the debate about my lecture got under way, the Labour government was struggling through its last, difficult months and was replaced by the Thatcher regime. Defeat was followed by some years of crisis and civil war within the Labour Party, during which the party almost foundered. My initial paper had touched on a number of sore spots and anticipated some of the debates that were to divide the left. In particular, it called on the left

> to do what Marx would certainly have done: to recognize the novel situation in which we find ourselves, to analyse it realistically and concretely, to analyse the reasons, historical and otherwise, for the failures as well as the successes of the labour movement, and to formulate not only what we would want to do, but what can be done.

It turned out that these were seen as fighting words by a section of the left in the circumstances of 1978 and the following years. So much so that I increasingly found myself drawn further into public political debate and polemic. The articles I wrote, most of them initially

1

published in *Marxism Today*, but several of them also republished elsewhere at home and abroad, were written for the occasion: to comment
on general elections or other important events such as the Falklands
war, or to coincide with Labour Party conferences or other occasions for
debate on the left, such as a Congress of the Communist Party or the
Labour Party's policy reviews. The idea of republishing them as a book,
together with some more general political or politico-historical studies,
came from Robin Blackburn, who also suggested that my contributions
to the 1982 book would usefully supplement them. Except for two
chapters, the pieces were originally written in English. The short paper
on 'Farewell to the Classic Labour Movement?' and a conversation
between myself and Peter Glotz, formerly General Secretary of the
German Democratic Party (SPD), have been translated from the
original German. The first was given at a colloquium organized to
commemorate the 125th anniversary of the SPD, which now chooses to
date its birth from the foundation of Lassalle's *Allgemeiner Deutscher
Arbeiterverein.* The second was part of a sort of double interview, of
which the other part, in which I interviewed Glotz, was published in
English in the August 1987 issue of *Marxism Today.*

If there is any justification for publishing these mainly occasional
papers as a book, it must be that they represent a reasonably consistent
point of view on issues which are of continuing relevance in British politics and in the international debate on the left. These issues are both
particular or national, and general or global.

Seen in a narrow or purely British perspective, the debates to which
my papers contribute were and are about the nature of Thatcherism (as
distinct from other Conservative governments in Britain or neo-
Liberalizing governments abroad), about possible ways of mobilizing and
uniting the non-Thatcherite majority of the country, which remained as
large in 1987 as it had been in 1979, and about the problem of leadership
and policy within the Labour Party, which is and will remain the only mass
party on the British left, and, alone or in coalition, the only party of alternative government.

Two of these debates have been settled by any criterion of rational
argument. The main point which *Marxism Today* argued over a number
of years and which my articles supported, can no longer be seriously
contested. Thatcherism is *not* 'just another bourgeois or Tory government' as so many on the blinkered left maintained. It is as much of a
break with the Toryism of Heath, Home, and Macmillan – to go no
further back than thirty years – as it is with Wilson and Callaghan. My
argument that it is the 1980s version of a government of the radical
right, or at least that it contains a decisive nucleus of such a regime, may
not be so universally accepted. Nevertheless, it is manifestly wrong to

see Thatcherism as essentially similar to other 'privatizing' governments in Europe or the Americas, an error into which many observers overseas tend to fall.

The second debate that has been settled is about the need for unity, including perhaps electoral unity, if Thatcherism is to be defeated. For most foreign readers this may be self-evident, given the nature of the British electoral system, but in Britain it arouses passionate and acrimonious feelings. At the time this introduction is being written the matter is off the political agenda, since no party, large, small, or diminutive, will entertain the idea of electoral arrangements, at any rate in public. All that can be said is that it will return to the agenda in one form or another, unless something rather improbable happens to the prospective electoral support of the main parties.

The third debate remains open. My papers are said to have contributed to it, though their role has been much exaggerated.* How far their republication can still contribute to it readers must judge for themselves.

Looked at in the broader or international perspective my papers are about the need for the left to reconsider its policies and outlook in a world very different from that envisaged by Marx or Lenin. This does not mean that Marx's analysis has ceased to be a guide to understanding the world, though his theory itself, like any other theory, must also be open to critical scrutiny. What it means is that we live in a world which in the thirty years after the Second World War was 'transformed so globally, so fundamentally, so radically and with such unprecedented speed, that all previous analyses, even when they remained correct in principle, simply had to be modified and brought up to date in practice' (see p. 160 below). It is as pointless for socialist fundamentalists to argue that nothing has changed since 1867 or 1939 because, after all, we still have capitalism, as it is for the cold warriors to argue that nothing has changed in the USSR since Stalin because there is still a one-party state. Times *are* different, and arguments to the contrary, however sophisticated, are not only unconvincing but self-blinding.

However, my papers are also interventions in a more permanent debate on the left: that between realists and what used to be called

*This may be the place to dismiss the baseless claim, passed from one journalist to another, that I functioned in any sense as 'Kinnock's guru'. My contacts with Neil Kinnock, whose election as leader of the Labour Party I naturally welcomed with enthusiasm, have been confined to two occasions. He took the chair at a meeting at which I spoke, organized by the Fabian Society on the eve of the 1983 Party Conference, and I interviewed him in 1984. Of course it is not unlikely that, in the course of his struggle against the 'hard left' in the early 1980s, Neil Kinnock found it convenient to cite against his opponents a writer whose track record as a man of the left was both long and undeniable. However, it cannot be supposed that Kinnock needed to read Hobsbawm in order to talk common sense about the Labour Party.

'impossibilists', the broad and the narrow, compromise and purity. The two sides are often (especially on the sectarian left) identified respectively with right and left in the movement, and reformism and revolution, betraying and maintaining the aim of socialist transformation. But this is not so. There are realistic radicals and revolutionaries and impossibilist ones. The political tradition to which my writings belong is that of the radicals who are also political realists, the tradition of Marx and Lenin, or, concretely, the Communist International's Seventh World Congress: of anti-fascist unity and peoples' fronts.

For this reason several of the papers in this book are directed against the sectarian or fundamentalist left. Not because its arguments are intellectually worth much effort – in fact they are today employed mostly in the form of incantation rather than reasoning – but because they are emotionally very powerful on the left, in ways which anyone who shares the socialist commitment will readily understand. Over half a century of such commitment has taught me how strong that emotional appeal is. It would be wrong to conceal that my rejection of so many 'hard left' attitudes is not shared by some old and valued friends and comrades. Nevertheless, a critique of left emotion by left reason is indispensable. For those who feel that it is not only simpler but better just to keep the red flag flying here while cowards flinch and traitors sneer, run the grave risk of confusing conviction with the pursuit of a political project, militant activism with the pursuit of social transformation, victory with 'moral victory' (which has traditionally been the euphemism for defeat), shaking a fist at the status quo with shaking it, or (as so often in 1968) gesture with action.

I do not believe, on grounds of socialist tradition, that babies should be left in bathwater that needs changing, but my papers are also directed against those who think, on grounds of realism, that new water requires a new baby. Rethinking socialist analysis and the socialist project may certainly lead to major, far-reaching, and, for some of us, painful modifications of long-held views: for instance, about the relation between Marx's analysis of the dynamics of capitalism and his predictions about the role of the proletariat as the agent of transformation, or about the historical justification of the split between Social Democracy and Communism, or the effects of the October Revolution. But it does not, or ought not to, undermine the classical socialist case against capitalism, the classical understanding of the socialist project, or the Marxist conviction that capitalism is destined to be a passing phase in mankind's long historical development.

Painting Adam Smith red (as some are inclined to do, even in the world of 'really existing socialism') is no more acceptable than painting nationalism red, another temptation against which one of my papers is directed. The global crisis of capitalism in the 1970s and 1980s has led to two equally paradoxical results. It has led to a revival of the belief in unrestricted private enterprise and unrestricted markets; a recovery of militant self-confidence by the bourgeoisie unparalleled since the late nineteenth century, and simultaneously to a sense of failure, an acute crisis of self-confidence, among socialists. While politicians of the right, probably for the first time, glory in the word 'capitalism', which they used to avoid or rephrase because of its associations with rapacity and exploitation, socialist politicians are now shy about using the word 'socialism' or claiming too much for it. But capitalism is still rapacious and exploitative and socialism is still good.

Lack of confidence is the spectre that haunts the left. It is not the object of this book to add to it. If we do not believe that the uncontrolled pursuit of private advantage through the market produces antisocial and conceivably catastrophic results; if we do not believe that the world today calls for public control, management, and planning of economic affairs, then we should not call ourselves socialists. But why should we not believe these things? They are obviously true. Surely, if Marx had lived to see the world of the late twentieth century, he would have modified some of his ideas. But equally surely, if he were living into the time when the unplanned and uncontrolled production of exchange-value, mostly in a few developed capitalist countries, puts the very physical environment of the globe, and with it human life as a whole, in immediate jeopardy, he would regard this as strengthening the case for the necessary supersession of this system, either by another one – or by a relapse into the ages of darkness.

PART I

Exploring the Problem

1

The Forward March of Labour Halted? (1978)

It is my privilege to give the Marx Memorial Lecture of 1978 and I want to use it to survey some developments in the British working class during the past hundred years. It is a long-established habit, on these occasions, to take the texts of Marx and Engels as our starting point, but I shall not do so for two reasons. In the first place, as it happens, neither Marx nor Engels said much about the British working class between the end of the First International and the 1880s, and to the best of my knowledge they said nothing whatever about it exactly one hundred years ago. In fact on this very day (17 March 1878) there appeared in an American journal one of a series of five articles by Engels on the European workers. This mentioned numerous countries from Russia to Portugal, but contained not one word about Britain. He remained totally silent – no doubt regretfully silent – about the admittedly uninspiring labour scene in this country a century ago. In the second place, and more to the point, what I wish to underline is something which a Marxist analysis alone will help us to understand, but which Marx's texts cannot; that the forward march of labour and the labour movement, which Marx predicted, appears to have come to a halt in this century about twenty-five to thirty years ago. Both the working class and the labour movement since then have been passing through a period of crisis, or, if you prefer to be mealy-mouthed about it, of adaptation to a new situation. Most of us, engaged in day-to-day struggle, have not paid as much attention as we ought to this crisis, though we can hardly fail to be aware of some of its aspects. My purpose is to see it in the long-term perspective of the changing structure of British capitalism and the proletariat in it. I see our task as Marxists, and mine as the Marx Memorial Lecturer, as applying Marx's methods and general analysis concretely to our own era, and I hope Marx himself would also have seen it that way.

It was taken for granted in the 1870s that the great majority of the British people consisted of manual workers and their families – and this meant manual workers outside agriculture. I need hardly add that the majority, even of the farming population, consisted of proletarians, that is, of wage-labourers. In both these respects Britain was then peculiar and probably unique: in the enormous size and percentage of its manual working classes and in the relatively small size and percentage of its agricultural population, and above all its insignificant peasantry. This had significant political consequences, which are still in some ways felt. Whereas in most other states at that period the introduction of a democratic voting system would still have left the manual workers in a minority, in Britain, so it was believed, they would immediately constitute a majority. In 1867, the statistician Dudley Baxter estimated the non-agricultural manual workers at just under 70 per cent of the population. So, from the point of view of the ruling classes, it was absolutely essential to gain or maintain the political support of an important section of the working class in one way or another. They could not hope to offset an independent class-conscious party of the proletariat by mobilizing the majority of peasants, petty craftsmen, and shopkeepers, whether with or against the working class. They had to come to terms with the fact of a working-class majority from the time of the Second Reform Act onwards.

I shall leave aside for the moment the question whether what was understood by 'manual workers' in the 1860s and the 1870s is what we would today call a working class or proletariat. However, whatever they were, they got their hands dirty, and for most of the past century the manual workers in this broad definition have not grown but declined. In 1911 they included about 75 per cent of the population, in 1931 about 70 per cent, in 1961 64 per cent, and in 1976 a little over half.

This does not, of course, mean that the percentage of proletarians in the technical sense has gone down, that is, of people who earn their living by selling their labour-power for wages, plus their dependants. On the contrary, in this sense proletarianization has, as Marx predicted, continued to increase. We cannot accurately measure the percentage of 'employers and proprietors' for the nineteenth century, but in 1911 it included less than 7 per cent of the occupied population and it has since gone down – after staying more or less stable until 1951 – to something like $3\frac{1}{2}$ per cent in the mid 1960s. So we have, over this century, growing proletarianization combined with the relative decline, within the wage-earning population, of the manual workers in the literal sense of the word.

This is a very general phenomenon in the industrial countries. However, in Britain the decline is particularly striking for a special historical reason. A hundred years ago the sector of white-collar work in the widest sense employed only a tiny number of wage-earners; probably relatively less than in other countries with a substantial bureaucracy, public and private. For instance, in 1871 'commercial occupations' as a whole occupied less than 200,000 out of about 12 millions, whereas by 1911 it already included 900,000. By 1976 about 45 per cent of the occupied population could be classified as non-manual.

Here, then, is the first major development of the past hundred years. But let us look more closely at the manual workers. A hundred years ago industry depended on manual labour to an extent we find difficult to grasp today, since the technology of the industrial revolution which Britain pioneered, and which made this country into the 'workshop of the world', was, by modern standards, extremely undeveloped; it was in fact, as Raphael Samuel has recently reminded us, a 'juxtaposition of hand- and steam-powered technology'. It was, to use the modern term, enormously labour-intensive. Craft skills of the kind associated with the pre-industrial artisans were no doubt to some extent supplemented or speeded up by power and machinery, but they were not yet to any extent replaced by it. Not until the end of the century were automatic machine-tools seriously introduced into British engineering workshops. Other operations, skilled or less skilled, relied almost entirely on manpower. Practically every ton of coal – which supplied the overwhelming bulk of power for all purposes – was got by men with picks and shovels.

These characteristics of nineteenth-century British production had two consequences. In the first place, growth of output was linked to an expansion in the workforce to an extent that is difficult to recall today. Thus between 1877 and 1914 the tonnage of coal produced in British pits just about doubled – and so did the number of coalminers. On the eve of the First World War something like one and a quarter million men (plus their families) were required simply to produce Britain's coal. Today the spectacularly larger energy requirements of Britain, including coal, oil, gas, electricity, and nuclear power, do not require more than a fraction of this enormous labour force. The army of labour was constantly growing. But in the second place, the relative backwardness of mechanization by twentieth-century standards gave the British workers whose manual skill and experience was indispensable – and this included others besides apprenticed craftsmen – considerable strength in collective bargaining. British trade unionism was therefore already strong or potentially strong, even in industries in which elsewhere, it was notoriously weak, as in cotton mills. Unionism was recognized by government a little more than a century ago, and – leaving aside particular areas and industries – no systematic and consistent attempt to smash it as a whole was made thereafter, or succeeded for any length of time. At the same time, the peculiar structure of British trade unionism also reflected – and still reflects – this historic past.

Thus unlike many other countries, our unions are not a small number of giants each covering in theory all workers within a specified industry. Though this pattern of industrial unionism was favoured, and at one time militantly advocated, by the socialists, it was not generally success-ful. Even on the railways, as we know, the rivalry between industrial and sectional unions has not been eliminated. Instead – or rather side-by-side with such industrial tendencies – we have the coexistence of craft unions and, a phenomenon peculiar on this scale to Britain, the great 'general unions' which gradually absorbed those not eligible for, or wanted by craft unions, those too weak to form them, and a variety of others. Furthermore, in some ways this tendency, which was first estab-lished in the period of the great dock strike of 1889, continues to re-assert itself. Smaller unions have increasingly tended to amalgamate into bigger ones; but while these amalgamations could be seen, in the first half of the present century, as steps towards a sort of industrial union-ism, in the past twenty years they have looked increasingly like the form-ation of new conglomerates of the 'general union' type – as with the merger of the AUEW with the foundrymen and the draughtsmen and the ETU with the plumbers. Conversely, the enormous potential strength of the 'craftsman' type of worker continued to be felt in union-ism, particularly in the great complex of metalworking, engineering, and electrical industries that went on expanding as the old nineteenth-century industries of mass employment, such as textiles, mining, and transport, contracted. When mass unionism came to these industries in the 1930s and during the war, it was initially through the craftsmen – often, as in the aircraft industry, men who still worked, and sometimes thought, in the old terms of craft pride. As late as 1939 the men at Harland and Shorts in Belfast still refused to accept piece-rates, as their grandfathers had done in the craft unions of Marx's day. These were the men who spread unionism into the motor industry; who kept the average engineering factory as a collection of separate craft unions; and, incidentally, who sent the women and the non-craftsmen to be organ-ized by the T & GWU, which has thus become the majority union in the motor industry. It was the persistence of multiple unionism in so many factories that made rank-and-file inter-union co-ordination by such people as shop stewards so formidable a force on the British industrial scene.

I have stressed these historic continuities. But they are combined with one major historic transformation. A century ago the working class was deeply stratified, though this did not prevent it from seeing itself as a class. The very people who were the backbone of trade unionism, perhaps with the exception of the miners, were, and were seen as, a labour aristocracy which looked down on the mass of those whom it regarded as unskilled and 'mere labourers'. But industrial change first threatened and then eroded this superiority from three directions. In the first place, the rise of tertiary employment – white-collar and professional employment – produced a new form of labour aristocracy which identified directly with the middle class. It is only since the Second World War – at least outside the public sector – that the white-collar workers and professional workers have organized as a mass in trade unions, and increasingly within the TUC, that is, the conscious labour movement. In the second place, modern technology increasingly created a stratum of professionals and technicians separately recruited from outside rather than promoted from those with workshop experience. So the gap between the labour aristocracy and the middle strata widened. On the other hand, modern technology and industrial organization threatened the privileged position of the labour aristocrat by increasingly turning him into, or replacing him by, the less skilled process worker operating specialized machines or carrying out specialized parts of an increasingly elaborate division of labour. In other words, as Marx had predicted and as the capitalists had always intended, skill was increasingly transferred from men to machines or to the design of the flow of production. In fact, the labour aristocracy was threatened with dilution. Thus the labour aristocrats were not only forced further away from the middle strata, but closer to the other strata of the working class, although their economic advantage (as distinct from their position in the social structure) was not seriously weakened before the First World War. They tended to be radicalized, especially in the great complex of industries in which mechanization, mass production, and similar changes in the organization of industry produced the most direct confrontation between the skilled worker and the new threats, in the growing complex of the metalworking industries.

Now I would like to note, in passing, that my explanation of this process is a little different from Engels's, though it does not actually conflict with it. Engels, who wrote about these problems in the 1880s (notably in the new Prefaces to his *Conditions of the Working Class*), stressed two things: first, the formation of a 'relatively comfortable' and ideologically moderate labour aristocracy in Britain; second, the world monopoly of British industrial capitalism which provided benefits for *all* British workers, though disproportionate ones for the labour aristocracy. But 'even the great mass had, at least, a temporary share now and then'.[1] He expected a radicalization of the British working class as a result of the decline in the British world monopoly, although he not foresee this happening among the labour aristocracy of the 'old unions', but rather by the emergence of labour-organization among the hitherto unorganized masses, whose minds were 'free from the inherited "respectable" prejudices which hampered the brains of the better situated "old" Unionists'.[2] What he did not appreciate sufficiently were the developments in capitalist production that were to radicalize the former labour aristocracy itself, at any rate in the growth industries of the twentieth century. But in the 1880s these were not yet very visible.

All this does not mean that the working class became a single homogeneous mass, although in many ways it was drawn more closely together, by a growing class consciousness, by political demands that united workers of all strata and sections – for instance, in the fields covered by local government, of education, of health and social security – by a common lifestyle and pattern, and, for a minority, by labour and socialist ideology. This common 'style', if I may so call it, of British proletarian life, began to emerge just about a century ago, was formed in the 1880s and 1890s, and remained dominant until it began to be eroded in the 1950s. I am thinking not only of the rise of the socialist movement and the Labour Party as the mass party of British workers, the changes in trade unionism, the enormous and unbroken increase in the number of co-op members from half a million in 1880 to three million in 1914, but also of the non-political aspects of working-class life; of the rise of football as a mass proletarian sport, of Blackpool as we still know it today, of the fish-and-chip shop – all products of the 1880s and 1890s, or at the earliest the 1870s; of the famous cap immortalized by the Andy Capp cartoon, which is, broadly speaking, Edwardian; and a little later – they had hardly developed much before the First World War – of the council flat or house, of the picture palace, of the *palais de danse.*

At the same time the nature of British capitalism has changed profoundly, in four ways. First, as suggested, it has been transformed as a system of production by technology, mass production, and the enormous concentration of the productive unit, that is, the plant in which people work. In 1961 about half of all workers in manufacturing establishments worked in plants of more than 500 workers, about a quarter in establishments of over 2,000, and less than 10 per cent in units of 50 or under. Second, the rise of monopoly capitalism with a massive public sector has concentrated employment even more, and in particular created a huge sector of government and other public employees such as simply did not exist a century ago. Today something like 30 per cent of all people work in the public sector – as employees of government, local authorities, nationalized industries – and the proportion is rising. That is to say, for every two people employed in the private sector (I omit employers and the self-employed) there is now roughly one in the public sector. Third, it follows that the factors which determine the workers' conditions are no longer, to any major extent, those of capitalist competition. The capitalist sector is no longer one dominated by the free market, since it is largely monopolized; and the public sector, as an employer, as the provider of all manner of social services and payments, and as the manager of the economy, very largely determines them, or at least the limits within which they are fixed. Political and not profit decisions determine public sector practice. And fourth, the actual standard of living of most workers has been revolutionized for the better. Several of these trends can be traced back to the period between Marx's death and the First World War, but the really dramatic transformation has occurred since 1939.

This has implied a number of changes within the working class, quite apart from the growing division between a manual working class which increasingly tended to vote for its class party and a white-collar stratum which, at least outside the public sector, was predominantly conservative, until the last twenty years or so during which it has also begun to organize itself on trade unionist lines, and – perhaps to a lesser extent – to turn politically leftwards. I shall mention some of them.

First, the organized working class a hundred years ago was almost entirely masculine, as Engels himself noted; except in the textile industry. In so far as women worked for wages, they did so primarily before and after marriage (in 1914 only about 10 per cent of married women were so employed) and were regarded as unskilled and treated as cheap labour. The largest by far – 44 per cent in 1881 – in any case worked as servants. Even in 1911, when service had already begun to decline as an occupation, there were still a million and a half maids. That was the 'Downstairs' of 'Upstairs and Downstairs'. Though there was already a remarkable influx of women into industry, and even more into office work and shop work in the quarter century before 1914, women continued to be treated as second-class workers, and the demand for equal pay did not make any serious headway until after the Second World War. And though the employment of married women for wages increased a little between the wars – in 1931, 13 per cent of all married women were so employed – the practice did not become normal until after the Second World War. Since 1951 the proportion of married women technically described as 'occupied' has gone up from about a fifth to about a half. This is a major change in the composition of the working class.

Geographically, the working class a century ago was, in spite of all migration and mobility, a collection of localized communities. It is still locally rooted to a much greater extent than the middle classes, as anyone can tell as soon as a trade unionist from Birmingham or Gateshead, not to mention Clydebank or Swansea, opens his or her mouth. But, on the whole, such local differences did not run counter to the sense of a single class consciousness, but were part of it. The differences between Lancashire and Yorkshire workers did not prevent – they may even have underlined – their common characteristics as workers. Even the growing differences – especially in the years separating the wars – between the old nineteenth-century industrial areas of the north, of Scotland and Wales, and the new industrial areas of the Midlands and the southeast, did not produce greater division of feeling and attitude. The one exception to this was nationality (or in the case of the main immigrant group, the Irish, nationality-cum-religion). Here, as Marx himself had realized, there was a force that did deeply split the British working class, at least potentially, and as witness there is the political history of Merseyside. And if the rivalries between the supporters of Sheffield United and Sheffield Wednesday, or of Notts. County and Notts Forest, did not so much divide as underline the basic unity of workers in those cities, we all know that the supporters of Rangers and Celtic, or Liverpool and Everton, or Hearts and Hibs, divided on national–religious lines. Still, the striking thing about the British working classes is how little – I would say how increasingly little – they were affected by such national splits until the 1950s, in spite of the very obvious fact that Scotsmen, Welshmen, and Irishmen were proudly conscious of *not* being Englishmen; and the other way round. Unlike, say, the Poles in imperial Germany, the Irish in Britain, if organized at all, joined the all-British unions and supported the all-British party of their class, at all events after Ireland had become independent. Until the labour movement as a whole entered upon its present crisis, there was no significant mass base for national parties in Scotland and Wales, and until the mass immigration from the former empire after the Second World War, one would have said that working-class racism was probably less significant in Britain than, say, in France – even allowing for anti-Irish, and from the early 1900s, some localized anti-Jewish feeling. If anything, it looked like a declining force for three-quarters of a century after 1878. Here is another significant and unwelcome development of the past quarter of a century.

But there are other divisions within the working class. A hundred years ago there were three main sectional differences within the working class: that between industries and particular branches, firms, or localities in an industry (Tyneside and the southwest); that between various grades and levels of workers ('craftsmen' and 'labourers'); and that between rival groups within the same level or grade, as between different groups of the skilled. As to the first, local and regional differentials were high and probably growing a hundred years ago. They have tended to diminish since 1900, though at times when some regions were relatively prosperous and others very depressed, as between the wars, they could remain very large in practice because of unemployment. In theory, the rise of state monopoly capitalism and employment in the public sector has tended to even them out. In practice, things are more complicated. This is not the place to discuss these problems in greater detail.

As to sectional differences between rival groups of the same level, these have a long history. They caused conflicts chiefly when groups tried to keep a monopoly of particular jobs for themselves against others, either because technical progress undermined their natural monopoly of long training and skill, or because in times of unemployment there was more pressure to fill a limited number of jobs. Thus bitter demarcation disputes in the northeastern shipyards reached a peak in the 1890s, and this industry and area is still familiar with them. As the old division of labour became technologically obsolescent, such rival or potentially competing groups of specialized workers have often tended to amalgamate – the merger of the boilermakers, shipwrights, and black-smiths, for example – but this kind of sectionalism is far from dead. Indeed it has increased inasmuch as modern industrial development cuts across trade sectionalism and makes it possible for different industries or groups of workers to carry out what are essentially the same or alternative processes. Thus in 1878 there could be no overlap between, say, compositors and journalists, but with the modern technology that enables a journalist to type straight on to the press, there can and is. Containerization produces potential and actual conflicts between dockers, lorry-drivers, and railwaymen which simply did not and could not exist in 1878 or even much later. And so on. Some coalminers would prefer the shutting down of the nuclear power industry, but workers in that industry presumably would not. Hence I would suggest that this type of sectionalism, after a period when it probably tended to decline, has been on the increase since the Second World War. This is a dangerous development.

The third kind of sectionalism, stratification, was kept largely out of sight a hundred years ago, and this was for two reasons. First, the favoured strata (such as the so-called labour aristocracy) were still rather successful at restricting entry to their trades or keeping themselves in a favoured position by being, on the whole, the only ones with access to effective organization. In fact, there is little doubt that at that period unionism reinforced exclusiveness. Only in the period of socialist leadership, at first very slowly, but then more rapidly from the great labour

unrest before the First World War, did trade unions come to be factors
for evening out rather than for increasing local, trade and grade differentials. Second, a hundred years ago wages and conditions were still
largely fixed by custom and convention, and only partly by pure market
calculation. The bourgeoisie paid as little as they could, but even when
they could afford more, they thought there ought to be a ceiling above
which worker's wages should never rise. They could think this because
workers themselves thought in terms of 'a fair day's pay for a fair day's
work', depending on the sort of workers they were. Their limit was a lot
lower than the sky. Now neither of these observations is any longer true.
The old hierarchies have been undermined by technological change and
differentials have been eroded, particularly by the development of
complex, not systematically planned, opaque, and unpredictable
changes in wage-payment, which no longer give an automatic advantage
to skill – payment by results, systematic overtime, and some of the
effects of productivity bargaining. Also (especially in the great boom
period after the Second World War) the workers learned that the limit
of their demands was a lot nearer the sky than most of them had ever
imagined, and the employers were willing to make concessions they
would earlier have regarded as unthinkable. These tendencies can, I
think, be traced back to the Edwardian period, for they can be detected
in some syndicalist arguments.

Now all this suggests that the old working-class stratifications should
lose their significance, and – with all the survivals of old divisions and
tensions – common working-class interests should increasingly prevail.
And this probably did happen in the first half of this century. But it
would be a mistake to think that this has made the working class more
homogeneous. On the contrary, it seems to me that we now see a growing division of workers into sections and groups, each pursuing its own
economic interest irrespective of the rest. What is new here is that their
ability to do so is no longer related to traditional criteria such as their
technical qualifications and their standing on, as it were, the social
ladder. In fact it now often happens (as sometimes occurred even a
hundred years ago) that groups of workers strike, not minding the effect
on the rest – skilled men on labourers, for example – and that the
strength of a group lies not in the amount of loss they can cause to the
employer, but in the inconvenience they can cause to the public, that is,
to other workers, by power blackouts or whatever. This is a natural
consequence of a state-monopoly capitalist system in which the basic
target of pressure is not the bank account of private employers but,
directly or indirectly, the political will of the government. In the nature
of things such sectional forms of struggle not only create potential friction between groups of workers, but also risk weakening the hold of the

labour movement as a whole. The sense of class solidarity may be further weakened by the fact that the real income of a family may no longer actually depend on a worker's own job alone, but even more on whether their wives or husbands also work and what sort of jobs they have, or on various other factors not directly determined by the union's struggle. In short, though there are plenty of material and moral reasons for solidarity, and a few dramatic examples of it – as over the Industrial Relations Act in 1970–71 and the miners' strikes – there is not much doubt that sectionalism is on the increase.

There is one final division within the working class, which in some ways recalls the divisions of a hundred years ago, though conditions are now quite different. It is between those who can take full advantage of the great economic and social improvements of the postwar era and those who cannot – if you like, those who would, a century ago, have been called 'the poor'. These are the people in persistently low-paid occupations virtually beyond the range of effective trade unions; the quarter of all households that get more than half their household income from social security and earn less than £40 a week; the people who live in private rented accomodation as against those who own houses and rent council housing – in 1975, 17 per cent of unskilled workers were private tenants as against 11 per cent of skilled workers; the poor who live worse and pay more. And when we consider these, let us not forget that, by international standards British wages have fallen behind others, and the British social security system, of which we were so proud in the immediate postwar years, has probably fallen even further behind the social security systems of several other European countries. It is the poor who are disproportionately worse off, and whom the established modes of labour organizations help least directly. A hundred years ago the labour movement recommended its forms of struggle and organization to everybody – trade unions, co-ops, et cetera. But it was then not accessible to everybody, but only to favoured strata of workers. Let us ask ourselves whether there is not a similar complacency among some sections of the movement today.

Now, how far does the development of the class consciousness of the British working class reflect these trends? Let us take the most elementary index of it, trade unionism. This has undoubtedly increased pretty steadily from a century ago, though we have no comparable figures before the 1890s: say from 13 per cent of the labour force in 1900 to 45 per cent just after the Second World War (1948). But thereafter it remained stagnant for quite a bit, or even dropped a little, and though it grew in the 1960s and 1970s, it is now only a little higher (as a percentage) than in 1948 – 46 per cent. And – a point we don't often note – it is much lower than in Denmark, Sweden, and Belgium, where it is around 70 per cent, and actually a little lower than Italy. Now of course the composition of trade unionism has changed – there are a lot more women and white-collar workers – but the point I wish to note regretfully is that 35 per cent of the employed are not in any trade union, and that this percentage has not declined for thirty years. And also, that Britain, the home of mass trade unionism, has clearly fallen behind some other countries.

If we look at the political expression of class consciousness, which means, in practice, support for the Labour Party, the picture is even more troubling. The number and percentage of Labour voters (including Communist ones) grew without interruption (except in 1931) between 1900 and 1951 when it reached a peak of 14 million or just under 49 per cent of all votes. After that it went down to 44 per cent in 1959 and 1964, rose again to just over 48 per cent in 1966, and then fell again. At the 1974 election it was well under 40 per cent. What is more, in *absolute* figures Labour (plus Communist) after 1951 barely ever got to within one million of its peak vote, and in 1974 it polled about 2.5 million less than in 1951, less than in *any* election since 1935. Of course this trend also affected the Conservatives who reached their all-time peak (13.5 million) in 1959, but that is no consolation.

There is no equally simple way of measuring shifts in the highest degree of class consciousness, namely socialist consciousness, but if we are to take the active membership of all socialist organizations as a very rough criterion – as distinct from trade union activism – then I also suspect that from some time after the early 1950s there has been a decline, perhaps broken in the late 1960s. However, in this most recent period, a very high proportion of the new socialist activists inside and outside the Communist Party and other Marxist groups, have probably been not manual workers, but students and white-collar or professional workers. Of course, we ought to note that until the 1950s very many and perhaps most of these new socialist activists, often from working-class and white-collar families, would not have been able to go to colleges.

It seems to me that for the first seventy years or so of the last century, Marx and Engels would have been neither very surprised nor very disappointed by the tendencies of development in the British working class. Not very surprised, because the tendencies were such as they predicted, or might have predicted, on the basis of Marx's own analysis of the development of the factory system, for example; though I think they would have been a bit surprised by the speed with which the tertiary sector developed, yet perhaps not so much by the formation of a new conservative white-collar labour aristocracy. Because they did not expect very much from the British working class beyond what actually looked likely to happen, they would not have been very disappointed by the growth of a mass political party based on class consciousness, separate from the parties of the bourgeoisie, and increasingly if vaguely committed to replacing capitalism by socialism. Of course, like you and me, Marx and Engels might well have wanted the British working class to be a bit more revolutionary and, like you and me, they would have been pretty contemptuous of the Labour leadership, but things did look as though they were moving in the right general direction. But in the past thirty years this movement seems to have got stuck, except for one trend: the 'new' labour aristocracy of white-collar technical and professional workers has become unionized, and the students and intellectuals – from whom it is largely recruited – have also been radicalized to a greater extent than before.

I have already suggested some of the developments in the economic and social structure of the country and its working population which might explain this. But Marxists are not economic and social determinists, and it simply will not do to say that this crisis of the working class and the socialist movement was 'inevitable', that nothing could have been done about it. We have already seen that the halt in the forward march began before the dramatic changes of the past twenty years; that even at the peak of the 'affluent society' and the great capitalist boom, in the middle 1960s, there were signs of a real recovery of impetus and dynamism: the resumed growth of trade unions, not to mention the great labour struggles, the sharp rise in the Labour vote in 1966, and the radicalization of students, intellectuals and others in the late 1960s. If we are to explain the stagnation or crisis, we have to look at the Labour Party and the labour movement itself. The workers, and growing strata outside the manual workers, were looking for a lead and a policy. They did not get it. They got the Wilson years – and many of them lost faith and hope in the mass party of the working people.

At the same time the trade union movement became more militant. And yet this was, with the exception of the great struggles of 1970–74, an almost entirely *economist* militancy; and a movement is not necessarily less economist and narrow-minded because it is militant, or led by the left. The periods of maximum strike activity since 1960 – those of 1970–72 and 1974 – have been the ones when the percentage of pure wage strikes have been much the highest – over 90 per cent in 1971–72. And, as I have tried to suggest earlier, straightforward, economist trade-unions consciousness may at times actually set workers against each other rather than establish wider patterns of solidarity.

My conclusion is that the development of the working class in the past generation has been such as to raise a number of very serious questions about its future and the future of its movement. What makes this all the more tragic is that we are today in a period of world crisis for capitalism, and, more specifically, of the crisis – one might almost say the breakdown – of British capitalist society. It is a moment when the working class and its movement should be in a position to provide a clear alternative and to lead the British peoples towards it.

We cannot rely on a simple form of historical determinism to restore the forward march of British labour which began to falter thirty years ago. There is no evidence that it will recover automatically. On the other hand, as I have already stressed, there is no reason for automatic pessimism. Men, as Marx said (the German word means men and women), make their history in the circumstances that history has provided for them and within its limits – but it is they who *make* their history. But if the labour and socialist movement is to recover its soul, its dynamism, and its historical initiative, we, as Marxists, must do what Marx would certainly have done: we need to recognize the novel situation in which we find ourselves, to analyse it realistically and concretely, to analyse the reasons, historical and otherwise, for the failures as well as the successes of the labour movement, and to formulate not only what we would want to do, but what can be done. We should have done this even while we were waiting for British capitalism to enter its period of dramatic crisis. We cannot afford not to do it, now that it has.

Notes

1. F. Engels 'Preface 1892', in *Marx and Engels on Britain*, Moscow & London 1968, p. 31.
2. Ibid., p. 32.

2

The Verdict of the 1979 Election (1979)

Since the very lively and serious discussion on 'the forward march of labour halted?' was started a year ago, it seems reasonable that the author of the original article should now comment on the debate.[1] I hope this will not be misunderstood as trying to have the last word. The discussion must and will go on. The questions it has raised are too important to be put on the shelf and, since the bitter experience of the last election, it is clearer than ever that the British labour movement has not yet found satisfactory answers to them. Nor is this second intervention intended to exaggerate the significance of the first article. This was originally given early in 1978 as a Marx Memorial Lecture, and it was not intended as a political statement (except in so far as all Marxists try to unite theory and practice), but as a historian's survey of what had happened to the British working class over the past century. There would have been no discussion at all, if people in the movement, and above all people with active responsibilities as union officials or shop stewards, had not recognized that important and urgent questions for our movement emerged from this survey, and if they had not taken them up.

What is at issue is not whether the forward march of labour has been halted in some respects, but whether this retreat is offset, or more than offset, by other developments in the British labour movement. About the halt there can, unfortunately, be no doubt. Some indications about the falling electoral support for the Labour Party, its declining membership, and the comparative stagnation of trade-union membership were given in the original article. They could have been supplemented by data about the declining support of trade unionists for the Labour Party, as indicated by the payment of the political levy. The general election of 1979 has unfortunately confirmed this analysis.

To put the matter briefly: Labour polled fewer votes than at any time since 1931, nor did any significant number of these lost votes go to other candidates of the socialist or Communist left. Labour only barely exceeded the Conservatives among the skilled working-class voters. Something like a third of *trade unionists* appear actually to have voted for the Tories. Since 1974 the swing to the Conservatives among trade unionists seems to have been something like 7 per cent, among unskilled workers 6.5 per cent, among skilled workers no less than 11 per cent. Almost 10 per cent of first-time voters swung right. These disastrous developments are not offset by the good showing of Labour in Scotland, by the immigrant vote, by the resistance of women to the appeal of the Tories (their swing was only 3 per cent compared to 9.5 per cent among the men), and by the interesting fact that the Labour vote actually rose significantly among the smallish professional and managerial group. (These data are taken from public opinion polls, but there is no reason to think that they are not roughly correct.) What makes these results even more disappointing is that the percentage of voters actually rose a little. People who had not bothered to vote previously went to the polls – and they chose the Tories. In short, there is no comfort to be got from the 1979 election.

As against these negative trends, several contributors to the debate, starting with Ken Gill, have drawn attention to positive developments. First, and in the most general sense, the British working class 'without itself exhibiting the will to power, has established that it cannot be governed in the old way' (Royden Harrison). This is clearly a fundamentally new factor in British politics since the war and, in so far as British capitalism is unable – or no longer able – to meet its demands, in the British economy. Second, and more specifically, there is the rising tide of militancy and industrial struggle, which reached a peak in 1970–74, but has continued or resumed at a high level. Third, there is the political power of this militancy as demonstrated by the role of the TUC in politics and by the fall of the Heath Government in 1974; people on the left are less inclined to cite the difficulties it caused the Labour Government in 1978–79. Fourth, it is argued that this militancy has led to a shift to the left in the leadership of the trade union movement, accompanied by a shift to the left within the Labour Party – even by the virtual abdication of the old Jenkinsite right wing within the parliamentary Labour Party. Fifth – the point has once again been made by Royden Harrison – there is the emergence of a new and politically more promising Labour left as typified by Benn.

In practice, therefore, the case for an advance of labour rests essentially on the industrial movement. In recent years this has been overwhelmingly a wages movement, and this is recognized in the discussion, which has dealt mainly with the character, possibilities, and limitations of trade union action. I do not want to discuss the political shift within the Labour Party and elsewhere on the left in detail. There has been an undoubted and welcome advance here. Most of the old Labour right has indeed been pushed out of the Labour Party or out of politics. Tony Benn's Labour left, unlike its predecessors for a very long time, actually has a policy, including a policy for tackling the economic problems of Britain. It is indeed the only such policy on offer from within a major party, other than the proposal by Mrs Thatcher and Sir Keith Joseph to turn the economic clock back to about 1865. The possibilities of united action by socialists and Communists are indeed better than they have been for many years, the chief obstacle being probably the sectarianism of some smaller groups on the unfortunately fragmented left. But at present these welcome developments represent what is happening within a badly defeated Labour Party, whose active membership is dangerously small – perhaps not more than 300,000 people – and not necessarily representative of its mass support; and a Communist Party and other groups on the left which are, to put it mildly, not growing. Moreover, with the recent shift to the right in the leadership of some unions which, as Stan Newens pointed out 'may yet produce dramatic setbacks in the higher councils of the TUC and the Labour Party', it is too early to start counting chickens. It is certainly wrong to overlook the prospects of a future advance, but they are in an as yet uncertain future.

On the other hand the trade union movement is powerful, effective, in recent years highly militant, and evidently changing and developing fast. Nor can it be denied that it has a powerful rank-and-file base. Indeed, the shift of the unions' centre of gravity from official structure to plant and shop floor is characteristic of the past twenty years – and until recently it has accelerated. The contrast between the weakness of the political side of the movement and the power and dynamism of the industrial side has been striking. It is natural that the left has been tempted to overrate the possibilities and underrate the limits of purely industrial action. There has been precious little else to cheer about.

Its achievements, particularly in the years 1969–74, have indeed been striking, and contributors to the discussion have been right to criticize me for not saying enough about them. It is probably true, as Steve Jefferys of the Socialist Workers Party has argued, that it has ensured the survival of the strong traditional kind of working-class consciousness (limited though this was and is) in spite of the decline of the old nineteenth-century industries which provided its main base and the numerical decline of the old (male) skilled worker who played such a crucial role in it; and in spite also of the great improvement in standards of living which middle-class observers in the 1950s expected to lead to

'bourgeoisification'. It has made it possible to integrate the rapidly growing non-manual and white-collar workers into the labour movement and
thereby to some extent into the working class. Though something like 40
per cent of unionists are today white-collar workers, this has not led to a
lowering of militancy. Today it is not only the traditional manual worker
who practises union solidarity and refuses to cross picket lines. It has
made it easier to integrate the enormously increased number of (often
part-time) working women in the organized labour movement. And it
made possible the victories of 1969–74.

And yet the limits of this renovated 'trade union consciousness' have
not been overcome. They have even been emphasized by the concurrent
decline in the *political* class movement. It has been argued that trade
union action has not been divorced from politics, because it has also
conducted non-economist struggles (such as that over pay beds in hospi-
tals) and because left-wing unions and activists take political stands. This
is true to some extent, though the overwhelming majority of political
strikes in recent years have actually been on economic issues, directly or
indirectly against government attempts to limit free bargaining and to
cut down union rights. It has also been argued that they are political in
the sense that they will in some unspecified way regenerate the political
movement, broaden mass support for a socialist policy, and unify the
working people of the country. So far there is not much evidence for
this.

It is not enough to say that 'in our time the "wages question" is being
transformed under our eyes from a *sectional* into a *class* question; from
an *industrial* one into a *political* one' (Royden Harrison). This has long
been so; capitalists and governments have acted on this assumption. But
there is an enormous difference between periods when the wage question in this form is part of a wider political upsurge of the working class,
as between 1918 and the General Strike (the Labour vote rose from
about two to about eight million between 1918 and 1929), and periods
like the present, when this is not the case. In short, trade unionism alone
is not enough, as Marxists ever since Karl Marx himself have argued
against syndicalists and others of their kind. And the present phase of
militancy is overwhelmingly trade unionist and economistic, mainly on
the issue of wages. There is no real disagreement about this. What is
unclear is 'the type of relation which exists between wages and the
political struggle' (Pete Carter), and how the wages struggle is to be integrated into the wider struggle of which it is only one part. I believe that
this is the crucial problem which faces the labour movement today.

For of course – as Roger Murray rightly reminds us – 'the wages
struggle will go on, regardless. . . . I think the denunciation of wages
struggles as economistic . . . while being accurate in some ways, is

unhelpful'. This needs to be said. It would be a curious kind of labour movement that paid no attention to what working people are actually fighting for – to what in crisis and inflation they are almost bound to fight for. But of course there is no danger of that. The danger lies rather in rationalizing militant economism into a general strategy.

Its limitations have been brought out in the discussion, not least by some of those active on the industrial front. There is sectionalism. 'The wages struggle in *isolation* and conducted *sectionally* can and does divide the labour movement, isolate it from other sections and assist the right-wing drift' (Roger Murray). Whether sectionalism is stronger in the trade union movement today than in the past, as I suggested, is an historical question on which I may well have been wrong. It is not worth discussing here. The fact remains that sectionalism – of a different kind from the past perhaps – exists *today*, and that (in Royden Harrison's words) 'under the conditions of state and monopoly capitalism the consequences of sectionalism are likely to become more disagreeable and more divisive'. We all know this, not least the comrades active in industry.

There is also the tendency of 'straight' trade unionism to take the capitalist system as given and to concentrate on getting the best terms within it. This has always been the weakness of the British trade union movement, 'an opposition which never becomes the government' as R.H. Tawney pointed out long ago, and of the characteristic 'trade unionist' form of British working-class consciousness which has prevented it from 'exhibiting the will to power' (Royden Harrison). It can easily lead to integrating itself into capitalism. At least one major strike of 1978 has been described in the discussion as 'an exercise of the market forces within the framework of capitalism' (Mike Le Cornu). There are great dangers here. The call for the abolition of all restraints on free wage-bargaining may at times be a crucial slogan, but we might remember that the call for the abolition of restraints on the free operations of the market (of which it is a special form) usually has very different political implications.

There is, thirdly, the fact that trade-union action – even militant action – can be quite divorced from political consciousness. The dockers who struck in solidarity with their imprisoned comrades in 1972 were the same men who had protested against Heath's sacking of Enoch Powell and who jeered Bernadette Devlin outside Pentonville Jail. The fact that over a third of trade unionists voted Tory in 1979, many of them no doubt participants in industrial action, is a sad reminder of this. All the more when we remember that there was a time when trade union membership or background and voting for Labour used to go together.

We may therefore conclude that trade union power and militancy alone, important though they are, have not offset, *and by themselves cannot offset,* the setbacks of the labour movement in other respects.

But what can be done about it? This must clearly be the subject of the next stage of the debate. The discussion so far has brought forward a number of general suggestions and some more specific proposals, mainly about how to link the industrial struggle with wider demands and struggles, but I don't think anyone believes that satisfactory answers have been found. They cannot be found by wishing the British working class and its movement were different from what it has historically been and become. They cannot be found by concentrating on its most advanced sections – whether the active members of the Labour and Communist parties or other parties and groups. The test of vanguards lies in their ability to lead armies. Answers cannot be found by concentrating on one aspect of the fight of labour – the industrial struggle, which has naturally formed a large part of the discussion – even if this is at present the nearest thing to a mass mobilization of the working people. There are, after all, today something like 350,000 shop stewards. They cannot be found by adding up various sections of the population who, for one reason or another, may find the left supporting their sectional demands.

A class party of labour (with all its limitations) became the mass party of the British working class (or, since we are a multinational state, the British working classes) by giving unity to the class consciousness of this class as a whole, and offering, in addition to the defence of material or other special interests, confidence, self-respect, and hope of a different and better society. How did this come about? Why did millions of workers and others after 1918 and again during and after the Second World War, turn to Labour? Why have, even today, certain groups — the Scots, women, a modest but growing section of the middle classes – in varying degrees resisted the turn towards Toryism? These questions have not been adequately analysed and studied by the left. Perhaps such study may help our movement to find its way forward again. The discussion in *Marxism Today* and elsewhere is welcome because it recognizes a serious crisis in the development of the movement. But there is no reason to believe that the faltering of Labour as a political mass movement is historically inevitable or cannot be reversed.

Notes

1. Contributions to the debate were collected as *The Forward March of Labour Halted?*, published by Verso in 1981, to which all following references refer.

3

The Debate on 'The Forward March of Labour Halted?' (1981)

The debate, initiated by my Marx Memorial Lecture in 1978, developed in *Marxism Today*, and collected in *The Forward March of Labour Halted?*, has mobilized not merely other academic intellectuals, which is common enough, but people involved at all levels in political and trade union activity, from local branch to parliament, and from the workshop floor to national leaders. This does not happen often, for theory and practice, the writers and the doers, are not as easily combined as they ought to be. The first point I would like to make is that this shows that theory does not have to be imprisoned in the overheated aquarium in which intellectual specialists swim about like some sort of tropical fish. Some theory does not confine itself to dealing with the real world as we know it, and with the palpable problems and tasks that confront those of us who want to improve and change it. But when theory faces this world and these tasks, the screen that divides those whose business is writing from the rest disappears. We all talk the same language and contribute to the discussion.

As for the main subject of this debate, nobody can seriously deny that the British labour movement today is in a considerable mess. It is in a state of deeper crisis and confusion than could easily be foreseen even three years ago. To this extent the basic argument of 'The Forward March of Labour Halted?' is not easily challenged, and in fact none of the new contributors to the debate have disagreed with it. Wherever the march of labour is going to take us in future, it has certainly not taken us forward since 1978. It has brought electoral defeat, followed by what is probably the most reactionary government of Britain this century, and certainly (barring Turkey) the most reactionary government in Europe at the present moment. It is also a spectacularly disastrous government, which has intensified the British part of the global capitalist crisis to the point where, unlike other capitalist countries, it is almost certainly already worse than the crisis of 1929–33.

Unemployment is already comparable to that of the years 1929–33 and will go on rising. Unlike the 1930s, the framework of British social welfare is being simultaneously dismantled – for example, schools and health service – while public and private housebuilding, which were then booming, have virtually ceased. The structure of British productive industry is being demolished almost beyond the hope of restoration. Few workers who voted for Thatcher don't bitterly regret doing so, and even large sections of British capitalists are desperately looking for someone else to back. In the circumstances one would expect a major surge of support for Labour, led by a united labour movement confident of victory.

Instead we find a confused and divided labour movement, torn by splits and internal squabbles, and isolated from many of its old supporters. Halfway through the course of a disastrous and deeply unpopular government in which nobody in Britain or abroad believes – not even most of its members – belief in Labour as an alternative government had also slumped. That at such a time Warrington, one of the most solid Labour constituencies in England, could almost be lost to the candidate of a third party that did not even pretend to put forward an alternative policy, and to a man personally associated with the EEC, which is certainly not a popular cause, amounts to a popular vote of no confidence in Labour. It is not to be explained away. So long as this situation lasts it would be absurd to claim that Labour has resumed its forward march, or looks like doing so.

While this is so, it is still as vital as it was three years ago to analyse dispassionately what has brought Labour to the present pass. There can be no reversal of Labour's fortunes, unless, in the words of Jack Jones, we 'avoid a repetition of slogans and generalizations from the past, allied with a refusal to assess realistically the facts of the present'. Are all the contributors to the present discussion ready to accept the facts of the situation and the results of a realistic diagnosis? I am not so sure.

In this instance the facts are too strong to be denied. Two apparent indications of labour advance have been or may be mentioned: British unions (as Steve Jefferys was right to point out) began to increase their membership again in the 1970s after a quarter-century of stagnation, and it may be that Labour Party membership has also lately begun to rise. As against this, the signs of decay accumulate. The national Labour vote forms a lower percentage of the electorate than at any time since 1931. In absolute figures it has inexorably drifted down from its peak of almost 14 million in 1951 to 11.5 million in 1979, except for a brief rise in 1964–66. If people don't vote Labour, there can be no Labour government, a fact sometimes overlooked by enthusiastic militants. The parties and groups to the left of the Labour Party have no significant electorate, national or even local. The Labour Party itself, in terms of its individual active membership, is not at present a mass party, even allowing for a recent influx of activists. It is probably less of a mass party at the moment than the Conservatives. Nobody can claim that the Communist Party and other Marxist parties and organizations are expanding significantly. The political radicalization of a section of the young after 1968 has not continued. At a representative meeting of perhaps 150 assorted leftwing intellectuals in the spring of 1981 there was not a single person under twenty-five. As for the unions, their power and capacity to resist attacks upon them remains, in spite of all, the most impressive part of the labour movement. Nevertheless their relative strength underlines the *political* weakness of the movement. For the first time since 1923 the national Labour electorate is today *smaller* than the number of unionists affiliated to the TUC: even in the disastrous year of 1931 it was larger. Labour today cannot mobilize even the members of the trade union movement to its cause. In 1979 a third of unionists actually seem to have voted Tory; and if the Warrington election is any guide, even if they won't vote for the Tories, many of them won't vote for Labour any longer.

In the 1970s it was this contrast between a declining and uncertain political labour movement and a growing, militant and apparently unbeatable industrial movement capable of resisting and defeating governments which encouraged a good many illusions about the latter's political potential. If we use the metaphor that Raymond Williams rightly challenged, people acted as though the bird of labour could fly on one wing, and indeed they were sometimes tempted to argue that the political wing could somehow be regenerated by the flapping of the industrial one. These illusions, which were accompanied by a certain idealization of rank-and-file action are not entirely dead, since they are based on the perfectly true observation that 'organization from below' is a necessary part of any political as well as industrial strategy of the left. But it is not enough to say that the road to Labour's recovery is to be found simply by 'really working on the basics: the respect of picket lines, collections for others on strike, solidarity action, rebuilding the independence of the shop-stewards' committees, building united rank-and-file organizations to generalize the anti-Tory fight' (Jefferys). Important as all these tasks are, they are not enough.

Nor can the great illusion of the 1970s, that militant unionism is enough, be saved by arguing that it would have been enough if only the unions had not been so narrow-minded: if we had not 'failed to harness the rank-and-file strength of the movement to clear class-wide socialist perspectives' (Jefferys again), or if unions had not 'neglected to be political in the sense of campaigning around the wider social needs of working people and other oppressed groups' (Wainwright). Certainly there could have been more harnessing and broader campaigning, though the need for both is not exactly a new discovery among socialists. But it is clear from the arguments of both Jefferys and Wainwright that the strength of militancy is 'not sufficient in the face of a world capitalist crisis and a Britain dominated by multinational capital' (Jefferys), and that the power of unions *by itself*, is essentially 'the power to bargain over the employment contract' (Wainwright) — one might add, on behalf of particular groups of workers. Therefore however much union action is widened politically, it can only be *one part* of labour's struggle, though a fundamental, crucial, and formidable part. Inevitably there is much of vital interest to workers as citizens, and to citizens not directly represented by unions, that cannot be dealt with by industrial action, adequately or at all, and which must consequently be fought for in other ways. Of course everyone recognizes this in principle, and (except for syndicalists) has done so ever since British unions, over eighty years ago, recognized that they needed a party, including the socialists, to supplement their action. It is certainly recognized today. Nevertheless, in practice, the temptation to think in purely industrial terms appears not to have been entirely overcome.

This temptation also leads people to underestimate or explain away possible contradictions within the industrial sector of the movement and also frictions between unions and other parts of the movement. Most of the debate on 'the forward march' has dealt with one aspect of these difficulties, namely trade union sectionalism. I do not want to prolong this debate, since *in practice* three things seem to be widely accepted by the participants. First, it is clear that sectionalism raises very serious problems, whether or not it has recently increased. Second, it is clear, not least from Jack Jones's valuable – and, coming from him, pretty authoritative – contribution, that there is no *automatic* way of spiriting away the differences between trade unions and the Labour Party, which have developed over the years and still exist particularly in times of Labour government. A concrete and limited set of policy objectives has to be hammered out to which both sides have to be committed, even when it does not represent what each would want if left to itself. And third, some contributors have admitted the unpalatable but undeniable fact 'that resentment towards trade union power has in fact grown' (Wainwright), even among supporters of Labour and probably within the membership of unions. We cannot pretend that this did not influence the defeat of the Labour government in 1979 nor deny, because such resentment has paradoxically continued even as trade union power has declined in a time of slump and unemployment, that it is still a significant political factor.

We might argue about a great many matters. Thus I believe that Jack Jones was right against Hilary Wainwright in his analysis of the political failures of the movement in the 1970s. The fault of the unions was not that they looked to Labour governments and councils to meet 'all the workers' other needs' beyond those with which collective bargaining could deal directly, *therefore* limiting themselves 'to fighting for the interests of the wage earners, full stop.' In itself this was sensible enough, since union action *alone* can achieve only limited, though indispensable, aims. Unions can, by their capacity to mobilize workers, greatly assist in wider campaigns, and by their peculiar position in the Labour Party, can help to shape the policy of Labour governments. Unions can, as the most massive form of citizens' self-organization, broaden the horizons of what we think of as 'politics' beyond the institutional and parliamentary or other representative (i.e. indirect) forms of political action, which act for and on behalf of (and sometimes against) people, but only occasionally allow them to act *for themselves*. But unions cannot replace the wider political movement of labour, of which they are only one part, though a crucial one. There must be some 'division of labour'. The fault of both unions and party in the period when there was a 'deepening division between the Labour Party leadership and the trade union movement' was that – in spite of efforts to the contrary by people like Jones – Labour leaders carried out a policy that workers did not expect from their party, and trade unions in turn pursued their own narrow interests irrespective of governments, including Labour governments, and thus helped to bring both Conservative and Labour governments to defeat.

However, though there is much more to be said about sectionalism and other problems of the trade unions, other aspects of Labour's difficulties are equally and perhaps more, urgent. They have not emerged so clearly in the discussion to date.

Since 1979 the illusion of salvation through union militancy has been replaced by another, and probably more dangerous, set of illusions, based on the fact that the only dynamic aspect of the movement of late has been the striking advance of the left within the organizations of the Labour Party. This is indeed a most impressive and welcome phenomenon. The present position of the left in the party, based on its strength and planned organization among activists in constituency parties and unions, and on constitutional changes such as the reselection of candidates and the new method of electing the party's leaders, would have been quite inconceivable even ten years ago. The next Labour victory, it is hoped, will bring into office a parliamentary majority of the left, under socialist leadership which is not only committed to a socialist policy by the party manifesto as formulated by Conference, but also no longer able to deviate from it once the new Labour government is in being. However, it is assumed that the party's turn to the left and its promise of staying true to its commitment will itself guarantee the next Labour victory.

This illusion is more dangerous than that of the 1970s, because it entirely bypasses the main problem, which is that the best and most leftwing party is not enough if the masses won't support it in sufficient numbers. Old and new Marxists in Britain, unfortunately, have plenty of experience of this. Trade unionism, with all its limitations, is never able to overlook the masses, because it organizes millions of them, has to represent them all the time, and has to mobilize them quite a lot of the time. But capturing the Labour Party for the left can be done in the short run without reference to the masses. It could, in theory, be achieved pretty well entirely by a smallish minority of a few tens of thousands of committed socialists and left Labour people by means of meetings, the drafting of resolutions, and votes. The illusion of the early 1980s is that *organization* can replace politics. There are today several tens of thousands of such activists, and their numbers are increasing because the successes of the left within the party encourage their hope. They are tempted, as I have suggested to Tony Benn, to look at the problem of resuming Labour's forward march 'in a little too narrow an organizational sense.'

But they are tempted to overlook – until electoral disaster dramatizes their oversight – the basic problem: how to get the British peoples, who reject Thatcherism utterly, to turn to Labour again. This they are visibly not doing at present, in spite of the fact that Labour is not only the party of the working people but the obvious alternative party of government.

There are three aspects to this problem. We need to analyse, first, what the basis of the forward march of Labour was between 1900 and the 1950s, and whether this basis is still sufficient to ensure its resumption. Second, we need to analyse the reasons for the decline in the political support for Labour, particularly in the past fifteen years. And third, we need to consider *politically* the ways of reversing this trend.

Basically Labour grew and became a party of government as what its name said it was, the party of the manual working class conscious that it needed a political class party. Most studies of why people vote Labour have come to essentially the same conclusion as McKenzie and Silver in 1968: 'When working-class Labour voters were asked what the parties were "like" they tended overwhelmingly to reply in terms of class'; or Westergaard and Resler: 'Asked why they vote as they do, manual working-class Labour supporters usually refer to the fact that the party is – or is supposed to be – the party of the working class.' For most of this century the manual workers formed a substantial majority of the British peoples, but while for half a century workers increasingly moved towards their class party, even, at the peak of Labour's fortunes (1945–66) between 35 and 40 per cent of them did not (yet) vote for the Labour Party. The decline in Labour's fortunes after 1951 was thus, at least initially, not to be explained by a numerical decline in the manual proletariat.

Nevertheless, Labour did not only rise as a party of manual workers. It appealed disproportionately to the minority peoples of Britain, not only because Scotland and Wales were proprotionately more industrialized than England, and the Irish in Britain were overwhelmingly workers, but also because the Scots, Welsh, and Irish are minority peoples. It also appealed to a small but growing section of intellectuals and 'progressive' middle strata, as the heir of a defunct liberal-radicalism, the party of education, reason, and progress, of a more socially just society, and largely as the party of peace. This was perhaps not of major electoral significance even in 1945, but the move 'forward from liberalism' is nevertheless not negligible, as witness the political history of families such as the Foots and the (Wedgwood) Benns. More significant was the turn of a growing number of the small salaried white-collar and lower professional employees to Labour, notably in 1945, for these groups (with some exceptions such as teachers) had previously kept aloof from the workers. In short, Labour also rose as a potential or actual 'people's party' of progressive change.

But there is a third element. Since 1918 the party has been committed to a socialist objective, and it is pretty certain that most working-class Labour supporters have also believed, however imprecisely, that capitalism ought to end and that not only a less unfair version of the present, but a newer and better society, should replace it. To this extent the British working class in politics, unlike the US working class, became – and one hopes has remained – socialist. The historians who have underestimated this aspect of Labour's rise, especially between 1918 and 1945, are mistaken. The argument of the Labour right, that Clause 4 was electorally damaging, was both disingenuous and wrong. It was bogus, because the right rejected the socialism of Clause 4 anyway, and not just because they thought it would lose votes; and it was wrong because it has not prevented Labour from winning general elections since the 1950s. Nor will it. On the contrary, it may be argued that Labour's greatest leaps forward have taken place when it was carried by great surges of hope for a better society, as in 1945 when the Labour vote rose by almost 50 per cent. Nor has or will the hope of a transformed Britain appeal only to manual workers. On the contrary, at a time of national crisis, almost of national despair, it can have the widest appeal.

Now the original basis of Labour's forward march has weakened. The manual working class of the old kind is now probably a minority and certainly a diminishing proportion of the people. So, even if we suppose that all the old working-class supporters flock back to the party, we would not get back to 1945. And while the 'new' working class of white-collar, technical, and lesser professional employees is now indeed largely organized in unions, and a part of them (especially in the public sector) have undoubtedly been radicalized, their 'class consciousness' is not necessarily the same as that of the old-style manual workers, and their spontaneous attraction to a 'party of the working class' is less. It is a safe bet that the percentage of ASTMS members who vote Labour is smaller than that of NUR and ASLEF members, even though the leadership of ASTMS is further to the left than that of the other two.

Moreover, even the 'old' working class is no longer what it was a generation ago, quite apart from the changes in its composition which my original article attempted to sketch. In general, as Jack Adams rightly pointed out:

> mass support for political advance and the assertion of class consciousness . . . have waned.... Among elderly people I frequently find a sympathetic response and a clear class understanding in discussion. These are less strong in later generations, although many young people are evidently looking for a radical alternative.

More specifically, there have been changes that discourage the old type of political consciousness. Thus the values of consumer-society individualism and the search for private and personal satisfactions above all else, have been daily taken into every living-room for a generation by the media (Adams was right to draw attention to the media, but I would stress not so much the distortions and bias of news and propaganda, as the constant atmosphere of apparently unpolitical advertising and entertainment breathed in by all of us). Moreover, the weakening of the hold of the old labour movement itself has made some workers less resistant to reactionary infections such as racism. For good or ill, we cannot simply go back to what Steve Jefferys rather offensively calls 'the Andy Capp class consciousness' of the 1940s. Incidentally, I never suggested that we could, though, with all my reservations, I regret it.

Moreover, we cannot simply expect the old calls for socialism to have the same resonance as in the past. Not many people today look to the various socialist countries as models for a socialist Britain, or are inspired as British workers once were by what they saw as 'the first workers' state' in the Soviet Union. After thirty to forty years of living with many nationalized industries, the call to nationalize some more may indeed be valid and necessary, but it no longer looks like an automatic solution to the workers' problems, as it did when Will Lawther proclaimed in 1944: 'What could be achieved through public ownership? It would win the complete confidence of the miners and their families. Generations of suspicion and hatred would be wiped out, and an entirely new attitude developed towards the coal industry.' The case for socialism is as strong as ever, but it has to be argued in a new way, with much clearer proposals concerning the sort of society we want and what socialism can achieve, rather than a repetition of old slogans which, however valid, no longer carry the same conviction. This point was rightly and forcefully made by Robin Blackburn. We cannot rely on our past.

These observations are enough to throw doubt on the proposition that all that stands between us and the next Labour government is a good leftwing programme for Labour and the proof that the party programme will not be betrayed. However, the view that this is the master-key to a resumption of Labour's forward march is based on a more specific diagnosis of Labour's defeat and crisis, which is mistaken. With the one exception of 1966 the Labour vote has continued to fall inexorably since 1951. The party has lost or won elections not because of the movement of its own support, but because of shifts in Tory and other party votes. Labour won in 1964 because the Tory vote fell by 1.7 million, lost in 1970 because it rose by about the same number, won in February 1974 and again in October because it twice fell by over a million, and lost in 1979 because the Tories' vote increased by over 3 million. Third party votes also went up and down like yo-yos. Labour's own vote did not vary by more than a couple of hundred thousand between elections (omitting 1966),[1] and drifted downwards all the time.

Whatever happened to Labour in the 1970s was clearly not due to dramatic reactions of the mass of *actual* Labour voters to Labour or other governments, but was the result of the reactions of people who ought perhaps to have been Labour voters, *but no longer were.* Labour governments have not been defeated because of secessions of Labour voters disappointed with their record: in 1951, two million more voted for Labour than in 1945, and even in 1979 the Callaghan government lost with a shade *more* votes than it had won with in 1974.[2] This reduces to folklore much talk about the betrayal of programmes as the reason for Labour's defeats. But there is one significant exception: the Wilson years of 1964–70. Here, and here alone we have a *rise* of 0.8 million in the Labour vote in 1966, followed by a slightly bigger fall in 1970. Why?

At no time did the Wilson governments have a programme worth the name, and hence they could hardly betray it. Labour got a majority because it offered the hope of change, and it lost, not only because, like all governments since then, it proved incapable of coping with the crisis of the British economy, but also because it did very nearly the opposite of what Labour voters and trade unionists expected from a Labour government. There is no denying the disappointment and demoralization of traditional Labour supporters. But once again, the crux of the problem lay not in the 'solid' Labour vote, which hardly changed between 1964 and 1970, but in the failure to seize the 1966 opportunity to widen Labour's support again, and even to hold the support then temporarily gained. Labour's forward march cannot be resumed so long as we think primarily in terms of people like those who form the large but declining block of men and women still within the field of the old loyalties, appeals, discourses, and arguments of 'the movement', or, still less, in terms of the devoted minority of activists. A vast mass of potential Labour voters, even among the members of the trade unions, are no longer among these.

How is the forward march to be resumed? That it can be done is proved by the recent examples of parties that have succeeded, at least for a time, in breaking out of the stagnation, decline, and political isolation which is not confined to British Labour. But it has been done by parties that have moved forward not *only* as class parties, and still less as sectional pressure groups and alliances of minority interests, but as 'people's parties' with which the majority of their nation interested in progressive reform and change can identify; as spokesman for the nation in time of crisis. This does not mean that they cease to be based on the labour movement. Unity between socialists and Communists, insisted on against opposition within and outside the French Socialist Party and underlined by Communist participation in President Mitterand's government, was the essential condition of its triumph. Nor does it mean that such a party retreats from its programme. The French Socialist Party (PSF) won an absolute majority with a programme to the left of anything so far suggested by the British Labour left. The Labour Party is potentially such a party. It must learn again to act like one.

This means that it should be and act as what Tony Benn himself sees as the first condition of Labour's revival, namely, 'a broad party' leading a broad movement. This does not merely mean a recognition of diversity within the party, but an acknowledgement of the diversity of the classes and other groups of the population, and of the aspirations and interests of those who make up the broad progressive front that must carry Labour to victory. This means not only that both left and right, however embattled, belong to a broad movement and have a right to be there, something that has been more readily recognized in the trade union movement than in the Labour Party. Terry Duffy and Tom Jackson are labour leaders as much as Alan Fisher, Arthur Scargill, and Ken Gill; they represent genuine currents of opinion within the movement, however much we may wish to change such opinions; and the movement as a whole would be weakened if the right or the left seceded.

But it also means that we must distinguish clearly between individual figures and bodies of opinion. I do not suppose anyone of the left grieves for those rightwing individuals who have, over the years, left the party and found a more congenial as well as presumably a more prosperous home elsewhere – the Shawcrosses, Robenses, and the rest. I do not suppose that the loss of Roy Jenkins, as a person, was much regretted. But it is a mistake to dismiss the collective secession of the Social Democrats and the foundation of a new party as good riddance. It represents the loss of a significant section of the left-of-centre middle class, which long looked to Labour, and in many cases actively worked for Labour *rather than* some other party. As is now clear, it potentially represents a significant electoral weakening of the Labour Party – how much so is still unclear. In short, it represents a lot of people who ought to support the Labour Party, and who must again be won for it, what-ever we think of the Gang of Four. And anyone who thinks a Labour Party without such supporters will at least be a stronger, more commit-ted and united force for socialism, should pause. Both as a historian and as a Marxist whose political memory goes back half a century, I have known plenty of strong, committed parties, great, small, and tiny, with admirable programmes, which have never built socialism or even been in government, except as occasional parts of coalitions in which they were much more shackled by their bourgeois partners than supporters of Benn need be by having to coexist with supporters of Healey. Moreover, the experience of the left unfortunately suggests that in these days even a committed socialist party will not escape internal divisions and quarrels.

As Jack Jones reminded us, the party that will resume Labour's forward march must think of politics in terms of ordinary people inside and outside the movement, and not primarily in terms of the activists who are untypical, if only because they spend far more time and energy on the movement than most men and women. We may or may not agree with Jones about the Social Contract, but he was surely right in stressing, time and again, that we need policies 'that workers can understand and fight for'; that it is disastrous when a Labour leadership does not put forward 'policies with much impact on working class opinion'; that 'because much of the critical work now going on is of the academic intellectual variety, there is not much understanding among the trade union rank and file about what has to be done'; that 'workers need to see and feel progress to gain confidence', that 'you gain mass interest by fighting for things that people see as justified and feasible'. Perhaps Jones concentrated a bit too much on the (necessary) campaigns around 'simple, clear, limited policies' which can be seen to bring immediate advantage. People want not only jobs for school-leavers, but a fairer and better world for their children, and confidence in a party which will work for it, beyond any immediate programme. And Labour needs to appeal not only to working people but to all who need such a better and fairer world. Yet, fundamentally, Jones was right.

The future of Labour and the advance to socialism depends on mobilizing people who remember the date of the Beatles' break-up and not the date of the Saltley pickets; people who have never read *Tribune* and who do not care a damn about the deputy leadership of the Labour Party, except (if they are Labour supporters) insofar as they are troubled by the fact that, as Britain founders after over two years of Thatcherism, the party seems to spend so much of its time on mutual laceration. They may be wrong, but the reason why these struggles are not just remote and incomprehensible has not been explained to their satisfaction. The future of Labour and socialism depends on men and women, blue collar, white collar and no collar, ranging from zero CSE to PhD, who are, regrettably, not revolutionaries, even though they want a new and better Britain and, if they can be shown that socialism can achieve this, a socialist Britain. In this century Labour has advanced with the support of such people, who have accepted the leadership of the left when it has made sense to them in their own terms. If Labour is to advance again, it cannot forget this. For if such people do not vote for Labour – which is the minimal index of political support – then Labour will not reverse its long-term decline.

There are only three possible ways of avoiding this conclusion. We may suppose that there is still a huge mass of men and women identified with 'the movement' who will automatically support *any* leadership and *any* policy because it represents Labour, when it comes to the point of voting. We would be unwise any longer to rely on this, however: millions will stay loyal, come what may, but they will not be enough. We may also suppose that somewhere there is a vast, unknown, untapped reservoir of left votes. There is no good evidence for this view at present. Lastly we may put our money on a breakdown of British capitalism and politics, leading to a crisis in which the masses will turn to the left. Since we are in such a crisis, in which British capitalism *is* breaking down, and since traditional politics and the system of class rule are visibly unable to carry on in the old ways, this is not an implausible scenario. But if this crisis has hitherto shown anything, it is that the masses have so far not turned to labour or the left, nor are they likely to do so automatically.

Even with a declining Labour vote, Labour could still form the next government, if the curious British electoral system produces a parliamentary majority because the anti-Labour vote is sufficiently split between Tories, Liberals, Social Democrats, and whoever else. No doubt the politicians, commentators, and swingometrists are already busy figuring out possibilities on their pocket calculators. In such circumstances, a committed Labour government could still achieve much. But let us make no mistake. In such circumstances the problems of reversing Labour's decline and resuming its forward march would not have been solved, or even tackled. The task would still be there to face us. And we would have no excuses left if we failed.

Notes

1. Except, curiously, when it just nosed ahead of the Tories in February 1974 with half a million fewer votes than in the year of defeat, 1970.
2. The really massive drop in the labour vote – 1.5 million – occurred during the Tory and cold-war years of 1951–55, and must be explained differently.

4

Looking Towards 2000:
the Politics of Decline? (1982)

For a century, the decline and fall of Britain has been confidently and correctly expected, with results depending on the prophets' tastes and hopes. Imperial Germany and the United States thought they would replace Britain as the world empire, having relegated her to the second division as an industrial power. Both dreamed of world power through navies. The twentieth-century model of American global control, now also rather shop-soiled, was modelled on the nineteenth-century British version ('Pax Americana'), as the British in its time was inspired by memories of another empire to whose decline and fall, in spite of Gibbon, they paid little attention.

Engels, first of a long line of hopeful socialists, expected the British proletariat to recognize its historic destiny once it was no longer cushioned by the profits or super-profits of global, and later imperial, monopoly. But whether one welcomed British imperial decline, or regretted it like the passionately anglophile liberal middle classes of central Europe (Sigmund Freud is a case in point), it seemed inevitable to all except most of the British, who could not quite believe it. Something was bound to turn up. It has not; and we now face the evident fact that the decline of Britain, dramatically accelerated in the past fifteen years – with considerable help from the British government since 1979 – has far-reaching consequences for the political and social affairs of this county. What are these?

The most obvious of them is de-industrialization. We are, of course, familiar with complete de-industrialization, which has been the frequent fate of old mining centres like Cornwall or North Wales, whose economy now depends on tourism. If it is difficult to conceive of this happening in Merseyside or Strathclyde, it is not because the ruins of ancient industry cannot be made attractive to tourists (think of Ironbridge and the ghost mining towns of Nevada), but because most of the archaeological interest was removed from British industrial areas by the property boom of the 1960s. It will take a century or so to develop sentimentality about the new Birmingham, though it ought to be said, in fairness to the Labour councils who so often presided over this vandalism, that a declining Blackburn is still a better and handsomer place to live in than a declining Wilkes Barre (Pennsylvania), which has been left to moulder by genuine free enterprise.

However, we are not faced with the complete reconquest of Britain by meadow, trees, and romantic ruins but with an industrial economy throttled by the fact that it is internationally less and less competitive, in spite of having become a lower-wage economy; by the fact that it is therefore only barely if at all profitable; by the fact that it can flourish only through heavy capital investment, which it can ill afford and which implies the shedding of workers, who swell the armies of the permanently unemployed, and whose maintenance cannot be easily afforded either. The great global boom of 1950–73, while undermining British as well as other western societies, bore the British economy, like them, into an unprecedented prosperity. That prosperity is now at an end.

This is a problem which faced and faces any British government. What is new is the recognition that the traditional post-1945 economic policy of moderate consensus, still represented by the Liberal–SDP alliance, has not worked and is unlikely to work. Its advantages were primarily social and political. It preserved the fabric of British politics and that social stability so envied by foreigners.

The depth to which consciousness of Britain's decline has penetrated is indicated by the fact that British politics has become increasingly dominated by two rival and equally desperate camps promising economic salvation. This is not because the situation in the mid 1970s was catastrophic in any immediate sense, but because the promises and policies of the past seemed to have lost all credibility for the long-term future.

These rivals recommend, respectively, a flight backwards into a utopia of competitive private enterprise, a sort of bourgeois anarchism almost equally hostile to state, public sector, and those large corporations so inclined to come to an understanding with the state; and, on the other hand, a flight forward into something described as 'socialism', which is certainly associated with a vast extension of public ownership and management. We need not at present consider the second of these alternatives, since those who propagate it most passionately appear to be making sure by their political behaviour that it will not be on the immediately foreseeable political agenda.

As for the first – unfortunately represented by the government – its economic failure can be taken as read. So can the scepticism of most economists, and indeed businessmen, about the chances of this policy reviving the British economy. But it is evident by now that this government expects its economic policy to be judged not by its results but by its *will.* It appeals as the government which has stood up to unions, Argies, and intellectual doubters, hunger strikers and wets, sociologists, the Common Market, and even civil servants: which doesn't just stand there but *does* something. Its achievements are not as important as the posture in which action is pursued. In short, the major effects of Thatcherism – apart from an accelerating deindustrialization – are likely to be social and political, rather than economic.

These effects may well be profound, since the temperament, ideology, and logic of its policies push this government towards radical changes in the British political system. It is, in fact, the nearest thing to a government of the radical right in British history. This reflects the crisis in the two-party system which has allowed the radical wings of each to become disproportionately influential, while driving out the more despairing champions of the old. (Far from 'breaking the mould' in politics, the SDP is trying to stick its shattered fragments together again.)

Political and social polarization was precisely what the traditional British rulers wanted, at all costs, to avoid. Ever since Burke, they feared that it would lead to revolution. For that very reason the radical left have always favoured polarization. Moreover, the Marxists among them have always predicted that the decline of Britain as an economic and imperial power would inevitably radicalize British politics. Unfortunately, they also rather took it for granted that this would benefit the left. At present this is far from being the case.

The transformation of Tory government, therefore, like the simultaneous crises which convulse the Labour Party, represents a dramatic break with old and deeply rooted British political traditions. It puts an enormous strain both on the fabric of the old class or establishment rule, and on the elaborately interwoven structure of private, semi-private, and public, of state and corporate interests, which was evolved in this century precisely to avoid class polarization.

That Establishment – or what the Italians call 'the political class' – ranging from traditional Tories to traditional Labour, is united in thinking the policies of the Thatcher government unrealistic to the point of irrationality, as witness its silent reaction – except for some of the top people's press and some reflexes of the BBC – to the Falklands affair. Conversely, the government bypasses the traditional establishment so far as possible, while appealing directly, over its head, to the masses. It is the first government which treats its own senior civil servants – the people who keep the show on the road – not as the politically neutered servants of *all* legitimate governments, but in the manner of 'class enemies'; distrusting them on principle as representing the state it wishes to dismantle.

The formal and informal structures of political rule are coming to pieces. I would bet that most of *Who's Who* (except perhaps for its military component) today consists of worried eyebrow-raisers, rather than of the operational power elites of old.

Politically, this restructuring of public life relies on two developments in British society. The first is the disintegration of old class structures and class loyalties, which took place in the course of the boom gener- ation, notably among the working classes, but also among the middle classes. This is not a specifically British phenomenon, though it has local colouring. Hence the appeal of Thatcherism has successfully crossed class boundaries. Its long-term prospects depend much more on the readers of the *Sun*, who were or would have been Labour voters, than on those of the *Express, Mail*, and *Telegraph* who were always Tories.

The second social development is visibly a reflection of Britain's decline, and may be compared – all precautions taken – with the mood of Weimar Germany. Anyone who knew that country, which also felt itself defeated, relegated, looked down on by foreigners, impoverished, and deprived of its old moral structures and certainties, knows the dangerous forces which such a situation can breed. Not least, national- ism on the right, a passionate radicalism on the extreme left (which turned out not to be shared by 'the masses' to whom it appealed), and on both sides the thirst for a regime which will *do* something: anything.

Prosperity can dampen these sentiments down, as it did in Germany from 1924 to 1929, and in Britain during the 1960s – when they merely took the form of uneasiness and a unique preoccupation with the glories and certainties of the past, from the Forsytes to the comforting memories of the Second World War. Nostalgia was (and is) the name of the national game in a country which has no better prospect than to look backwards, like ancient supporters of Accrington Stanley.

Depression allows these forces to flare up. Britain now finds itself living through the dangerous combination of resentment and slump, under a government ready to exploit both resentment and nostalgia. Absurd though it would be to push the analogy with Weimar Germany too far, the rapid erosion of the traditional structures of British politics brings danger. This arises primarily from the logical consequences of pursu- ing policies which are patently unrealizable. Thus it is increasingly obvious that a government devoted to dismantling the state has inevitably streng- thened it, since only the state can impose the utopia of *Daily Telegraph* editorials on the recalcitrant reality largely consisting of people and institu- tions employed by, subsidized by, or otherwise dependent on, public funds.

Since the dream of an economy and people entirely independent of the Treasury is unreal, and government must continue to supply finance, the state must henceforth – in the interests of withering away – give ever more precise directions about what its funds should and should not be spent on. Thus, universities, whose autonomy was once carefully guarded against direct government interference, now come under encroaching centralized, politico-bureaucratic orders. Central power and command are not diminishing but growing, since 'freedom' cannot be achieved except by bureaucratic decision. The scope for democracy and local liberties are inevitably restricted.

Politically the danger arises out of the isolation, within the Establishment world, of the Prime Minister and her smallish group of unconditional supporters. This is partly concealed by the suicidal fragmentation and impotence of the opposition, the traditional reluctance of Tory dissidents to break with their party, and the fact that *some* Thatcher policies have wide support even beyond the Tory ranks – for instance, the weakening of the unions. Yet the Thatcherites are visibly beleaguered by a vast force of ministers, politicians, administrators, businessmen, experts, and general-purpose intellectuals who do not like the drift of her policies, and whose opinions range from utter scepticism through to despair.

Thatcher is neither loved nor expected to succeed. Moreover, the policies do not work. The deeper the government's commitment to them, the greater the scepticism surrounding it. Like Napoleon, she has to keep winning battles. Or seem to. There can be immediate triumphs: public declarations of firmness, victories over unions, strikers, or Argentines, preferably with the suggestion that all are equally enemies of the Union Jack. There have been enough of these triumphs to lend credibility, if not to the claim that national regeneration is under way, or that the old British empire in all its glory can be reconstituted round some depopulated islands near Cape Horn, then at least to the conviction that Mrs Thatcher is not a politician like all the others. And to the belief that she is calling for a crusade.

For what? Against what? For the mobilization of undefined but powerful beliefs and symbols: patriotism, national pride, social order, law, morality, independence, self-respect, the good old days. In short, for beliefs which are held by the majority of citizens, often in combination with very different beliefs (such as class consciousness), but which, in isolation, are most easily manipulated by the right. The last time these beliefs were adequately mobilized on behalf of the left was when they were combined with anti-fascism and the hope of a fair society in the Second World War.

And *against*? Against enemies abroad and also at home; including the 'strangers' in our midst – heterodox minorities, subversives, or those who can be presented as such, the disturbers of conventional morality, doubters and softies, the ever unreliable intellectuals, those who fail to salute flag and uniform or to sing *Rule Britannia* with the required zeal.

In short, we are seeing the mobilization of the usual forces of the radical right (except for the churches, which have shown a regrettable tendency to prefer God to this particular Caesar) against its habitual targets. The incentive to press on with this crusade grows as the gap between the promises and the results of policies widens. The logical result of such demagogic populism of the right would be to put an intolerable strain on the constitutional and institutional structures of British politics.

However, two things chiefly distinguish this kind of crusading politics from the fascisms of the past. In the first place, it emerges from neither an organized movement nor a formed ideology. At most, the logic of politics nudges politicians who certainly have no sympathy for the destruction of British democracy, in a direction which is dangerous to it. And perhaps towards the point where a total conviction of *rightness* and the need to regenerate Britain – when confronted with the loss of effective political support – might consider that truth must be made to prevail against opposition, parliament, or other 'temporary' obstacles, by *any* means.

In the second place, the commitment to financial orthodoxy and free-market enterprise deprives the crusaders of some of the most powerful assets of demagogy. And unlike fascism during the last world depression, the economic record is against this sort of politics. Unlike Hitler three years after his arrival in office, Mrs Thatcher has seen unemployment not sharply decline but rise to the highest figure ever recorded in this country. The main successes of her government belong to the realm of public relations, rather than to that of reality. Her main achievements have therefore been simply to enjoy rather more public support in the fourth year of government than was to be expected, against a divided and demoralized opposition. Their weakness lies in the growing gap between rhetoric and results.

A rather expensive little war, maliciously described by *Le Monde* as 'a Clochemerle of the South Atlantic', left the international position and problems of Britain quite unchanged, though clearly demonstrating that she possesses formidable, efficient, and professional armed forces. Nothing has changed in Northern Ireland. There is not more law and order but less, not least in parts of the increasingly well-paid and well-praised police.

And the future? De-industrialization will be the inevitable background to British politics. We shall certainly continue to live in a tottering and mangled economy, which nobody quite knows how to revive, and which cannot rely on anything as simple as an economic upturn, even if good times were to return to the world economy. In any case, that is unlikely for the rest of the decade. Too much has been destroyed when, as happened recently, with the Carron Company in Scotland, a firm of ironmakers which survived good times and bad since 1760, finally went out of business.

Granted this, the future of politics will depend on the rate at which the traditional institutions and practices of politics continue to be eroded and undermined, that is, the extent to which the familiar machinery ceases to work. Its ability to survive, and remain operational, should not be underestimated so long as the masses (as distinct from the ideologues, fringes, and militants) have not arisen to the calls of right, left, or nationalist separatism. And, until now, they have not.

It is even possible that the old structure of relatively conciliatory centre governments may revive in one form or another – as traditional Butskellite Toryism or Labour, as 'national government', or as coalitions of various groups and blocs operating in the space between the radical-ized political extremes. Like it or not, this is still the largest political space in Britain. The details of such rearrangements do not matter, except to lobby correspondents. While this would provide no solution, it would probably be the least disagreeable way for most people to live the continued decline of their country. In retrospect the dying decades of the Habsburg monarchy look better to most people, in the parts of Europe it once occupied, than what came after.

It is possible, however, that the political machinery for ruling Britain or keeping its citizens quiet, will seize up for one reason or another. Speculations about future military coups at least indicate a deep sceptic-ism about the prospect for the political system. Such developments can no longer be excluded. Experience has shown that, when politics become unmanageable in the West or East, armed men are apt to step in.

Short of apocalyptic daydreams, only three things can reasonably be said about coups. They are, first of all, not in themselves solutions to a country's problems. There is plenty of evidence for this, from Poland and Argentina to Brazil. Second, European armies (at least so long as their professional interests are satisfied) are extremely reluctant to inter-vene, especially against legitimate governments, even when they are politically out of sympathy with them. There is good evidence for this too, as the King of Spain is able (so far) to testify.

Finally, politicians who either call on men in uniform to intervene on their behalf, or explain that they will inevitably intervene against them-selves, are simply testifying to their own failure or refusal to do their job. This is particularly relevant to the prospects of a radicalized Labour

Party which, given the débâcle of Thatcherite policies, may yet get its chance. If it did, then in spite of all its efforts to the contrary, it could potentially command a very great deal of the broadest support as the last untried enterprise of national regeneration. If it were to act on the assumption that the entire apparatus of government, business, and public force, from the Crown to the last copper on the beat, was dedicated to defeating Labour's effort, it would not only be mistaken, but would guarantee its own defeat. The militants could then retire, if still allowed to, behind clouds of maximalist rhetoric, to the familiar entrenchments of opposition. But the best available chance for the slow, difficult, and uncomfortable process of giving Britain a new start, would recede.

Would it return? History does not guarantee solutions for its problems. It merely guarantees that society and its institutions will go on in some form, short of a nuclear holocaust which would deprive even this platitude of realistic meaning. If this far from impossible catastrophe happens, speculations about the future of British politics are pointless. If it does not, there is hope.

Peoples have survived both short-term cataclysm and slow-motion historical landslides. Still, in fifty years from now, it is very unlikely that many inhabitants of Britain will look back with any satisfaction on the 1970s, 1980s or, probably, the 1990s.

5

Falklands Fallout (1983)

More has been talked about the Falklands than about any other recent issue in British and international politics and I fear many have talked nonsense. I don't mean the great bulk of the people, whose reactions were probably considerably less passionate or hysterical than those whose business it is to write and formulate opinions.

I want to say very little indeed about the origins of the Falklands war because that war actually had very little to do with the Falklands. Hardly anybody knew about the Falklands. I suppose that the number of people in this country who had any personal relations with the Falklands or even knew anybody who had been there, was minimal. The 1,680 natives of these islands were very nearly the only people who took an urgent interest in the Falklands, apart of course from the Falkland Island Company, which owns a good deal of it, ornithologists, and the Scott Polar Research Institute, since the islands are the basis of all the research activities in the Antarctic. They were never very important, or at least they hadn't been since the First World War or perhaps just the beginning of the Second World War.

They were so insignificant and so much out of the centre of interest, that parliament let the running be made by about a dozen MPs, the Falklands lobby, which was politically a very, very mixed lot. They were allowed to stymie all the not very urgent efforts of the Foreign Office to settle the problem of the islands' future. Since the government and everybody else found the Falklands totally without interest, the fact that they were an urgent concern in Argentina, and to some extent in Latin America as a whole, was overlooked. They were indeed far from insignificant to the Argentines. They were a symbol of Argentine nationalism, especially since Peron. We could put the Falklands problem off for ever, or we thought we could, but this was not true for the Argentinians.

Now, I'm not judging the validity of the Argentine claim. Like so many nationalist claims it can't bear much investigation. Essentially it is based on what you might call 'secondary school geography' – anything that belongs to the continental shelf ought to belong to the nearest country – in spite of the fact that no Argentines had ever actually lived there. Nevertheless, we're bound to say that the Argentine claim is almost certainly rather stronger than the British claim and has internationally been regarded as such. The Americans, for instance, never accepted the British claim, whose official justification changed from time to time. But the point isn't to decide which claim is stronger. The point is that, for the British government, the Falklands were about as low as they could have been on its list of priorities, and it was totally ignorant of Argentine and Latin American views, which are not merely those of the junta but of all Latin America.

As a result, by withdrawing *The Endurance*, the one armed ship which had always been there symbolically indicating that you couldn't take the Falklands over, it managed to suggest to the Argentinian junta that the UK wouldn't resist. The Argentine generals, who were patently crazy and inefficient as well as nasty, decided to go ahead with the invasion. But for mismanagement by the UK government, the Argentine government would almost certainly not have decided to invade. They miscalculated and did so, but it is perfectly clear that the British government actually precipitated the situation, even though it had not meant to. And so, on 3 April the British people discovered that the Falklands had been invaded and occupied. The government should have known that an invasion was imminent, but claimed that it didn't; or at any rate if it did know, it took no action. This is of course what the Franks Commission was set up to investigate.

But what was the situation in Britain when war broke out and later, during the war itself? Let me try and summarize it fairly briefly. The first thing that happened was an almost universal sense of outrage among a lot of people, the idea that you simply couldn't accept this, that something had to be done. This was a sentiment which was felt at all levels right down to the grass roots and it was unpolitical in the sense that it went through all parties and was not confined to the right or to the left. I know of lots of people on the left within the movement, even on the extreme left who had the same reaction as people on the right. It was this general sense of outrage and humiliation which was expressed on that first day in parliament when the pressure for action actually came not from Thatcher and the government, but from all sides, from the ultra-right in the Conservatives, from the Liberals and Labour, with only the rarest of exceptions. This, I think, was a public sentiment which could actually be felt. Anybody sensitive to the vibes knew that this was going on, and anyone on the left who was not aware of this grass roots feeling, and did not grasp that, at least at this stage, it was not a creation of the media but a genuine sense of outrage and humiliation, ought seriously to reconsider their capacity to assess politics. It may not have been a particularly desirable sentiment, but to claim that it didn't exist is quite unrealistic.

This upsurge of feeling had nothing to do with the Falklands as such. We have seen that the Falklands were simply a far-away territory swathed in mists off Cape Horn, about which we knew nothing and cared less. It had everything to do with the history of this country since 1945, the visible acceleration of the crisis of British capitalism since the late 1960s, and in particular the slump of the late 1970s and early 1980s. So long as the great international boom of western capitalism persisted in the 1950s and 1960s, even a relatively weak Britain was to some extent gently borne upwards by the current which pushed other capitalist economies forward even more rapidly. Things were clearly getting better and we didn't have to worry too much although there was obviously a certain amount of nostalgia around the place.

And yet, at a certain stage, it became evident that the decline and crisis of the British economy were becoming much more dramatic. The slump in the 1970s intensified this feeling and of course since 1979 the real depression, the de-industrialization of the Thatcher period, and mass unemployment, have underlined the critical condition of Britain.

So the gut reaction that a lot of people felt at the news that Argentina had simply invaded and occupied a bit of British territory could have been put into the following words: 'Ours is a country which has been going downhill for decades, the foreigners have been getting richer and more advanced than we are, everybody's looking down on us and if anything pitying us, we can't beat the Argentinians or anybody else at football any more, everything's going wrong in Britain and nobody really quite knows what to do about it and how to put it right. But now it's got to the point where a bunch of foreigners think they can simply march troops onto British territory, occupy and take it over, and they think the British are so far gone that nobody's going to do anything about it. Well, this is the straw that breaks the camel's back and something's got to be done. By God we'll have to show them that we're not really just there to be walked over.' Once again, I'm not judging the validity of this point of view but I think this is roughly what a lot of the people who didn't try and formulate it in words felt at that moment.

Now in fact, we on the left had always predicted that Britain's loss of empire, and general decline would lead to a dramatic reaction sooner or later in British politics. We hadn't envisaged this particular response but there's no question that it was a reaction to the decline of the British

Empire of the kind we had predicted for so long. This is why it had such very wide backing. In itself, it wasn't simply jingoism. But, though this feeling of national humiliation went far beyond the range of jingoism, it was easily seized by the right and taken over by Mrs Thatcher and the Thatcherites in what I think was a politically brilliant operation. Let me quote her classic statement of what she thought the Falklands war proved (from a 1982 press release after the end of the war):

> When we started out there were the waverers and the faint-hearts, the people who thought we could no longer do the great things we once did, those who believed our decline was irreversible, that we could never again be what we were, that Britain was no longer the nation that had built an empire and ruled a quarter of the world. Well, they were wrong.

In fact the war was purely symbolic, it didn't prove anything of the kind. But here you see the combination of somebody catching certain popular vibes, and turning them in a rightwing (I hesitate, but only just, to say semi-fascist) direction. That is why from the rightwing point of view it was essential not simply to get the Argentinians out of the Falklands, which would have been perfectly practicable by a show of force plus negotiation, but to wage a dramatic victorious war. That is why the war was provoked by the British side whatever the Argentine attitude. There's little doubt that the Argentinians, as soon as they discovered that this was the British attitude, were looking for a way out of an intolerable situation. Thatcher wasn't prepared to let them because the whole object of the exercise was not to settle the matter quickly but to prove if only in a symbolic fashion that Britain was still great. At virtually every stage the policy of the British government in and out of the United Nations was one of total intransigence. I'm not saying that the Junta made it easy to come to a settlement but I think historians will conclude that a negotiated withdrawal of the Argentinians was certainly not out of the question. It wasn't seriously tried.

This provocative policy had a double advantage. Internationally, it gave Britain a chance to demonstrate her hardware, her determination and her military power. Domestically, it allowed the Thatcherites to seize the initiative from other political forces within and outside the Conservative Party, it enabled a take-over by the Thatcherites not only of the Conservative camp but of a great area of British politics. In a curious way the nearest parallel to the Thatcherite policy during the Falklands war is the Peronist policy which, from the other side, had first launched the Falklands into the centre of Argentine politics. Peron, like Mrs Thatcher and her little group, tried to speak directly to the masses using the mass media, going over the heads of the establishment. In our case that included the Conservative establishment as well as the opposition. She insisted on running her own war. It wasn't a war run by parliament. It wasn't even run by the cabinet; it was a war conducted by Mrs Thatcher and a small war cabinet, including the chairman of the Conservative Party. At the same time she established direct lateral relations with the military, a move which I hope will not have long-term political effects. It was this combination of a direct demagogic approach to the masses, bypassing the political processes and the establishment, with the forging of direct lateral contact with the military and the defence bureaucracy, that was characteristic of the war.

Neither costs nor objectives counted, least of all the Falklands themselves, except as symbolic proof of British virility and something which could be put into headlines. This was the kind of war which existed in order to produce victory parades. That is why all the symbolically powerful resources of war and empire were mobilized on a miniature scale. The role of the navy was paramount anyway, but traditionally public opinion has invested a lot of emotional capital in it. The forces sent to the Falklands were a mini-museum of everything which could give the union jack particular resonance – the Guards, the new technological strong men, the SAS, the paras; all were represented down to those little old gurkhas. They weren't necessarily needed but you had to have them because this was, as it were, a recreation of the old Imperial durbars, or the processions at the death or coronation of British sovereigns.

No war is a farce. Even a little war in which 250 Britons and 2,000 Argentinians get killed is not a matter for jokes. But for foreigners who didn't realise the crucial role of the Falklands war in British *domestic* politics, the war certainly seemed an absolutely incomprehensible exercise. *Le Monde* in France called it a Clochemerle of the South Atlantic recalling that famous novel in which the right and the left in a small French town come to enormous blows over the question of where to situate a public convenience. Most Europeans simply could not understand what all the fuss was about. What they did not appreciate was that the dispute was not about the Falklands at all and not about the right of self-determination. It was basically an operation concerned with British politics and with the British political mood.

Having said that, let me say firmly that the choice was not between doing nothing and Thatcher's war. I think it was politically absolutely impossible at this stage for any British government to do nothing. The alternatives were not simply an acceptance of the Argentine occupation by passing the buck to the United Nations, which would have adopted empty resolutions, or on the other hand, Mrs Thatcher's intended replay of Kitchener's victory over the Sudanese at Omdurman. The pacifist line was that of a small and isolated minority, if indeed a minority with a respectable tradition in the labour movement. Politically that line was simply not on. The very feebleness of the demonstrations which were being organized at the time showed this. The people who said the war was pointless, and should never have been started, have been proved right in the abstract, but they themselves did not and aren't likely to derive any political benefit from having been proved right.

The next point to note is more positive. Thatcher's capture of the war with the aid of *The Sun* produced a profound split in public opinion, but not a political split along party lines. Broadly it divided the 80 per cent who were swept by an instinctive patriotic reaction and identified with the war effort, though probably not in as strident a manner as the *Sun* headlines, from the minority which recognized that, in terms of the actual global politics concerned, what Thatcher was doing made no sense at all. That minority included people of all parties and none, and many who were not against sending a task force as such. I hesitate to say that it was a split of the educated against the uneducated; although it is a fact that the major hold-outs against Thatcherism were to be found in the quality press, plus of course the *Morning Star*. The *Financial Times*, the *Guardian*, and the *Observer* maintained a steady note of scepticism about the whole business. I think it is safe to say that almost every single political correspondent in the country, from the Tory ones right through to the left, thought the whole thing was loony. Those were the 'faint-hearts' against whom Mrs Thatcher railed. The fact that there was a certain polarization but that the opposition, though it remained quite a small minority, was not weakened, even in the course of a brief and, in technical terms, brilliantly successful war, is significant.

Fortunately for Mrs Thatcher the war was won, very quickly and at a modest cost in British lives. With it came an immediate and vast pay-off in popularity. The grip of Thatcher and the Thatcherites, of the ultra-right, on the Conservative Party unquestionably increased enormously as a consequence. Mrs Thatcher was on cloud nine and imagined herself as a reincarnation of both the Duke of Wellington, (without that Irish realism which the Iron Duke never lost) and Winston Churchill (without the cigars and, one hopes, without the brandy).

Now let me deal with the effects of the war. I shall mention only briefly the short-term effects, on the period between now and the general election. The first of these concerns the debate on whose fault it is. The Franks Commission is at present inquiring into precisely this. It is certain that the government, including Mrs Thatcher, will come out badly, as they deserve to. The second issue is the cost of the operation and the subsequent and continuing expense of maintaining the British presence in the Falklands. The official statement is that it is going to be about £700 million, but my own guess is that it will almost certainly run into thousands of millions. Accountancy is a form of creative writing, so exactly how you calculate the cost of an operation of this kind is optional. However it is done, it will turn out to be very, very, expensive. Certainly the left will press this issue and they ought to. However it is unfortunate that the sums are so large as to be meaningless to most people. So while the figures will go on being much quoted in political debate, I suspect this issue won't be very prominent or politically very effective.

The third issue is the bearing of the Falklands on British war policy, or defence policy as everybody now likes to call it. The Falklands war will certainly intensify the savage internal warfare among admirals, air marshals, generals, and the Ministry of Defence which has already led to one post-Falklands casualty, the Minister of Defence himself, Nott. There is very little doubt that the admirals used the Falklands affair to prove that a large navy, capable of operating right across the globe, was absolutely essential to Great Britain – whereas everybody else knows that we can't afford it and, what's more, it just isn't worth keeping a navy of that size in order to be able to supply Port Stanley. These discussions will certainly raise the question of whether Britain can afford both a global navy and Trident missiles, and what exactly the role and importance of independent British nuclear weapons is. To this extent, they can play a part in the development of the campaign for nuclear disarmament which should not be underestimated.

How about the future of the Falkland Islands themselves? This too is likely to be of little general interest since to most Britons the Islands will again cease to be of any serious interest. But it will be an enormous headache for civil servants, for the Foreign Office, and for anybody else involved because we have no policy for their future. It wasn't the object of the war to solve the problems of the Falkland Islands. We are simply back to square one, or rather square minus one, and sooner or later a permanent solution will have to be found unless British governments are content to keep a permanent and enormously expensive commitment for ever, and for no good purpose, down by the South Pole.

Finally, let me deal with the more serious question of the long-term effects. The war demonstrated the strength and the political potential of patriotism, in this case in its jingoistic form. This should not perhaps surprise us, but Marxists haven't found it easy to come to terms with working-class patriotism in general and English or British patriotism in particular. British here means where the patriotism of the non-English peoples happens to coincide with that of the English; where it doesn't coincide, as is sometimes the case in Scotland and Wales, Marxists have been more aware of the importance of nationalist or patriotic sentiment.

Incidentally, I suspect that while the Scots felt rather British over the Falklands, the Welsh didn't. The only parliamentary party which, as a party, opposed the war from the start was Plaid Cymru and of course, as far as the Welsh are concerned, 'our lads' and 'our kith and kin' are not in the Falklands, but in Argentina. They are the Patagonian Welsh who send a delegation every year to the National Eisteddfod in order to demonstrate that you can still live at the other end of the globe and be Welsh. So as far as the Welsh are concerned the reaction, the Thatcherite appeal on the Falklands, the 'kith and kin' argument, probably fell by the wayside.

Now there are various reasons why the left and particularly the Marxist left has not really liked to come to terms with the question of patriotism in this country. There's a particular historical conception of internationalism which tends to exclude national patriotism. We should also bear in mind the strength of the liberal/radical, anti-war, and pacifist tradition which is very strong, and which certainly has passed to some extent into the labour movement. Hence there's a feeling that patriotism somehow conflicts with class consciousness, as indeed it frequently does, and that the ruling and hegemonic classes have an enormous advantage in mobilizing it for their purposes, which is also true.

Perhaps there is also the fact that some of the most dramatic and decisive advances of the left in this century were achieved in the fight against the First World War, and they were achieved by a working class shaking off the hold of patriotism and jingoism and deciding to opt for class struggle; to follow Lenin by turning their hostility against their own oppressors rather than against foreign countries. After all, what had wrecked the Socialist International in 1914 was precisely the workers' failure to do this. What, in a sense, restored the soul of the international labour movement was that after 1917, in all the belligerent countries, the workers united to fight against the war, for peace, and for the Russian Revolution.

These are some of the reasons why Marxists perhaps failed to pay adequate attention to the problem of patriotism. So let me just remind you as an historian that patriotism cannot be neglected. The British working class has a long tradition of patriotism which was not always considered incompatible with a strong and militant class consciousness. In the history of Chartism and the great radical movements in the early nineteenth century we tend to stress the class consciousness. But when in the 1860s one of the few British workers actually to write about the working class, Thomas Wright the 'journeyman engineer', wrote a guide to the British working class for middle-class readers (because some of these workers were about to be given the vote), he gave an interesting thumbnail sketch of the various generations of workers he'd known as a skilled engineer.

When he came to the Chartist generation, the people who had been born in the early nineteenth century, he noted that they hated anything to do with the upper classes, and would not trust them an inch. They refused to have anything to do with what we would call the class enemy. At the same time he observed that they were strongly patriotic, strongly anti-foreign and particularly anti-French. They were people who had been brought up in their childhood in the anti-Napoleonic wars. Historians tend to stress the Jacobin element in British labour during these wars and not the anti-French element which also had popular roots. I'm simply saying you cannot write patriotism out of the scenario even in the most radical period of the English working class.

Throughout the nineteenth-century there was a very general admiration for the navy as a popular institution, much more so than the army. You can still see its mark in all the public houses named after Lord Nelson, a genuinely popular figure. The navy and our sailors were things that Britons, and certainly English people, took pride in. Incidentally, a good deal of nineteenth-century radicalism was built on an appeal not just to workers and other civilians but to soldiers. *Reynolds' News* and the old radical papers of those days were much read by the troops because they systematically took up the discontents of the professional soldiers. I don't know when this particular thing stopped, although in the Second World War the *Daily Mirror* succeeded in getting a vast circulation in the army for precisely the same reason. Both the Jacobin tradition and the majority anti-French tradition are thus part of English working-class history, though labour historians have stressed the one and played down the other.

Again, at the beginning of the First World War the mass patriotism of the working class was absolute genuine. It was not something that was simply being manufactured by the media. It didn't exclude respect for the minority within the labour movement who failed to share it. The anti-war elements and the pacifists within the labour movement were not ostracized by the organized workers. In this respect there was a great difference between the attitude of workers and of the petty bourgeois jingoists. Nevertheless, the fact remains that the largest single volunteer mass recruitment into any army ever, was that of British workers who joined up in 1914–15. The mines would have been empty but for the fact that the government eventually recognized that if it didn't have some miners, it wouldn't have any coal. After a couple of years many workers changed their mind about the war, but the initial surge of patriotism is something we have to remember. I'm not justifying these things, simply pointing to their existence and indicating that in looking at the history of the British working class and our present reality, we must come to terms with these facts, whether we like them or not.

The dangers of this patriotism always were and still are obvious, not least because it was and is enormously vulnerable to ruling-class jingoism, to anti-foreign nationalism and of course, in our days, to racism. These dangers are particularly great where patriotism can be separated from the other sentiments and aspirations of the working class, or even where it can be counterposed to them: where nationalism can be counterposed to social liberation. The reason why nobody pays much attention to Chartist jingoism, is that it was combined with and masked by an enormous militant class consciousness. It is when the two are separated, and this can be easily done, that the dangers are particularly obvious. Conversely, when the two go together to harness, they multiply not only the force of the working class but its capacity to place itself at the head of a broad coalition for social change, and they even give it the possibility of wresting hegemony from the class enemy.

That was why in the anti-fascist period of the 1930s, the Communist International launched the call to wrest away national traditions from the bourgeoisie, to capture the national flag so long waved by the right. So the French left tried with some success, to conquer, capture, or recapture both the tricolour and Joan of Arc. In this country we didn't pursue quite the same object, but we succeeded in doing something more important. As the anti-fascist war showed quite dramatically, the combination of patriotism with a genuine people's war proved to be politically radicalizing to an unprecedented degree. At the moment of his greater triumph, Mrs Thatcher's ancestor, Winston Churchill, the unquestioned leader of a victorious war, and a much greater victory than the Falklands, found himself, to his enormous surprise, pushed aside because the people who had fought that war, and fought it patriotically, found themselves radicalized by it. The combination of a radicalized working class movement and a peoples' movement behind it proved enormously effective and powerful. Michael Foot may be blamed for thinking too much in terms of 'Churchillian' memories of 1940, of Britain standing alone of the anti-fascist war and all the rest of it, and obviously these echoes were there in Labour's reaction to the Falklands. But let us not forget that our 'Churchillian' memories are not just of patriotic glory, but also of victory against reaction both abroad and at home: of Labour triumph and the defeat of Churchill. It's difficult to conceive this in 1982 but as an historian I must remind you of it. It is dangerous to leave patriotism exclusively to the right.

At present it is very difficult for the left to recapture patriotism. One of the most sinister lessons of the Falklands is the ease with which the Thatcherites captured the patriotic upsurge which initially was in no sense confined to political Conservatives let alone to Thatcherite ones. We recall the ease with which non-jingos could be tagged, if not actually as anti-patriotic, then at least as 'soft on the Argies'; the ease with which the union jack could be mobilized against domestic enemies as well as foreign enemies. Remember the photograph of the troops coming back on the troopships, with a banner saying 'Call off the rail strike or we'll call an air strike'. Here lies the long-term significance of the Falklands in British political affairs.

It is a sign of very great danger. Jingoism today is particularly strong because it acts as a sort of compensation for the feelings of decline, demoralization, and inferiority, which most people in this country feel, including a lot of workers. This feeling is intensified by economic crisis. Symbolically jingoism helps people feel that Britain isn't just foundering, that it can still do and achieve something, can be taken seriously, can, as they say, be 'Great' Britain. It is symbolic because in fact Thatcherite jingoism hasn't achieved anything practical, and can't achieve anything practical. *Rule Britannia* has once again, and I think for the first time since 1914, become something like a National Anthem. It would be worth studying one day why, until the Falklands period, *Rule Britannia* had become a piece of musical archaeology and why it has ceased to be so. At the very moment when Britain patently no longer rules either the waves or an empire, that song has resurfaced and has undoubtedly hit a certain nerve among people who sing it. It is not only because we have won a little war, involving few casualties, fought far away against foreigners whom we can no longer even beat at football, and that this has cheered people up, as if we had won a World Cup with guns. But has it done anything else in the long run? It is difficult to see that it has, or could have, achieved anything else.

Yet there is a danger. As a boy I lived some formative and very young years in the Weimar Republic, among another people who felt themselves defeated, losing their old certainties and their old moorings, relegated in the international league and pitied by foreigners. Add depression and mass unemployment to that and what you got then was Hitler. Now we shan't get fascism of the old kind. But the danger of a populist, radical right moving even further to the right is patent. That danger is particularly great because the left is today divided and demoralized and above all because vast masses of the British, or anyway the English, have lost hope and confidence in the political processes and in the politicians: any politicians. Mrs Thatcher's main trump card is that people say she isn't like a politician. Today with 3,500,000 unemployed, 45 per cent of the electors at Northfield, 65 per cent of the electors at Peckham, don't bother to vote. In Peckham 41 per cent of the electorate voted for Labour in 1974, 34 per cent in 1979, and 19.1 per cent today.

I'm not talking of votes cast but of the total number of people in the constituency. In Northfield, which is in the middle of the devastation zone of the British motor industry, 41 per cent voted for Labour in 1974, 32 per cent in 1979 and 20 per cent today.

The main danger lies in this de-politicization, which reflects a disillusionment with politics born of a sense of impotence. What we see today is not a substantial rise in the support for Thatcher and the Thatcherites. The Falklands episode may have temporarily made a lot of Britons feels better, though the 'Falklands factor' is almost certainly a diminishing asset for the Tories; but it has not made much difference to the basic hopelessness, apathy and defeatism of so many in this country, the feeling that we can't do much about our fate. If the government seems to hold its support better than might be expected, it is because people (quite mistakenly) don't put the blame for the present miserable condition of the country on Thatcher, but, more or less vaguely, on factors beyond her or any government's control. If Labour hasn't so far regained enough support – though it may still just do so – it isn't only because of its internal divisions, but also, largely, because many workers don't really have much belief in any politicians' promises to overcome the slump and the long-term crisis of the British economy. So why vote for one lot rather than another? Too many people are losing faith in politics, including their own power to do much about it.

But just suppose a saviour were to appear on a white horse? None is likely to, but just suppose someone were to appeal to the emotions, to get that adrenalin flowing by mobilizing against some foreigners outside or inside the country, perhaps by another little war, which might, under present circumstances, find itself turning into the big war, which, as we all know, would be the last of the wars? It is possible. I don't think that saviour is going to be Thatcher, and to that extent I can end on a slightly up-beat note. Free enterprise, to which she is committed, is not a winner, as fascist propaganda recognized in the 1930s. You can't win by saying: 'Let the rich get richer and to hell with the poor.' Thatcher's prospects are less good than Hitler's were, for three years after he had come to power there was not much unemployment left in Germany, whereas three years after Thatcher came to power unemployment is higher than ever before and likely to go on climbing. She is whistling in the dark. She can still be defeated. But patriotism and jingoism have been used once to change the political situation in her favour and they can be used again. We must be on the lookout. Desperate governments of the right will try anything.

6

Labour's Lost Millions (1983)

Five years ago in *Marxism Today* the question was raised whether 'the forward march of Labour' had been halted. This led to a long debate, later elaborated into a book. Looking back on this debate from late 1983, two things strike me about it: first, the sheer refusal of some of the left to look unwelcome facts in the face, even though they were already obvious to any unblinkered observer, and second, the failure of even the gloomiest among us to appreciate the rate and distance of Labour's imminent retreat. The Labour vote, while slowly eroding over the years, had not usually dropped by more than a couple of hundred thousand between elections, win or lose. There was no reason to suppose that it would suddenly collapse.

Yet this is exactly what has happened. And before some of us have quite managed to retreat into an imaginary world behind the screens which self-delusion is already erecting to shelter us from the grim sight of reality, it is important to remind ourselves just how terrible a beating the labour movement took at the 1983 election. It is not just that Labour lost one in five of its already low number of votes. It is the massive defection of supporters of *all* classes, ages and genders.

In 1983 Labour is larger than other parties only among unskilled/semi-skilled workers, the unemployed, and trade unionists, *but had majority support among none of these groups*, not even the unskilled/semi-skilled workers and the unemployed. They have lost support since 1979 among all three. Only 35 per cent of skilled workers voted Labour: down by more than a quarter. Only 39 per cent of trade unionists supported the party they had founded: a similar drop. Women had shown a slight swing to Labour in 1979, but in 1983 they abandoned the party at a greater rate than men. 41 per cent of the young (first-time voters aged 18–22) had chosen Labour in 1979, a modest enough result for a party which ought to be able to inspire young people. But in 1983 the situation is quite disastrous. Only 17 per cent of first-time voters chose Labour, 3 per cent less than chose the Alliance, 11 per cent less than the Tories – while almost *half* did not bother to vote at all. Of those who bothered to vote only 29 per cent put their cross against Labour candidates.

In short, there is not a glimmer of comfort in the results of this election. As has been correctly said: 'The Labour vote remains largely working-class; but the working class has ceased to be largely Labour.' The surviving stock of Labour voters consists largely of people living in Scotland and the North (but Wales is no longer the stronghold it was), or in decaying inner cities, of people employed in the traditional and rapidly declining industries of Britain's past and/or in the public sector, and is more apt than not to be elderly, or black, and council tenants. The most that can be said is that the geographical concentration of the Labour vote makes it likely that the party will continue to send a substantial block of members into the Commons even if it sinks further, and that it will still be in a position to control a number of important local authorities. If this were not so, it could *already* have been reduced to a couple of dozen or so seats, like the Liberal–SDP Alliance, which, after all, has a comparable, if slightly smaller number of votes. In any case, on present showing, Labour is living on declining assets.

The disaster which has struck the party is underlined by the fact that Thatcherite Toryism has done quite poorly itself. True, it has held far more of its 1979 support than it could have been expected to do, but it lost ground nevertheless. The Tory vote is lower than in 1979, much lower than under Heath, and it has mobilized just under 31 per cent of the total electorate, counting those who did not want or bother to vote at all. This is a smaller share of voters than at any time since 1923. The triumph of Thatcher is the by-product of the defeat of Labour. That is the measure of the task which now confronts us.

The long-term reasons for Labour's decline, discussed at length in the debate on *The Forward March of Labour Halted?*, are clear enough. But while they suggested that Labour's decline would continue, unless the party did some drastic rethinking, they did not suggest an imminent catastrophe. Arguments rage about why Labour fell apart so dramatically, but unfortunately most of them are superficial, and a lot of them are self-serving, wishful dreams, and quite unverifiable. There is not much point in arguing the toss about the precise importance of the redistribution of seats, the anti-Labour bias in the media, or the effect of polls, about the lack of money and the competence of our campaign propaganda, the image of the party leadership, the weakness of constituency organization, or the visibly growing despair and demoralization of

Labour's national spokesmen as the campaign advanced. Actually some of these weaknesses were not so much contributory causes as symptoms of the party's impending defeat. There is no point at all in arguing whether candidates of the right or left did significantly better or worse. So far as one can tell, whether candidates did (relatively) well depended overwhelmingly on the location and social composition of the constituency. The chances of any Labour candidate, right or left, in the industrial towns of southern England, which we had once won and should have won again, proved to be virtually zero. The chances of a Labour candidate in Strathclyde were good, whether or not he or she supported Tony Benn. The party looked like losing before the campaign started, and it was clobbered.

Only two things can and must be said about the election, and said very firmly. The first is that far too many people in the opposition parties were *not seriously trying to defeat Thatcher*, whatever their official rhetoric. Perhaps initially, after 1979, many believed that the combination of mass unemployment on so vast a scale and an economic policy which looked as though it simply could not work, was automatically bound to put paid to a government that was widely disliked and distrusted even within the Tory establishment. But as time went on, it became increasingly clear that the opposition parties were engaged in a civil war rather than in fighting the right. They acted as though the next election was already lost in advance, and indeed I have heard people on the left privately say as much. The fight was about the nature of the opposition to the second Thatcher government, or the next-but-one election.

On the right wing of the opposition, the Social Democratic Party knew quite well that its foundation weakened the major force of anti-Thatcherism, the Labour Party. That, after all, was its primary intention. The SDP–Liberal Alliance did not seriously expect to form a government, or aim to. Its major strategic object was and is to hold the balance between Tory and Labour, and then sell its support to a government for the price of proportional representation, which would give it a permanent and substantial parliamentary presence and decisive bargaining strength. As it happens, its very success in weakening Labour has made this impossible for the time being: governments with huge majorities don't need to bargain.

But it also became more and more evident that the main question at issue on the left was not: what government? but: what Labour Party? To put it brutally, for many, a Thatcher government was preferable to a reformist Labour government. Since very few, even on the wilder fringes of the left, genuinely believe that Denis Healey is actually worse than Norman Tebbit, various theories were invented to delude ourselves. The old-style Labour Party could not win. A proper socialist Labour Party could win, because somewhere out there, millions of radical leftwing voters were abstaining, waiting only to flock to candidates and programmes of the left. The election was lost anyway, so it didn't much matter that potential Labour voters were puzzled and demoralized by the sight of party leaders and activists tearing each others' guts out in public for years on issues difficult to see the point of. And so on. However, the basic fact cannot be denied, that a large body of the left acted as though another Labour government like the ones we have had before from time to time since 1945 was not just unsatisfactory, but worse than no Labour government. And this means that it would be worse than the only alternative government on offer, which was Mrs Thatcher's.

This attitude raises grave problems of political judgment. Not only did it (as is now totally obvious) grossly misread the attitude of the voters to the Labour Party, but it also, and more dangerously, under-estimates the historical novelty of Thatcherism and the seriousness of the threat it represents. Past Tory governments were based on the principle for avoiding class confrontation in order to prevent a radicaliz-ation of the working class, which represented the substantial majority of the British people. Therefore, with occasional, mainly verbal, conces-sions to their backwoods-people, they shared a basic approach to policy with the 'moderate' reformist leadership of Labour ('Butskellism'). Give or take a few changes in emphasis, and allowing for the growing problems of the British economy and the gradual obsolescence of the reformist structures built between 1944 and 1948, until Thatcher, intervals of Conservative government did not make any serious differ-ence to the prospects of Labour governments.

This is no longer so. Thatcherism is committed to a radical and reactionary change in British capitalism, and indeed in the British political system. It is pushing ahead with this new, militant, and formid-able policy of class struggle from above, and the dismantling of the past reformist consensus with all the more confidence, because it has discovered that the weakening of and divisions within the working class and the self-ruination of the Labour Party make it apparently much less risky than the old Toryism had supposed. Thatcherism aims to transform Britain irreversibly in its own way, not just to keep the system on an even keel. To defeat it is therefore more than the routine demand of any opposition when it happens not to be in government. It is the condition of survival for a decent Britain, and of such chances as exist of advanc-ing to a better society.

The second point which must be hammered home is that Thatcherism won because the anti-Thatcher majority was split. And it was split because great masses of people who had previously voted Labour, who would have found it inconceivable *not* to vote Labour, or who might have been confidently expected to vote Labour chose, on grounds which seemed good to them, not only to stay at home but to vote for other parties. For the first time since the original decline of the Liberal Party, from which Labour benefited, British workers think they have a choice between rival anti-Tory parties or political alignments. The anti-Tory vote is roughly split down the middle (28 per cent, 26 per cent). So long as this is so, the chances of defeating Thatcherism must be remote, unless there is a really spectacular collapse of the Tory vote in favour of one opposition group to the left of Conservatism. For, given the approximately even split between the two parts of anti-Tory vote, the Conservatives could drop about a quarter of their total vote and still come first past the post.

It is vital to keep this point in mind for the next five years, because the prospect of defeating Thatcher hinges on it, whatever else the labour movement does to recover. If, at the next election, Thatcherism is everywhere opposed by two or more candidates competing for each other's votes, the Tories can look forward to being in power well into the 1990s. Some way of uniting the majority of the British people which is opposed to Thatcherism must be found.

This will be difficult, both for subjective and objective reasons. The mere suggestion that Labour and Social Democrats/Alliance might come to an electoral arrangement is likely to produce apoplexy on both sides, whether or not it is today a realistic proposition. That is natural enough. Relations between the two sides are unlikely to become more relaxed, since both will spend much of the next years fighting for each other's supporters. Moreover, it is already clear that each side will have trouble maintaining effective unity – of right and left within the Labour Party, between Liberals and Social Democrats, as well as within each of these far from united parties. But the issue of electoral unity will have to be faced nevertheless.

More seriously, it may be misleading to assume that all anti-Tory opinion, whatever the differences, is at least objectively united by anti-Thatcherism. This is to underestimate the basic shift in British politics which Thatcherism has systematically set out to achieve – and has already gone some way to achieving. Take John Maynard Keynes, whose ideas symbolized for a generation the underlying reformist consensus of British big business and the leadership of the Tory, Liberal, and Labour Parties. In this year, the centenary of his birth, he is almost a forgotten man. The mixed economy, the welfare state, economic management through a large public sector, the 'acceptable face of capitalism', stability through arrangements between state, business, and official labour, are out. This does not mean that there is much sympathy outside the Thatcherite sector of the Tory Party for what Andrew Gamble has called 'the blooming of a thousand exotic ideological flowers and rank weeds' which flourish on the radical right, and find know-nothing tycoons, ambitious intellectuals, and media hacks to cultivate them. But it does mean that much of what started as a purely Thatcherite speciality is now widely shared outside the Tory Party: for instance hostility to public bureaucracy, to state economic management (identified with 'state socialism'), to unions, a rabid anti-Marxism, as well as a reversion to pseudo-imperial flag-waving. From now on there is a Thatcherite element in the opposition (one thinks of David Owen), as well as a Thatcherite government. To this extent it is not enough to say: all we need to do is to unite the 57 per cent who voted against the Government. Nevertheless, the problem of uniting the majority remains fundamental.

What must be done to give Labour a chance of making a comeback? Two things. Labour must, of course, recover the support of the working class as a whole, but Labour must also become, once again, the party of *all* who want democracy, a better and fairer society, irrespective of the class pigeon-hole into which pollsters and market researchers put them: in short, to use the old Labour phrase, 'all workers by hand and brain' – and that includes not only the vast majority of Britons who earn wages and salaries. It is an error to see this as a matter of making opportunistic concessions to win votes. There is nothing opportunistic about the belief that a nuclear arms race is the way to disaster, and in saying so Labour is already appealing for support across class lines. It is not opportunistic to believe that we can and should appeal to *all* women and *all* young people, even if we may not expect much success today among the ladies who attend Ascot, or among the Sloane Rangers. (But some of us remember that in the 1930s anti-fascism had a mass base in such strongholds of the ruling class as Oxbridge.) It is not even opportunistic to take account of quite reasonable demands of bodies of people who are not satisfied that at present they are adequately met by Labour – of home-owners, of people who are dissatisfied with their children's schooling, or those who are worried about law and order. For one thing, they include a lot of workers.

Anyway, Labour was never *only* a class party. Britain in the past was so overwhelmingly a country of manual workers that it is often forgotten that Labour marched forward by mobilizing not only the proletariat as a proletariat, but a wide *coalition of forces*. It mobilized the women, the minority nations and ethnic minorities of the United Kingdom (except in Ulster); the Welsh, the Scots, the Irish in Britain, the Jews. It mobilized the intellectuals, academic or otherwise. It took over most of the heritage of nineteenth-century liberalism, which had exercised a similar wide appeal in its day. And until quite recently it has shown a continued capacity to win non-workers. For instance, as late as 1979, the minority among the higher managerial and professional, and the lower manageri- al and administrative groups which supported Labour (about 20 per cent and 25 per cent respectively), was still distinctly on the increase. We cannot abandon this tradition of being a broad people's party, for if Labour were to recover *only* the support of the manual working class, it would probably no longer be enough to give it victory, given the decline in its numbers and the rate of deindustrialization.

Nevertheless, unless Labour can once again become the party of the majority of the working class it has no future, except as a coalition of minority pressure groups and interests. There is only a modest future for a party which represents only such groups and social forces on the decline. If Labour cannot get back the sort of communities represented by Stevenage, or Harlow, or Swindon, or Slough, we can forget about the British or any other realistic road to socialism.

Why has Labour lost these and many other places? Certainly not simply because of the numerical decline of the working class and the growing sectionalism which, as Thatcher realized, can divide its votes. The long-term erosion of Labour's traditional position as *the* workers' party cannot explain the spectacular loss of 20 per cent of Labour's vote in four years. Nor will it do to blame the workers, or any one or more sections of them. Millions of people who might have been expected to vote Labour, abandoned the party in 1983, not because they suddenly ceased to see themselves as workers, but because they felt the party did not represent their interests and aspirations adequately or effectively. The solution lies not in changing the workers, but the party.

The body of party activists and more or less fully engaged politicians (which is now very different in social composition from the body of Labour voters), has been slow to recognize what is implied by the need for the party to change. For, in spite of what historians, sociologists, and political scientists were already saying in the 1970s, they still assumed that for most workers the party was 'our team', which they supported the way one supports Arsenal or Spurs, irrespective of what happens on the pitch. Sixty per cent or so of workers identified with Labour, and until the late 1960s almost all of them would vote Labour, rain or shine – though of course that wasn't enough. Naturally this meant that these workers assumed that Labour, broadly speaking, stood for what they wanted and would act in their interests when in government, but they were little bothered about the details of the programme, which few of them read, or about the embittered divisions, purges, and personal rivalries which have plagued the party almost since its foundation, or about the image and charisma of its leaders. Labour's greatest triumph was scored under Attlee, who had the charisma of an average building society branch manager, against Churchill, who had star quality to give away.

While this was so, it did not seem to matter too much, in the short run, what happened among the few hundred Labour politicians and the few tens of thousands of Labour activists and militants[1] who fought over party constitution, policy, and strategy, since at least ten million supporters would cheer on the team, never mind who was appointed as manager. In the long run, of course, it mattered a great deal, since reversing Labour's retreat and the prospects of a better Britain depended on the outcome. But, until the 1980s, few seriously believed that the usual solid minimum support would not line up behind any candidate, any leadership, or any programme that carried the label of the workers' party. After all, as R.H. Tawney had once said, solidarity was the name of the working-class game. The question was not whether this basic support could be relied on, but whether it was enough.

It was *not* enough. And, above all, it can no longer be relied on. The working class has changed. The country has changed. The situation has changed. And, let us not forget, the party too has changed and quite a few of its old supporters do not recognize themselves so readily in it. If these changes were not very substantial, Labour could still hope to poll 60 per cent of the vote in Wales and win all but four seats, as it did in 1966, instead of being down to 37 per cent of the vote and 12 seats out of 38 in 1983. And Wales, let us remember, was a country in which everything combined to create a Labour and socialist stronghold: a massive, organized, and militant working class, national sentiment, almost universal anti-Toryism and democratic egalitarianism, a tradition of peace movements, a passion for education, and, not least, an inspiring roll-call of great names, socialist and Communist, which belonged to the valleys: Keir Hardie, A.J. Cook, Arthur Horner, Aneurin Bevan, Michael Foot. But all this has not been enough.

Because Labour activists have been reluctant to admit this, a widening gap has developed between themselves and their supporters who can still be mobilized by the call of the old bugles, and those who no longer can be. During the election campaign enthusiastic meetings of the first lot cheered a party manifesto designed for them – it was, in fact, practically unreadable for anyone else – and failed to notice that the other lot, which consisted of millions of workers, were simply not convinced of Labour's case. They needed reasons for voting which persuaded *them*, not just flags behind which to rally.

Concretely, they needed convincing under four heads. First, that they actually wanted what Labour stood for. The old words are no longer enough. Thus for convinced socialists it is enough to call for socialism, but not for men and women who associate the word, no doubt with the enthusiastic assistance of the media, with more state power and public bureaucracy, which they have learned to distrust, with more nationaliz- ation, of which we already seem to have plenty, and – let us admit it – with countries in which workers are less well-off and less free than in the non-socialist countries with which they are most familiar. We have to show once again how and why the kind of fair, free, socially just, and prosperous society they want requires socialism.

Second, that Labour's policy is not only desirable, but realistic. Like it or not, we must answer Thatcherite and similar arguments which have by now spread widely ('who is to pay for it all?' etc,) in terms which they understand. We cannot afford to promise to create a few million jobs in five years if we cannot convince people, however much they would love to see it happen, that any government is capable of achieving this under present world conditions. And in fact, we did not convince them.

Third, that Labour is the party of all workers, not merely of some sections of them. No doubt we had a policy which appealed to tenants, but the many workers who are buying their own homes, or want to, also need to feel that Labour has a policy for them. And the party, in turn, must be as aware as the workers themselves are that the sectional interests of some groups are not merely different from others, but sometimes in conflict. This creates genuinely knotty problems which cannot simply be waved away.

Finally, and this is perhaps the most difficult task, that Labour has a chance. If workers were to stop seeing Labour as the alternative to Thatcherism, even more of them would vote, with or without regret, for candidates or parties who seem to have the best chance of beating the Tories. Already there are too many seats where Labour is the third party, and often a rather poor third. But the future of the party cannot rest on this or any other tactical or pragmatic appeal. The Liberal Party has survived, in spite of its negligible electoral prospects over many years, because it never lost a substantial body of people who would vote Liberal regardless of practical considerations or advantage: because they believed in liberalism. The most dangerous symptom of Labour's sick- ness is that in 1983 its vote went to pieces in many places, most notably in England, where it had never had much chance of electing more than the odd councillor, but where men and women nevertheless voted Labour out of conviction: because they thought Labour was right. But if they are to do so again, the party must be such that they can believe in it again.

All this requires some fundamental rethinking of Labour's struggle and objectives, for the situation is desperately serious. The danger, especially on the left, is not only that the activists may be unaware of their and the party's isolation from ordinary people, but that they may not care. They may actually give up the struggle for the workers as a whole, not to mention other sections of the people who do not happen to agree with the 'correct' policy or the way the party is run. They may choose their supporters to fit their convictions, in which case it is likely that the others will look elsewhere. For instance, they may see their most congenial constituency as 'the dispossessed', in 'the centre of a big decaying city', cosmopolitan and racially mixed, and look for a parliamentary seat in preference in such a place. 'It would be a mistake to stand in a safe seat with a solid white skilled working class . . . I wouldn't be happy there anyway' (Ken Livingstone). Would it be surprising if the sort of people who have formed 'the historic spine of the Labour Party' (Bea Campbell) would not be happy with such a candidate either? The strength of the labour movement has always been that it could represent *all* parts of the working class – both Stepney and the Fife coalfield – and it did not discriminate against any. If Ken Livingstone, who is one of the ablest, most prominent, most attractive and strategically placed figures in the party, feels really at ease with only some kinds of the inhabitants of Greater London – is it not reasonable to fear that it will be difficult for him to realize his own and his party's political potential in Britain's greatest city?[2]

Or again, how can we say: 'Though it would be foolish to ignore *wholly* the view of the electorate, it would be fatal if the Labour Party now started to fish around for a set of policies that upset no one and thus changed nothing'?[3] Are we going to be in a position to change anything if we do not pay attention to the 16 per cent of trade unionists who have stopped voting Labour since 1974, to the 71 per cent of youngsters who voted, but refused to choose Labour, to the 72 per cent of women who voted Tory or Alliance? To pay attention to them is not to betray socialism, but an essential condition of any likely socialist advance in this country. May there not be good as well as bad reasons why they have stopped looking to Labour?

Every traditional labour and socialist mass movement in the west has seen a certain erosion of its traditional support since the 1950s, and all for very similar reasons. The Labour Party is a particularly dramatic case, but not the only one. All have been faced with the task of doing something about it. Much the worst option is that proposed in some quarters of the Labour left (or the ultra-left which has colonized the empty spaces in the organizations of the movement left by the withdrawal of the masses from the party). This is to establish a 'correct' position and wait for the British people to recognize how wrong they are in not agreeing with it. As for those who show their disagreement by voting with their feet or the ballot-papers, good riddance to bad rubbish. History is full of sects, both religious and political, who have taken such a view, and are still waiting – even if they haven't, like the old ILP after the 1930s, practically disappeared from sight. There is no future in turning the Labour Party into a body of this kind. It would just go on declining, until in the end it risked even that unique asset of British labour, a single trade union movement affiliated to a single political party. It could not even turn into the clear-headed and unified socialist party we would all want, because its various left components, now united against the right, would quite surely go on battling each other to the death over their various and conflicting ideas of what constituted the 'correct' positions.

Two other strategies have been tried, with greater prospects of success. The first is what may be called 'neo-socialism', as it exists in France and Spain. This implies abandoning the traditional character of such parties as mass parties, based on mass organizations, especially those of the working class, and turning them into common electoral fronts of all who are, for one reason or another, opposed to reaction, interested in reforms, and prepared to sympathize with progressive appeals. This strategy has certainly succeeded in restoring the fortunes of parties which had fallen much lower than the Labour Party, for example, the French Socialist Party, which was in steep decline fifteen years ago, and the Spanish Socialist Party, which was virtually a shell company ten years ago. It has proved capable of striking electoral triumphs, some of them with strong leftwing programmes, as in France and Greece. Moreover, Mitterrand's government in France has done much to carry out its programme, so far as this has been within its power.

The weakness of this strategy lies in the instability of the political support gained in this manner (this is also evident in France), the lack of activity and feedback from the citizens, the undoubted temptations of opportunism which it encourages, and the lack of any organic base for the policies of such parties. They may sometimes be radical, but they do not have to be, and are not even very likely to be. If socialists can welcome and sympathize with Mitterrand in France, they can at best retain an open mind about the government of Felipe Gonzalez in Spain. They will almost certainly take a dim view of the (mainly anti-left) manoeuvres of the Portuguese Socialist Party of Mario Soares, and an even dimmer view of the combination of backstairs dealing, corruption, mafia tactics, demagogy, and opportunism by which the Italian Socialist Party of Bettino Craxi has tried to rebuild itself. The Labour Party can certainly learn *something* from the experience of neo-socialist parties, notably that elections can be won without necessarily compromising one's programme, and that comebacks are possible – but this is not a model which invites uncritical imitation.

The other strategy has no equally striking triumphs (unless we count the splendid comeback of the Swedish Socialist Party under Palme, in alliance with the Communists and with a good programme), but is more immediately relevant; for the Italian Communist Party (PCI), which can serve as illustration, *is and wishes to remain* a classical mass socialist labour party, attempting to rally the widest range of forces around its essential core of the organized working class. It has tried to do so through an era when Italian society has been spectacularly transformed – including its working class – and against powerful competition from both left and right, not to mention under conditions of systematic exclusion from national government. Yet it has gained ground over the decades, and while it dropped back a little between 1976 and 1980, it has been stronger than ever before since the middle 1970s. It has long been the unquestioned second party in the country, and is today running the Christian Democrats, the party of government since the war, closer than ever in the past (30 per cent against 33 per cent). This is not an unimpressive record.

It has succeeded not because its basic body of support has been unswervingly solid, but because it has known how to hold that loyalty, win back some or all of its losses, and extend its support to new social strata and groups, in new conditions. Since 1950 it has from time to time lost, and recovered, much working-class support in the northern industrial cities. In recent decades it lost quite heavily in the more backward south. Its most solid stronghold, central Italy (Tuscany, Emilia, Umbria), strikingly, in the region of Naples, where it has also recaptured the industrial zones it had lost. It is today the first party, ahead of the Christian Democrats, in almost all the major cities of Italy, north and south. Its most solid stronghold, central Italy (Tuscany, Emilia, Umbria) has changed out of recognition socially and economically. It is today a prosperous belt of dynamic, small and medium industrial enterprise, as well as commercial farming, and is probably the spearhead of Italy's economic development: the sort of area to which, if it were in California, Thatcherite propaganda would point as model of a go-ahead economy. If this zone is still as solid and red as ever, it is not because its inhabitants are blindly loyal, but because the party has shown, largely through its policy in local and regional government (which is recognized as a model – Bologna must be one of the best administered cities in Europe), that the left can have a policy for this kind of development. In Bologna and Florence even businessmen would be worried if the Christian Democrats took over: for one thing, because they would be strikingly more inefficient and corrupt.

The contrast here is not only with the Labour Party, but also with some other Communist parties which have failed to halt the recently accelerating erosion of their mass base among workers and intellectuals, as in France. The PCI has had its share of mistakes and poor analyses, and its own record of failing, from time to time, to keep in touch with changes in its own country, including in the working class. But it has not lived in and on its past; it recognized realities and social changes when they became inescapable, it has never written off its former supporters, and it has avoided sectarianism above all. It has never forgotten that the party of the working class must also be the party of the people. Its policy is certainly open to serious criticism, and this has not been stifled within its ranks or even within its leadership. But it has, at least, been able to demonstrate that the way of a classical socialist labour party in the late twentieth century does not necessarily have to be downhill.

Yet the PCI, and indeed practically all other socialist and Communist parties in countries with real elections, have lost, or never had, the major asset enjoyed by the Labour Party in the past, namely the capacity to win an election and form a government single-handed. That is why the arguments about the policy of Labour governments and the British road to socialism have had a unique urgency in this country. Parties which are incapable of winning single-party majorities (if only because their electoral systems make this practically impossible) can speculate about the prospects of socialist transformation, but under conditions of democracy their governments will almost invariably be at the mercy of coalition partners who will act as brakes on them.

The ability to form a single-handed socialist government is not, of course, enough. In the first place, the best government today is at the mercy of the world situation – for instance in economic affairs. No single nation has any real control over this, except perhaps the USA which can unload its problems on other and weaker economies abroad. The transformation of society today, whatever its shape, must have an international dimension. In the second place, the best socialist government has to be re-elected. It must maintain support. The idea that socialism can be irreversibly installed in five years is a fantasy, and the idea that socialist governments, once established, should abolish genuine elections is, or should be, unacceptable. Still, the position of the Labour Party in the past was unusually favourable, and hence disappointment with the performance of Labour governments is understandably, and justifiably, sharp.

The immediate and crucial question before us is whether Labour, which seems to have lost this unique position, can regain it. If the party cannot do that, then it will be useless to console ourselves with the thought that a large permanent minority has voted for a sounder socialist programme than in the days of Wilson, or will stop that programme being betrayed if there is another Labour government. For there will be none. If a minority Labour Party gets into government, it will be on terms negotiated with some other partner – Liberals, SDP, or whoever – and by their consent. If Labour refuses to enter government on those terms, as it reasonably might, it will be a permanent opposition. The perspectives of such an opposition, like it or not, cannot be to change society, but only to make it less intolerable. It will have no option but to be, in practice, 'reformist', or to make noise, or to wait for a near-miracle.

This means that Labour will have to win back those who switched from Labour to the Alliance, those who stayed at home, and a lot of those who are increasingly opting out of politics. Or, alternatively, it will have to learn how to lead a broad front of other parties or their supporters into backing Labour's policy. This is not impossible. But it means, first of all, understanding why the people who left us or stayed away did not wish to vote Labour. If we are to lead them forward, we have to get them to vote or support Labour for reasons which seem good to *them*, even if we do not like their reasons. That, by the way, is how socialists once built the Labour Party and eventually got it committed to a socialist objective. They started with a working class and others who were Liberals, Conservatives, or something else and who did not vote for Labour because no more than a small minority were attracted by socialism or knew what it was. They learned as they struggled – but the socialists were with them to help the learning. Rebuilding Labour, or building a broad front around Labour, will once again be like that. We think the masses need Labour, but if we ask them to come to us on *our* terms, they won't. Not any more. Then the chances are that they will never find out what Labour could do for them.

And neither will we.

Notes

1. P. Whiteley, 'The decline of Labour's Local Party Membership and Electoral Base, 1945–79', in D. Kavanagh, ed. *The Politics of The Labour Party*, London 1982, p. 115, estimates the real number of Party activists in the whole of Britain at around 55,000 in 1978.

2. The quotations in this paragraph are from his interview with Bea Campbell in *City Limits*, 1–7 July 1983, p. 10.

3. Tony Banks, MP, in the *Guardian*, 17 August 1983 (emphasis added).

Labour: Rump or Rebirth? (1984)

Marxists and other leftwing socialists – for many of them can hardly be regarded as Marxists, even when, as today, they advertise themselves as such – have never been happy about the Labour Party. Before 1918, it did not claim to be socialist at all. Since then it has, but many will agree with Ralph Miliband that 'it is reasonable to see [labourism] as an ideology of social reform, within the framework of capitalism, with no serious ambitions of transcending that framework, whatever ritual obeisances to "socialism" might be performed by party leaders on suitable occasions.'[1] Or, to be more polite, that what most Labour leaders have meant by 'socialism' is rather different from what is in the minds of socialists.

Consequently the left has, historically, had two views about the Labour Party. Some have written it off and attempted, from time to time, to form another, truly socialist, party of the working class in competition with it. This appears still to be the position of some Marxist groups such as the Workers' Revolutionary Party and Socialist Workers' Party, and was also that of independent socialists like Miliband who argued that

> the hope of the Left to transform the Labour Party . . . was illusory, and that, far from representing a short cut to the creation of a mass socialist party in Britain (which has never existed), it was in fact a dead end in which British socialists had been trapped for many decades – in fact since the Labour Party came into being.[2]

History has shown this to be a non-starter. None of the organizations which have followed this line between 1900 and 1983, from the Social Democratic Federation via the Communist Party at some periods of its history, and the Independent Labour Party in the 1930s, has got

anywhere. Nor do the present advocates of an independent socialist/
Marxist mass party look promising. In Britain there has been only one
genuine mass party of the left, based on the working class and its
movement: the Labour Party.

Most socialists, and today the great majority of Marxists, have
accepted this as a fact of life. Like it or not, the future of socialism is
through the Labour Party. This has been the basis of Communist Party
policy since its programme *The British Road to Socialism* in the early
1950s, and was implicit in its policy since the middle 1930s. Other
Marxists have moved into the Labour Party either as individuals or, like
the Militant Tendency, as collective 'entrists', thus, incidentally, making
the Communist Party's long-held hope of winning collective and open
affiliation to the Labour Party difficult to the point of impracticability. A
great body of socialists have always regarded the Labour Party as their
natural home and operated as a left within it.

However, there is a fundamental distinction within this body of
Labour-oriented socialists, and it lies at the root of the arguments about
the Forward March of Labour, presently being conducted with much
passion and some bad temper. Some on the left – probably a majority –
believe that the time has come when the Labour Party itself can be
transformed into the truly socialist mass party which we would all prefer.
To quote the admirably lucid Ralph Miliband again, their scenario is:

> the continuation of the struggles in which the left has been engaged, with the
> purpose of achieving predominance and turning the Labour Party into a
> socialist party free from the constriction hitherto imposed on it by its leaders.
> It must be presumed that many leading figures in the Labour Party would then
> want to leave it and seek political homes elsewhere. . . . In fact it would be
> essential that such people *should* leave the Labour Party, for just as the left
> makes life difficult for a leadership which is opposed to it, so could deter-
> mined right and centre parliamentarians make life difficult for a party in which
> the left had acquired predominance.[3]

The Labour Party might lose some members but would gain others. It
might even lose unions which wished to disaffiliate from a party that
went beyond labourism, but only in some cases.

The other view – which I share – holds that this is a dangerous
daydream. Certainly the future lies in a Labour Party which moves to
the left, not only under the influence of the socialists within and outside
it, but because its members and supporters recognize the need for it to
do so – just as formerly Liberal and non-political Labour supporters
came to see themselves as socialists earlier this century. But Marxists
must begin by taking the Labour Party as it has actually come into being
and developed to be the mass party of the British left. In the first place,

it has not developed as an ideologically homogeneous or unified party, but as *a broad class and progressive front*, containing a wide range of views from the centre to the revolutionary left. In fact, Lenin (whose *Leftwing Communism, an Infantile Disorder* repays careful reading even today) stressed 'the unique character of the British Labour Party, the very structure of which is so unlike the ordinary political party on the continent.'[4]

In the second place, and even more to the point, it has unfortunately *never* been true that the only thing which has prevented the Labour Party from being the party of our dreams, was the 'constriction hitherto imposed on it by its leaders'. The British workers, even the workers politically advanced enough to join a party committed to socialism and to defend its commitment against the Gaitskellite attacks on 'Clause IV', were never an army of leftwing socialists held back only by blind loyalty to rightwing leaders who betrayed their faith at every opportunity. The millions of Labour voters fitted this image even less. They have indeed often been misled and betrayed by those they trusted – not least by Attlee and Bevin who committed them to a cold-war policy they would certainly not have chosen in 1945–47, and also British nuclear weapons which they would not have wanted had they known about them. They have certainly often been disappointed by their party – more than ever since the disastrous 1960s – and by many of its leaders. They have, bitterly, seen a succession of men and women whom they trusted as people devoted to their cause, abandon them for the anti-Labour parties or reveal themselves as ambitious or money-hungry careerists. But, by and large, they have been content with a 'labourism' which stood for something much more modest than socialism in practice, even if it held out the hope of a socialist society. That is still the case.

To accept this is not opportunism, but realism. Still less does it mean that the Labour Party cannot move to the left. Indeed, it has done so to a notable extent since the days of Gaitskell and Wilson. What it does mean is that the political evolution of the party will fail if it takes place without considering the masses, without whose support it is lost. To quote Lenin again:

Change is brought about by the political experience of the masses; never is it brought about by propaganda alone. 'To march forward without compromise, without turning from the path' – if this is said by an obviously impotent minority of the workers . . . then the slogan is obviously mistaken. It is like 10,000 soldiers going into battle against 50,000 enemy soldiers – when it would be wise to 'stop', to 'turn from the road' and even 'enter into a compromise' in order to gain time until the arrival of the reinforcements of 100,000.[5]

How 'impotent' is the movement today? How fundamental are the changes it needs to undertake? Where must it look for its 'reinforcements'? The debate on my article 'Labour's Lost Millions' has concentrated on the third question, because, after the June 1983 elections, not even the most blinkered of sectarians were prepared to claim in public that Labour had not suffered a disastrous defeat or that nothing was wrong with the conduct of the party which finished four years of Thatcherism by losing a fifth of its supporters. Yet the debate shows that in fact the depth of Labour's crisis has not sunk in. People like me, say some, are just indulging in pessimism and 'the left's current passion for slinging mud at itself'.[6] We echo, say others, the Labour centre and right of the 1950s, which thought there was no future for a working-class-based party, and look how wrong they were.[7] Hobsbawm can only think that Labour's forward march has been reversed, says Royden Harrison, because he overlooks the 'wonderful, painful, indispensable, transition from mere Labourism to Socialism' which has been taking place within the Labour Party, though it is not yet complete.[8] This last statement reminds me of the oarsmen in a boat which is being swept towards the rapids who congratulate themselves, no doubt correctly, on rowing much better than they had ever done before.

As for the changes which have to be made, everybody agrees in principle that there is a lot to be done. Yet in practice it is denied that the profound changes in the social and economic structure and situation of Britain since the 1950s, to which I have tried to draw attention for the past five years, make a corresponding rethinking of the movement's political approach necessary. Eric Heffer argues that the 'working class', the traditional base of the party, is not declining, though the decline of 'the manual working class based on heavy engineering, the mines, shipyards, the docks etc.' is not denied. 'It is not true to say the working class has overall diminished. It is a different working class.'[9] *Socialist Worker* agrees: 'The working class is the overwhelming majority of the population.'[10] It is obviously true that the bulk of the population of working age, in so far as they are not unemployed, are in one way or another employed for wages or salaries, though it would be interesting to penetrate the statistically undocumented and almost certainly growing cloud of the 'black' or 'unofficial' economy, in which the difference between bosses, workers and what historians of the Victorian era call 'penny capitalism' are much less clear-cut. If a study of the changes within the working class aims to discover the new ways of mobilizing this mixture of old and new, but in all cases transformed, sections of the employed, then it is useful. Westergaard, who agrees that 'a labour movement dedicated to radical and constructive opposition to inequality can no longer hope to swing a majority behind it by appealing to class loyalties', has done a very good job of this kind.[11] But if such work merely asserts that the transformation of the working class proves that we should go plugging on in the old way, then it is not helpful. Of course there is also the view, recently expressed by Tony Benn and which I record without comment, that 'all this analysis of a fundamental change which means that everything is different is designed to demoralise and defeat'.[12]

The question arises why, if the Labour Party has basically been on the right lines (give or take a failure here and there) it suffered such a spectacular defeat in June 1983. And why those who believed it was did not predict what was going to happen, as the realists did, who are now labelled as 'pessimists' for having been patently right. Or, for that matter, why all the participants in this debate are arguing so furiously about the future of Labour.

I need say little about contributors who divert attention from the problems at issue by criticising me for not discussing the problems of the Communist Party and the revolutionary left, or for a bias against women.[13] As for the question of feminism, what was said on the subject in 'Labour's Lost Millions' can only be read as meaning that the women's movement and the problem of mobilizing women can *not* be treated as a mere sub-department of the working-class struggle, but that women and their movement are forces in their own right. The argument is in no sense anti-feminist. No doubt as Anna Coote points out, 'there may be a problem involved in appealing to the interests of women and men at the same time', though in the past labour movements have nevertheless succeeded in appealing to both with fair success. In the 1930s, for example, a consistent 41 to 42 per cent of the individual members of the Labour Party were women.

As socialists we simply have no option but to believe as a minimum that socialism is consistent with the aspirations of women.[14] If we thought it could not satisfy half the human race, how could we be socialists? In the meantime the task is enormous: 72 per cent of voting women in June 1983 chose the Alliance and the Tories, whose feminist records are hardly impressive. As for my article, I have genuine difficulty in understanding how it can be read as an example of male bias, or part of a 'Great *Male* Moving Right Show', even assuming it recommends a move to the right, which it does not. It is, of course, undeniable that, for reasons beyond my control, it was written by a man.

The Communist Party was not the subject of 'Labour's Lost Millions', though its problems are inseparable from the prospects of Labour, as are those of the rest of the socialist left, Marxist or not. However, critics are right in pointing out that the views expressed about Labour's future prospects by myself and others in *Marxism Today* are in a way, 'an up-to-date version of the Popular Front'[15] and that, in my own case, 'Popular

Frontism, in one form or another (has) characterize(d) his politics over five decades'.[16] This is not only the nostalgia of someone formed in the anti-fascist 1930s for the period which, after all, achieved the greatest advances of the left in Europe since the Russian Revolution, ranging from Labour triumph in Britain to, in some countries, autonomous social revolutions. It is because we were able to discover in practice how right Dimitrov was to tell us:

> We want to find a common *language* with the broadest masses for the purpose of struggling against the class enemy, to find ways of finally overcoming *the isolation of the revolutionary vanguard* from the masses of the proletariat and all working people, as well as overcoming the fatal *isolation of the working class itself* from its natural allies in the struggle against the bourgeoisie, against fascism.[17]

Situations change, and so do the styles of political discourse. But what Dimitrov said and what we learned in the school of politics, not least that the masses 'must be taken as they are, not as we should like to have them', made sense then and still makes sense.

So what changes have to be made? The debate about 'Labour's Lost Millions' has concentrated so overwhelmingly on one incidental suggestion, namely that under certain circumstances an electoral arrangement among anti-Thatcher forces might have to be envisaged, that I am probably now known to the large part of the left simply as 'the man who wants a coalition of Labour and the Liberal/SDP Alliance.' Just to have it on the record, let me say, once again, that I did *not* recommend either an electoral coalition or a coalition government, and still less that the Labour Party 'must abandon in advance the goal of forming a majority government' and seek a coalition instead.[18] I have *never* said that Labour 'can only really make progress if it makes some electoral or other arrangements with the . . . Alliance.'[19] I have simply raised the question of what happens at the next election if Labour's recovery is not sufficient to beat Thatcher single-handed. However we answer this question, someone has to ask it, because it does not go away if we shut our eyes. My own answer, in print, is that I regard 'the need to unite the anti-Thatcher forces by electoral arrangements in four years' time as the second-worst outcome in British politics', but nevertheless as 'preferable to the worst outcome, another Thatcher victory.'[20] But that was *not* what my earlier article was about. It was about the ways to avoid either of these two outcomes.

Why the debate has homed in so overwhelmingly on this one point, brings us back to the basic attitudes of the left to the Labour Party. Most of the critics who reject the suggestion, merely express an understandable outrage. But behind it, I think, there lies an approach similar to

Miliband's, and which Raymond Williams has put into the form of a careful argument in his article 'Socialists and Coalitionists'.[21] He accepts that those who take a similar view to myself do not want a coalition, but a Labour government. But, he argues, they are prepared to entertain the idea of a common front of centre and left, because they see even the Labour Party itself, as it has developed, as such a coalition, and so they find a wider common front acceptable, if by any chance a victory of Labour (the 'narrow coalition') is impossible. But, he argues, this side-steps the crucial question of the *socialist* character of its policies. So indeed, he agrees, do others on the left, who have accepted the Labour policies of 1983 as 'left' and 'socialist', though there is actually nothing specifically socialist about most of them. Nor does such a programme become more socialist by being combined with 'a bold announcement of a commitment to socialism', or by assuming that we only need to follow 'the answers . . . already known and advanced by the left in the Party . . . (which) is the way to a repetition of a merely divisive factionalism.' All the same, the so-called 'coalitionists' (little or big) are basically content with another version of the old Social Democratic policies, and socialists cannot be.

This undoubtedly puts its finger on a crucial question: what policies the labour movement and Labour governments should pursue if they want to do more than make the best of a bad job, and give capitalism 'a human face' – which, of course, many non-socialists also want to do. And behind this lies the even more crucial question, just how we envisage a British socialism. But these questions have two sides. They certainly require 'in the next four years . . . the radical reconstruction of all the main directions of policy in the light of the most open and informed socialist analysis.' But we also have to face the problem of how people whose interest in politics, or for that matter unions, is not socialist, and not necessarily identified in their minds with the struggle for socialism, can be convinced that socialism, and a socialist Labour Party, is for them. This is the wider problem of the politics of Labour, which includes, but is not the same as, the narrower problem of its programme and policies.

It is not a new problem, though it is today very much more difficult than during Labour's 'forward march' in the first half of the century, when we could rely on a growing number of workers accepting the equation: class equals support for the workers' party equals being against capitalism, equals for socialism. Even that was not enough, as the history of the Labour Party shows. But today we can't rely on the automatic growth of class consciousness with these implications any more. We can no longer even rely on the skilled workers, the traditional 'spine' of the labour movement, staying unconditionally loyal to Labour as 'their team'. And even where we can still rely on such loyalty which automatically identifies class, party, and (more doubtfully) socialism, we cannot overlook the masses who no longer have it, either shopping around among other parties, or alienated from politics, or even drawn away by Thatcherite propaganda. Let us not forget that the mass support for the Tories has not significantly diminished since 1979, and remains at the level of June 1983 even today, nine months after the election. So the problem of building a foundation for the advance of socialism, even among workers, simply cannot be treated as something internal to the Labour Party. And when we consider other parts or cross-sections of the people who can and must be mobilized for the transformation of Britain, then it is even less possible to think of it in this limited way.

If we can't win, or win back, these masses, then there is no foreseeable way forward. There is only the prospect of rallying a minority of convinced socialists who hope against hope that at sometime something will turn up; in fact, the prospect of writing off any hope of making Labour a force for socialist advance. Raymond Williams, it seems, is close to such pessimism – but then, he sees the past history of the Labour Party, in the very period when it became a party committed to socialism and millions rallied to it as such, namely 'during the generations of Liberal decline', simply as 'the only realistic left-of-Tory coalition'. 'Labour's Lost Millions', which rejects this view, was not a call for a retreat into opportunism and making the best of a bad job, but a call for *advance*. It did not even see the broad anti-Thatcherite front which is surely quite essential today, as a mere defence against encroaching reaction. It is that, certainly – but the history of the anti-fascist struggles shows that those purely defensive struggles were the foundation of major advances of the left – not least in Britain. It was not a call for a more moderate approach against the 'more radical tactics' of Williams and others, but against the sort of short-sighted and sectarian 'radicalism' which Lenin, for one, criticised, and which, to put it mildly, has done the Labour Party no good. *And which therefore has weakened the left.* For it is a historical fact that, since 1917, the Left (including, notably, the Marxist left) and support for the Labour Party have tended to grow and fall *together*, and not at each other's expense.

'Labour's Lost Millions' was about changing Labour's approach and the general lines of its future work, rather than specific activities or policies. As to the general 'model' for the future, it suggested learning something from the Italian Communist Party, just because 'it is and wishes to remain a classical mass socialist labour party, attempting to rally the widest range of forces around its essential core of the working class.' I would agree with Westergaard that we can also learn from the

Swedish Social Democrats who won their way back to power in 1982 with a programme 'to ease economic power out of private hands – and won, despite signs of a creeping erosion of traditional class allegiance.'[22]

This is not the place to discuss further what Labour should and can do concretely. But it is certainly essential in conclusion to remind ourselves of two things which must *not* happen. The first is the resumption, *from any side*, of the suicidal civil war within the Labour Party. It isn't likely that the existing leadership of the party will be directly challenged at present, since the 1983 Conference so clearly reflected the party's desire for unity and an end to fratricide, and since the new leadership has so obviously increased the party's support – as registered in the polls – by a third. But it is more than likely that local committee room battles to select and de-select delegates and candidates will have the same effect. This would be a disaster. The right must not indulge in scandalous wangles such as the attempt to keep Tony Benn off the shortlist for Chesterfield, which fortunately failed. Benn, quite apart from his personal qualifications, represents an important element in the Labour Party, which has the right to be represented in parliament. Just so (like them or not) Healey and Hattersely represent something in the party, not to speak of MPs like, say, Frank Field who are not, and are not even regarded as, standard-bearers on the Labour right, but who risk being de-selected because some faction or current wants their seats. If the politics of civil war are allowed to re-enter the Labour Party by the back door, it is lost.

The second thing which must not happen, is complacency. True, as Michael Meacher says, 'a consistent presentation of unity and a new charismatic leadership suddenly propelled the party (after the 1983 Conference) from third place in recent polls to neck-and-neck with the Tories.'[23] (Well, not quite . . .) But while this showed that millions demoralized by the sight of Labour aiming to score own goals, wanted nothing better than to support a credible Labour Party, it is not and will not be enough. It merely means that, if these people can be held – and they can go away as fast as they returned – the fight to recover and extend Labour's support does not have to start as far back as it looked in June 1983. It will still have to be won. It will be very difficult to win it. We cannot rely on automatic disillusionment with Thatcher or the Alliance to do the job for us. The Labour Party and all other parts of the labour movement have a very full agenda for the next four years. Now that the reasons for Labour's defeat have been debated, it is time to concentrate on it.

Notes

1. R. Miliband in R. Miliband and J. Saville, eds, *The Socialist Register 1983* (SR), London 1983, p. 109.

2. Ibid., p. 116.

3. Ibid.

4. V.I. Lenin *Selected Works* Vol. x, London 1979, p. 131.

5. Ibid., p. 127.

6. D. Massey, L. Segal, and H. Wainwright, 'And Now for the Good News', in J. Curran, ed., *The Future of the Left*, (FL), Oxford 1984.

7. J. Westergaard, 'Class of '84', *New Socialist* (NS), Jan–Feb 1984; R. Miliband, SR, pp. 104–5.

8. R. Harrison in *Labour Herald* (LH), 28 October 1983.

9. E. Heffer, 'Labour's Lost Millions II', *Marxism Today* (MT), December 1983.

10. *Socialist Worker*, 15 October 1983.

11. J. Westergaard, NS.

12. T. Benn in *City Limits*, 20–26 January 1984.

13. On the left, E. Heffer, MT., R. Harrison, LH; on women, Anna Coote, 'The Wrong Debate', in *Marxism Today*, January 1984 and D. Massey, L. Segal and H. Wainwright, FL.

14. See the important article by Tricia Davis, 'Feminism is Dead? Long Live Feminism', *Marxism Today*, October 1983.

15. E. Heffer, MT.

16. N. Carlin and I. Birchall, 'Kinnock's Favourite Marxist: Eric Hobsbawm and the Working Class', *International Socialism* 21, Autumn 1983, p. 90.

17. G. Dimitrov, *Selected Speeches and Articles*, London 1951, p. 113.

18. A. Freeman and D. Minns in the *Guardian*, October 1983.

19. E. Heffer, MT.

20. The *Guardian*, 2 November 1983.

21. Raymond Williams 'Socialists and Coalitionists', *New Socialist*, March–April 1984.

22. J. Westergaard, NS.

23. M. Meacher, 'Wide Ranging Reappraisal', *Marxism Today*, November 1983.

8

The Retreat into Extremism (1985)

For some years *Marxism Today* has been associated with a particular immediate political strategy for the Left in Britain: a united labour movement in broad alliance with all who can be mobilized against Thatcherite Toryism, which can be seen as, for the moment, the main enemy, and isolated as such. This does not represent a single coherent ideological doctrine or 'school' of 'Marxism Today-ism' or 'the Newer Left', as is sometimes argued. Many of those who have put forward such views in this journal are Marxists in the Communist Party, but that does not mean that they agree among themselves on all important points. In any case, to suppose that the articles in *Marxism Today* represent some sort of concerted factional doctrine is to misunderstand what 'a theoretical and discussion journal' is. It discusses.

Basically, the 'broad anti-Thatcherite' strategy represents the practical consensus of a lot of people on the left, that this sort of line *can* set Labour back on its forward march, whereas the strategies pursued on the hard and sectarian left have led to far more defeats and retreats than victories over the last few years. Such a view is compatible with a variety of ideological and theoretical positions. One does not have to agree on all points with Ken Livingstone to hold that the campaign in defence of the Great London Council is a model of exactly the sort of broad anti-Thatcherite mobilization that we have in mind. And one certainly doesn't have to be a Communist to see that the strategy put forward in *Marxism Today* makes sense, and that there is a shortage of other strategies on the left which take much account of political realities. That is why the *Marxism Today* articles have been so widely discussed and influential on the left, far beyond the usual range of Communist Party literature today.

Four major lines of argument have been put forward against this strategy. (I leave aside simple name-calling.) First, it is claimed that the situation of the labour movement isn't really as bad as all that. The movement hasn't really had serious setbacks, mainly because the unions are in excellent shape.[1] This is baloney. Anybody who actually believes this in April 1985 – anybody who believed it even at the peak of the miners' strike – is living in a time-warp. Britain has a uniquely strong, militant, and an extraordinarily heroic trade union movement. I don't think it is national chauvinism to say that the miners' strike of 1984 to 1985 would have been inconceivable today in any other country in the world. The British working class and its movement are the rock which will be the foundation of any broader movement or alliance. But it is an insult to the intelligence as well as to the devotion, loyalty, and heroism of British union militants to pretend that they haven't taken a good few beatings over the past six years. By now even the Socialist Workers' Party has got around to noticing that the unions on the whole aren't exactly on the offensive. We need not bother further with this argument.

The second argument is equally surprising. It denies that there is any special reason to regard Thatcherism as a particularly acute danger to the working class, saying that the Thatcher government is just a bourgeois government like all the others, except that 'the weakness of the British economy limits the potential manoeuvres available to bourgeois social democracy.' It is certainly not 'the focus of an unambiguous shift to the right in British society.'[2] Two distinguished and rather ancient members of the Communist Party have cited, as 'typical of the incessant counter-propaganda of *Marxism Today*' against what they regard as Communist principles, the thesis that 'Thatcherism is committed to a radical and revolutionary *change* in British capitalism.'[3]

Are comrades Rothstein and Arnot, Fine, Harris, Mayo, Weir, Wilson, and the rest who appear to believe this, living in the same country – even on the same planet – as most of us? Of course in one sense capitalism is always capitalism, and we are opposed to it whether it sails under the flag of Butskellism or Thatcher or the late William Ewart Gladstone. The Tories are always the Tories, and the left is against them, whether their leaders are Thatcher, Heath, Macmillan, Baldwin, or the late Benjamin Disraeli. And of course it is always possible to find an even more radical and reactionary change which capitalism could go in for, and which Thatcherism does *not* represent. For instance, she is not Adolf Hitler. In fact, a familiar conjuring trick in the arguments against *Marxism Today* is to suggest that we say that Thatcherism is like fascism, and because it obviously isn't, this means that there is no qualitative difference between Mrs T and Harold Macmillan (sorry, Lord Stockton), who is now so hostile to her that he is calling for the defeat of this Conservative government.[4] Actually, I cannot think of any

Marxism Today article which says that Thatcherism is fascism or the preparation of fascism, and several, such as Dave Priscott's and my own,[5] have quite specifically said it wasn't. Actually, the broad alliance strategy in Britain in the 1930s was not directed against British fascism, but against the national government, which was a great deal less reactionary than Thatcher. And those who formed the popular front certainly didn't abandon the traditional objects of socialism. However, the point is not to decide whether Thatcherism is or isn't like something in the 1930s, but whether it is committed to radical changes qualitatively different, more dangerous and disastrous – within the limits of a continuing monopoly capitalism – than other bourgeois and conservative regimes in Britain in this century.

It seems amazing that after six years of Thatcherite government, there can even be serious argument about such a proposition. In the first place, the Thatcherites have loudly, clearly and persistently declared their *intention* to change British capitalism radically, that it to say, among other things, to break with the traditional British ruling-class policy of avoiding open class confrontation. Of course, we do not have to believe that politicians mean what they say, but the difference between all other Tory governments and this one is that the others all claimed that they were against any radical change, or any change except what was unavoidable, and this one wants a radical break with the past.

In the second place, Thatcherism clearly has done a lot of transforming of Britain since 1979, incidentally leaving much of the British economy, the social infrastructure and welfare state, and the traditional system by which the British ruling class ruled, in ruins as a result. What other government since 1875 has seriously wanted to eliminate unions from the economic scene, and actually shackled them legally more than any other government for over a century? (Certainly more than after the General Strike.) What other government has set out to sell off the public parts of the economy wholesale, on principle, including not only what Labour and Keynesians have nationalized, but what had been nationalized by the public demand of those Victorian and Edwardian businessmen whom Mrs Thatcher claims as her inspiration, for example the telephone system? What other government this century has been as persistent an enemy of the welfare state and health service, of public education at all levels, of scientific research, of *any* public service (other than police and military) and independent local government? As a government of the right, Thatcher has no parallel, at least in twentieth-century Britain. Every historian will confirm this.

In the third place, Thatcherite policies clearly represent a style of politics, of ideology, and rightwing demagogy, which is new in British governments, though it has long been found in some press lords. It represents, with unprecedented frankness, the will to wage the class struggle against the workers ('the enemy within'), and a contempt for those who need help, for human and social considerations in policy, combined with flag-waving: one might call it 'I'm all right, Union Jack'. It represents the feelings of social climbers and hard-faced people who have done, or hope to do, well out of free enterprise ('get on your bike'). Insincere though Tory breast-beating about the unemployed may sometimes have been in the 1930s, it would have been inconceivable for a government of that era to have gone on for five years of mass unemployment before even beginning to wonder whether four millions out of work may not be a worse problem than whether inflation was 5 per cent or 6 per cent. Not this lot.

Finally, the unprecedented nature of Thatcherism is indicated by the unprecedented revolt against it of the traditional 'establishment', the very people and institutions the British ruling class used to rely on to keep the system running smoothly. This is the first Tory government which can expect the House of Lords to vote it down every so often; the first whose senior civil servants leak to the press; the first since the early nineteenth century which has seen a jury of the 'respectable' middle class (and vetted to ensure its 'respectability') acquit against the government in a political case; the first to have its prime minister publicly humiliated by the most ancient and Tory University, Oxford.

Coming from where they do, these are, by god, not gestures of social revolution. Almost certainly only a minority of the 1,000-odd Oxford dons who voted, by a majority of some 700 to 300 to refuse Margaret Thatcher an honorary degree, had ever been Labour supporters. Quite possibly most of them had been Tory voters. But whatever we read into such demonstrations, they clearly show that many pillars of Britain's traditional ruling structures themselves regard Thatcherism not as a continuation of the old ways by other means, but as a striking and worrying innovation.

There can't really be any doubt about this. The only question is whether Thatcherism is in a position to construct the Britain of which it dreams – and which would, quite surely, *not* be a Britain any previous Tory administration would have wanted, if only because the results of Thatcherism are so disastrous, even from a ruling-class point of view. Fortunately it does not look as though she will be able to, though she will have reduced much of Britain to a scrapyard in the process of trying. Thatcher will fail, partly because her aims, for example in economics, cannot objectively be achieved at all – at any rate by Thatcherite policy – and partly also because the force of resistance against Thatcherism, active and passive, will prove too great. But what is the nature of the forces which can be, and which are being, mobilized against it?

This brings us to the third argument against the broad alliance strategy, namely that it does not represent 'class politics', being 'a shift away from, or even an abandonment of, the central role of class and class conflict in the analysis and formation of political strategy'.[6] In the literal sense, this is nonsense. Anyone who reads at least this writer's articles in *Marxism Today*, any and all of them, can see with one eye that they try to do what Marxists were told to do, no doubt more than once, namely 'to use Marxist–Leninist analysis effectively, by carefully studying the concrete situation and the grouping of class forces, and making their plans for action and struggle accordingly.'[7]

But the accusation is not supposed to be literally true. 'Class politics' is just a label to stick on one kind of politics (the good one) to distinguish it from brand X (the bad one). In the sense in which it has been used in this debate, it is not a term of Marxist analysis, but a swearword.

But 'class', 'class analysis', and 'class politics' are too important for Marxists to be devalued into rhetorical labels. So it must be said clearly and firmly that the issue is not whether politics is 'class politics' but *what* particular kind of class politics best serves the interests of the class. It is about this that there can be and are different opinions. In case this is not clear, let me give some illustrations.

First, from the other side. 'Wet' and 'dry' Tories today, Chamberlain's appeasers of Hitler in the 1930s and Churchill's resisters, are or were equally committed to a bourgeois and capitalist Britain. None of us would be fool enough to argue that one lot did not represent the politics of their class, for example that Churchill's alliance with the USSR, or a House of Lords vote in favour of the GLC, were class betrayals. (There are of course Tory sectarians who might accuse Heath or Macmillan of class treason, but they are to be taken no more seriously than their leftwing sectarian opposite numbers.)

To come nearer home. The ultimate in 'class politics' by label was the so-called 'class against class' line of the Communist International in the late 1920s and early 1930s. It was class politics all right, only unfortunately the wrong kind, for it led the international Communist movement to disaster at the very time when the International expected that the world slump of 1929, which it had correctly predicted, would put the preparation of socialist revolution on the immediate agenda. It didn't. It brought Hitler. By early 1934 the movement (outside the USSR) was almost certainly weaker than at any time before or since.

Looking back, this is not very surprising. The 'class against class' line demanded 'an end to constructing a contradiction between fascism and bourgeois democracy, or between the parliamentary forms of the dictatorship of the bourgeoisie and the openly fascist forms.' It established the thesis that Social Democratic parties were 'social-fascist', seeing the entire development of Social Democracy as 'an uninterrupted process of evolution towards fascism'. It further observed that this process of fascisation extended to the very lowest rungs of the reformist organization. Thus – to quote the outline history of the Communist International prepared by the Institute of Marxism–Leninism of the Central Committee of the Communist Party of the Soviet Union:[8]

> the tactics of 'class against class' were in practice directed not only against the right-wing socialist leaders, but also against the rank-and-file functionaries of the reformist organisations. Such a sharpening of the 'class against class' tactics led to anything but the winning of influence on the rank-and-file of reformist workers. On the contrary, it led to increasing tension between them and the communists.

All this, as the Soviet history of the Comintern puts it, with restraint, meant that 'the communist movement did not immediately take account of the changed situation, and the consequent necessity to concentrate all forces, in the first instance, on the solution of the tasks of strengthening democracy in general and opposing fascism'. In fact, the radical slogan 'was as yet a long way from having won the support of the majority of the working class and others engaged in labour.' In short, class politics is not necessarily *good* class politics.

Did the line of broad anti-fascist unity which replaced 'class against class' mean the abandonment of class politics? The Communist International did not think so, and neither did those of us who got our political education and experience in the Communist parties during the 1930s and 1940s. What we read in Dimitrov was not a goodbye to class politics, but a goodbye to: 'sectarianism, satisfied with its doctrinaire narrowness, its divorcement from the real life of the masses; satisfied with its simplified methods of solving the most complex problems of the working-class movement on the basis of stereotyped schemes.'

What we thought we were learning to do was to conduct successful as distinct from unsuccessful class politics. And who will say that we were wrong? The broad alliance strategy led not only, and almost immediately, to the recovery and growth of the Communist parties in many countries. During and after the victory over fascism many of them reached the point of their greatest strength and influence. It undoubtedly produced a political radicalization of the workers and other strata, thus giving British Labour its greatest triumph. And, let us not forget, that in many places it raised the political struggle – for the first and only time in some West European countries – to the level of armed struggle, and produced ten new states setting out to construct socialism. Name any other strategy with comparable results.

The broad alliance line of those years can certainly be criticized, not least for being excessively skewed to serve the state interests of the USSR as seen by Stalin, sometimes at the expense of working-class interests in particular countries: for instance, by favouring the mainten-ance of the Conservative–Labour coalition in Britain after the end of the war in Europe.[9] But what it cannot be criticized for is an inability to serve class politics. To judge by results, it was by a long way the most effective strategy Communists have ever discovered in countries such as ours.

But why should anyone suppose that the 'broad alliance' strategy is incompatible with class politics? Practically all socialist movements from Marx on, in practically all countries, including *all* where successful revolutions were made, had to think in terms of alliance politics all the time, because in *none* of them (with the major exception of Britain) did the proletariat by itself form a majority of the people. In some the organized working class was a larger minority than in others, but in none of them could it hope to get very far without, in the words of that well-known revisionist the late Palme Dutt, 'win[ning] to its side the interme-diate strata, the petty-bourgeoisie, the peasantry, and also the backward workers.'[10] Today Britain is also in the same position as other countries, since we can no longer rely on an absolute majority of proletarian Britain to sweep a Labour government in single-handed. Actually, we never could, because British socialists, relying on the solid proletarian preponderance, overlooked the fact that *even at the peak of its forward march*, in 1951, they had failed to convert a third of the British workers, and since then Labour's working-class support has plummeted. As has lately been pointed out, continental working-class parties, polling 70–80 per cent of their class even today, did much better than British Labour, which failed to build itself either as the mass party of *all* workers, or as a broad front built on and around a class movement.[11] Britain used to be so overwhelmingly a proletarian nation that Labour could sometimes win in spite of its weaknesses. But now, when it no longer can, its problems and the strategies of socialists, revolutionary or otherwise, are no different from what they have always been.

Marx and Lenin themselves worked out their strategies on the assumption that the workers acted as leaders of a broad class front, being 'acknowledged as the only class capable of social initiative', even though in the minority.[12] In fact, when Marx thought what the strategy of a successful Paris Commune should be – the nearest thing to a proletarian revolution in his lifetime – he saw it in terms of what we would today call a 'popular front', and what he called 'the revolution of the Commune as representative of all classes of society which do not live off others' labour'.[13] And Lenin, between February and October 1917, convinced that it was essential to detach 'the broad masses of the petty-bourgeois population' from the provisional government, insisted that the Bolshevik programme should state that 'the immediate duty of the party of the proletariat is to fight for a system of state organisation which will best guarantee the economic progress and rights of the people in general.'[14] 'All classes of society'? 'Economic progress and rights of the people in general'? What kind of language is this? Hands up, those who think Marx and Lenin betrayed class politics! Broad alliances are the necessary complement to class politics, not an alternative to it.

The fourth argument is that the *Marxism Today* strategy abandons socialism. This is in the minds of the ancient monuments of our movement who mutter 'Bernstein', and those who accuse the supporters of the broad alliance of forgetting 'the immediacy of socialism itself'.[15] In a way, this accusation lies behind all the other arguments against the broad anti-Thatcherite strategy.

Let us first get rid of the argument that anything except unconditional loyalty to the USSR means the abandonment of socialism. This is obviously an issue in discussions within the Communist Party but (a) it has nothing to do with the broad alliance – in the 1930s Communists were both for such an alliance and totally loyal to the USSR, and (b) it is not of major concern outside the Communist Party. There are opponents of the broad alliance who also opposed the tanks in Prague 1968, and supporters who sympathize with General Jaruzelski and can see why the USSR went into Afghanistan. So let us keep the issue of loyalty to the Soviet Union out of the argument. All of us, including non-Communists, can agree that systematic anti-Sovietism, in other words, 'the notion of the Soviet Union as enemy', weakens the cause of peace and the left.[16] This has been recently demonstrated in France. We can also all, or most of us, agree 'that this does not preclude criticism of the Soviet Union.'[17] One would hope that most of us would see the USSR as a socialist country, though we wouldn't necessarily want our socialism to be like theirs; that we appreciate the support it has given to liberation movements in the Third World; that we recognize the October Revolution as the monumental historical event it is. No Communists can be indifferent to the USSR, but the present state of the international Communist movement is polycentric. Let us leave it at that.

But there is another, less specialized but fuzzier, meaning of abandoning socialism. Some are for its 'immediacy', others allegedly not. But what does 'the immediacy of socialism itself' mean? In practice nobody believes that socialism is on the immediate agenda of the movement, if only because all we can do right now is to argue whether it should be there or not. Even the infant school theory, which sees a radical socialist Labour government coming to power, dissolving the House of Lords, smashing the state apparatus and media power in six weeks or so, and then building the New Jerusalem like a 1960s tower-block, does not actually suppose that this can be done until there is such a Labour government. This is not on the immediate horizon.

Others, a bit less unsophisticated but opposed to the 'broad alliance', don't actually disagree that socialism in Britain at present, alas, looks rather a long way off. 'Socialism is not . . . a "long-term perspective"' says Roger Hallam, who tries manfully to wrestle with words in the *Morning Star*, because 'like all perspectives it is immediate': that is to say, it allows us to see *now* that 'the alliances of today lead towards the distant but real possibility of – if one may be excused for saying it – a revolutionary transformation of our ailing society.' Of course we'll excuse him. He's saying exactly what we are, even if he doesn't like it. Neither do we. The truth is that nobody disagrees about the comparative remoteness of a socialist Britain in March 1985. All socialists agree that the object of our strategies, whatever they are, is to bring it closer.

Nevertheless, let us not dismiss the fears that socialism is being flushed down the drain, however easy it is to dismiss simple-minded expression of it. These fears are real. All socialists, including the supporters of the 'broad alliance', ought to be worried that at a time when the contradictions of capitalism are more visible and potentially catastrophic than ever, in Britain and the world, there is no agreement on the left about what ought to be done or could be done; that our movements are weak and tearing themselves to pieces; that even governments of the left which came in with large majorities and high hopes, are on the defensive. It is also worrying that we do not have a clear idea of just what the future socialist economy is to be like and how it should be structured. For even if we survey the countries of 'really existing socialism' from the USSR to Yugoslavia, from the GDR to China, we see a variety of models and policies undergoing change. As for the other institutions of a future socialist society, who can discern their shape in the fog of argument about them?

It is understandable, in such circumstances, that many socialists should take refuge in ideological sermons. To tell ourselves, and to testify to the world, that we are for the class struggle, revolution, and socialism, and will have no truck with anyone who isn't, is at least some comfort and encouragement, and some protection against doubt and uncertainty. And it unquestionably helps to inspire militants to wage the long, arduous, and frustrating struggle for a goal which does not seem to come any nearer. It always has been so. As Brecht put it in the greatest poem ever written about Communist revolutionaries:

> Our forces were slight. Our goal
> Lay far in the distance
> It was clearly visible, though I myself
> Was unlikely to reach it.
> So passed my time
> Which had been given to me on earth.[18]

Unfortunately, morale-building is not enough. Our problem is, in the first instance, to get to the point where we can do something effective about our conviction that only socialism can solve the problems of humanity. This is not achieved by arguing which of us wants socialism most and soonest. We need to work out what to do next, *and how this can advance us on the road to socialism.* This is what writers in *Marxism Today* have done and are trying to do. We have at least some claim to attention as Marxists, since we diagnosed, before others did, the halting and reversal of Labour's forward march. Some of us, criticizing the political illusions arising out of the union militancy in the 1970s, and the policies which led to civil war within the Labour Party, predicted that they would lead to serious setbacks and defeats for the movement. Unfortunately we were right. We are proposing concrete strategies. Let these be discussed on their merits.

The merits of the 'broad alliance' line are so obvious that it is embarrassing even to have to argue them. To put it, once again, in the words of the celebrated revisionist Palme Dutt: 'Finance capital seeks to isolate and crush the working class vanguard. . . . And the answer of the working class to this is and must be . . . to isolate finance capital.'[19] The front of people and groups, who for one reason or another would wish to see Thatcherism defeated, is extraordinarily wide and getting wider by the month. It is no more necessary to agree with our potential allies on anything except opposition to Thatcher, than it was necessary for Britain and the USSR from 1941 to 1945 to agree on anything except opposition to Hitler. After the war, as we know, both resumed their disagreements, just as Ken Livingstone and the House of Lords have clearly not commited themselves to a lifelong alliance.

Ought we to hesitate over making such alliances for fear that in the end our allies will benefit more than we? Well, unless Thatcherism is defeated, none of us will benefit at all. But anyway, why the nervousness? The chances of the labour movement benefiting from a broad alliance are excellent, for two good reasons. First, because, in spite of what SDP journalists say, Labour remains the main force of opposition, and is likely to remain so – unless the sectarians have their way and reduce it to yet another rump sect, which is – luckily – no longer very probable. The most plausible form of a broad anti-Thatcherite mobilization is therefore one which had Labour as its base and central component. And the Labour Party, thanks to developments since the late 1970s, is, after all, a party which has moved considerably to the left from the Gaitskell, Wilson, and Callaghan days. And second, experience shows – certainly it did in the 1930s – that the broad front line increases the strength of the labour movement and the left within it.

As there is, in practice, no alternative line which has any practical chances of success, or is based on anything except declarations of faith and condemnations of sin and apostasy, it is difficult to consider the merits of the competition. Nor is arguing against sectarianism to the point. It is understandable that old comrades, in times when the cause to which they have devoted their lives is not doing so well, should resist anything that looks as though it might undermine their old, and justified, convictions. Alas, the world is no longer what it was when we and the Great October Revolution were young, and it is not right for Marxists to behave as though it was. Again, it is natural that young comrades, mobilized for the first time in the great struggle against capitalism, should express, above all, their detestation of this awful society, their determination not to have any truck at all with its compromises and corruptions. They are right. Lenin tore Willie Gallacher's 'infantile leftism' to shreds in the famous pamphlet on Radicalism (who reads it nowadays?), but not before he had paid tribute to the *spirit* behind the militants' left sectarianism.

The tragedy of the present situation is that these young or relatively young revolutionary socialists no longer find anywhere a school in which they can learn to combine conviction and non-sectarian political action adequately. Such a school the Communist Party provided for generations of workers and intellectuals, men and women. It has long lost its position as the unique centre of such political education, but it had, until now, maintained at least some presence as a political educator.

The strangest thing about the present debates within the Communist Party is that (apart from the issue of loyalty to the USSR) there is nothing specifically Communist about them. The arguments of the Communist Party's hard left are substantially like the arguments of the various Trotskyist, and non-ideological or non-Marxist Labour hard lefts. Tony Benn gives his blessing equally and generously to the Stalinists in the Communist Party (who don't seem to know who first used their anti-popular-front arguments) and the Militant Tendency. I suppose it could also be argued that there is no substantial difference between the arguments of *Marxism Today* and others who stand for a 'broad' line outside the Communist Party, but at least we can claim that, by general agreement, it was *Marxism Today* that launched these arguments. In fact, today the only contribution to theory and practice in Britain which is specifically identifiable with the Communist Party is the policy of the *British Road to Socialism*, which the 'broad alliance' strategy is based on.

The Communist Party is a small party – always has been – and has served the British labour movement well. It could still do so, as is shown by its contribution to the rethinking of the movement's strategy and struggles in the past few years. The British labour movement – any labour movement – needs Marxist analysis, by which I don't mean the ready-made set of slogans chanted by photo-fit hard-liners who would fit as readily into one left-wing sect as into another. The next few months will decide whether the Communist Party in this country has any future. It ought to have one.

Notes

1 'We recognise a considerable strengthening, unity and militancy in the workforce as organised in trade unions at the point of production. This has not been reflected electorally in the fortunes of the Labour Party, with the renewal of the Tory government and the rise of the SDP. It has revealed the extent to which the Labour Party is out of touch with and has failed to respond to developments in the trade union movement.' B. Fine, L. Harris, E. Mayo, A. Weir, E. Wilson, *Class Politics: An Answer to its Critics* (CP), pp. 62–3.

2. Ibid p. 63.

3. A. Rothstein and R. Page Arnot, *Morning Star*, 4 January 1985. The emphasis is Rothstein and Arnot's. Their quotation from my article 'Labour's Lost Millions' is wrong. What I wrote was that 'Thatcherism is committed to a radical and *reactionary* change in British capitalism, and indeed in the British political system' (my emphasis).

4. 'The idea of Thatcherism mistakes it with such a sharp break with the past that it opens up the spectre of fascism.' They disagree 'that a defensive alliance must be built against the dangers of fascism in which the traditional objects of socialism are abandoned.' Fine, Harris *et al.*, CP, pp. 2, 63.

5. Eric Hobsbawm's 'Labour's Lost Millions' and Dave Priscott's 'Popular Front Revisited', *Marxism Today*, Oct 1983.

6. Fine, Harris *et al.*, CP, p. 5.

7. Dimitrov in *Inprecorr*, 1935, p. 1649. He added, for good measure: 'We must get rid, once and for all, of a situation where communists who have neither the ability or the knowledge to make a Marxist–Leninist analysis, replace the analysis by vague phrases and general slogans, such as "a revolutionary solution to the crisis", without making any half-way serious attempt to explain under what circumstances, with what relation of class forces, and at what degree of maturity on the part of the proletariat and the working masses in general . . . [this] would be possible.' Amen.

8. Berlin 1970. The above quotations are from the Eleventh Plenum of the ECCI (April 1931) as cited in this work, pp. 377–8. My translations from the German text.

9. Everyone, and especially old and experienced comrades, knows quite well where the pressure to do this came from. That is why the accusation by Rothstein and Arnot/CP, that the *Marxism Today* line amounts to 'Browderism' is so odd. It is true that Earl Browder, then leader of the CPUSA, proposed that it should dissolve itself in 1944, a step followed by some Latin American parties at the time. Most of us could not understand this and thought it was mistaken. The dissolution was revoked in 1945. But the idea that in 1944 any Communist Party leader would propose, let alone carry out, the dissolution of a Communist Party without the approval, or indeed the instruction, of Moscow, is absurd. 'Browderism' reflected too much and not too little loyalty to what is at present called 'proletarian internationalism'.

10. *Inprecorr*, 1935, p. 1476.

11. See two excellent articles by Gareth Stedman Jones and G. Therborn in J. Curran, ed., *The Future of the Left*, Oxford 1984.

12. Marx, 'Civil War in France' draft I (*Werke* vol. 17, pp. 544–6).

13. Ibid., p. 533.

14. *Selected Works* VI, London 1979, p. 116.

15. Roger Hallam, 'Seeing what Divides the Communist Party Itself', *Morning Star*, 7 March 1985.

16. Fine, Harris *et al.*, CP, p. 47.

17. Ibid, p. 62.

18. B. Brecht, 'On those who come after' in J. Willett, ed., *Collected Poems*, London 1976.

19. *Inprecorr*, 1935, p. 1,476.

PART II

The Intelligence of History

9

Fifty Years of Peoples' Fronts (1985)

Fifty years ago, in 1936, the first popular front governments were formed in France and Spain; that is to say, coalitions of Communists with Social Democrats and certain middle-class parties which were not seen as the immediate preliminary to revolution and working-class power. Such governments before then had always been condemned by the revolutionary left. They were regarded as typically Social Democratic, likely to be dominated, directly or indirectly, by the bourgeoisie, and therefore likely to divert the movement from its real task, which was to make revolution. The only major exception to this might occur in colonial and semi-colonial countries, where – according to the Programme of the Communist International (1928) – the dictatorship of the proletariat was not the immediate aim of the Communists, but a more or less rapid transition from a bourgeois democratic to a socialist revolution would have to take place.

Without going into the complex history of earlier Communist discussions, let me simply say that people's front or coalition governments of the kind I have sketched were quite new and shocking in the 1930s, and raised serious debates within the revolutionary movement which have not ceased to this day. Before the war, two popular front governments failed. The French never overcame its internal contradictions and the half-heartedness of the socialists who led it, and faded away in 1938. The Spanish was faced with Franco's rising, and went down in defeat in 1939. But people's front governments, in the form of governments of anti-fascist unity in the war against Hitler, were formed during and after the war, if anything on an even broader basis than had been envisaged in the 1930s. In 1946 there were few countries which did not have them. They were the rule in the People's Democracies (which were so-called precisely because they were not then supposed to be exclusively

Communist governments), and in the west there were Communist ministers in Austria, Belgium, Denmark, France, Italy, and Norway until they were expelled or resigned with the coming of the cold war. In the colonial and semi-colonial countries governments of a broad anti-imperialist front were, of course, also common and less controversial.

For several years after 1947 people's front governments – outside the areas of colonial liberation – were neither practicable nor encouraged, but since the 1960s there has been a return to this type of perspective, notably in Italy, France, and Spain. Since the mid 1970s the major issue in Italian politics has been the entry of the Communist Party into government, either as part of a majority of the united parties of the left or as part of a grand coalition, a sort of national government excluding the neo-fascists and the extreme right. So the issues raised by such governments are not merely historical but belong to practical politics.

Revolutionary Perspectives after the First World War

The international Communist movement was founded on the assumption that a world revolution, or at least a revolution in important regions of the world, was both practicable and imminent. That revolution would not necessarily take the Russian form, but nevertheless the October Revolution was in a profound sense the model both of what ought to and would happen, and of the strategy, tactics, and organization for making it happen. This is why the new Communist International insisted on the most rigid and exclusive conditions for joining it. It wanted an effective world party of revolutionaries. It obviously wanted to exclude from this movement and its national sections the right-wing Social Democrats who had betrayed proletarian internationalism in 1914, and revealed themselves as deeply committed to capitalist society or even – as in Germany – as its main saviours. However, it also wanted to exclude anyone even partly committed to the non-Bolshevik way, anyone unwilling to break with Social Democratic tradition and organization in the most total and public manner.

In the excitement of the moment there were, after 1918, plenty of people and parties willing to declare themselves Communists, or even carried away by the mood of global revolution or the radicalization of the masses, to affiliate with the Communist International. What the International wanted, however, was not an influx of the miscellaneous left, but an international Bolshevik party. It thus deliberately rejected most of those wanting to join it, leaving the quite important group of leftwing socialist parties – or at least those unwilling to make the total break – to float vaguely in the space between Social Democracy and the Comintern. Several of them tried briefly to organize themselves into the so-called 'Two-and-a-Half International' or Vienna Union before drifting back to Social Democracy after 1922, for want of anywhere else to go.

This approach made sense only on the assumption that the Russian revolution would soon be followed by other revolutions, or that an international crisis offering similar perspectives would very soon recur. In 1918–20 this seemed a perfectly realistic assessment. It is quite unhistorical to blame Lenin, in the light of hindsight, for setting up an International on the basis of splitting the old international movement – or what remained of it – on the narrowest and most exclusive basis. The situation looked, and was, revolutionary. In such a situation the masses would follow the most consistent revolutionaries. The vital thing was to see that these were consistently and effectively revolutionary, rather than to convert a larger percentage of the old-non-Bolshevik socialist parties into Communist ones at the cost of compromise.

Exploring Alternative Strategies

Hardly had the Comintern established itself effectively when it became clear that its original hopes would not be realized. From the early 1920s it had to operate in a non-revolutionary situation, at least in most of Europe, though in much of the colonial, semi-colonial, and dependent world a revolutionary situation could be said to exist, or to be probable or even imminent. However, at this stage the great majority of Marxists did not regard the colonial revolutions as the immediate forerunners of the 'dictatorship of the proletariat' and socialist construction. As the programme of the Communist International put it in 1928:

> as a rule, transition to the dictatorship of the proletariat in these countries will be possible only through a series of preparatory stages, as the outcome of a whole period of transformation of bourgeois-democratic revolution into socialist revolution.

We need not here discuss the debates, mainly centred on the Chinese revolution, which were eventually to lead to a different view of the political prospects of colonial liberation.

From 1921, the Comintern thus found itself in the difficult situation of having to work out a strategy on the assumptions that further October Revolutions were not in fact likely to take place. This was awkward. As

Karl Radek put it at its Fourth Congress (1922): 'It is particularly difficult in a period when there are no popular revolts to pursue a Communist political policy.' It was doubly awkward, since the very principles on
which the International had been constructed now made it more difficult
to mobilize, and co-operate with, those large sectors of the movement
which it had been designed to exclude. The Comintern found itself in a
position rather like that of an army equipped for offensive, breakthrough, and pursuit, which suddenly and unexpectedly finds itself
obliged to settle down to a lengthy siege.

To do it credit – and the Communist International receives little
enough credit nowadays – it set about seriously rethinking its European
strategy almost immediately, with the launching of the United Front
policy in 1921. However, the discussions about the new strategy and the
new perspective were confused by four important factors. First and fore-
most, the hope of a European – or at least a German – October were
not abandoned but only postponed; at first briefly, but after the failure
of insurrection in Germany in 1923, for a longer period – perhaps until
the next capitalist crisis. Alternative strategies were therefore still largely
seen as something designed to fill in time until a new revolutionary crisis
made a new and better prepared October possible.

Second, opinion within the new Communist parties was divided and,
on the whole, unenthusiastic. Those who had joined them had done so
precisely because they wanted revolution and a total break with the old
Social Democratic tradition. They were ready to follow the line, but left
to themselves, most of them sympathized with what was increasingly
clearly a sectarian position. This was very marked in the German
Communist Party (KPD).

Third, the divisions and arguments within Communist parties were
unfortunately but necessarily entangled with the internal struggles and
debates within the Soviet party in the 1920s. This was particularly
evident in the period 1928–34, when a policy of almost suicidal sectarianism was imposed on the parties from Moscow. That such a policy had
some support within the parties is undoubted; but I don't think it would
have established itself in the British Communist Party, for example,
without Moscow.

Fourth, and more defensibly, the task of turning the new Communist
parties, so largely composed of former Social Democrats, syndicalists or
small leftwing sects, into proper Leninist parties, remained. After all, the
case for Lenin's type of party (with or without its Stalinist developments
or deformations) was not simply that such a party was required to make
insurrection. It was required for any form of effective struggle for, and
construction of, socialism.

Popular Front Strategy

So, though alternative strategies were explored within the Comintern in the 1920s and occasionally surfaced, it was not until the 1930s that they were systematically developed. The movement had, vaguely, looked forward to the coming world crisis of capitalism as something which would somehow automatically produce a revolutionary situation. Instead it produced the most staggering and undeniable débâcle, assisted, without any doubt, by the ultra-sectarianism of the Comintern line after 1928.

In early 1933 the entire European perspective of the International lay in ruins. Hitler was in power in the country to which Lenin had once hoped soon to transfer the headquarters of international socialism, and the KPD was in exile, in concentration camps, or a hunted, illegal rump of cadres. Italian fascism felt strong enough actually to let some Communists out of jail in an amnesty in 1932. The only other Communist Party in Western Europe with major support, the French (PCF) had been reduced to 28,000 members and 12 seats in Parliament. It was no longer possible to deny that the failure of the world revolution to occur in 1917–20 had been more than a temporary setback. The defeat of 1928–33 was clearly of more lasting significance, even though for another year or more the Comintern officially maintained that all was well, though with an increasingly strained air. What was more to the point, the movement was not only beaten but pursued. Fascism was advancing on all fronts. Something had to be done, if only to mobilize an effective defence.

It is not necessary to repeat the way in which the International came to adopt the popular front strategy, or the elements in earlier discussions within the Communist movement which anticipated it and from which it was developed. We know that it was pioneered in France in 1934, and officially adopted by the International at its Seventh Congress – the first for seven years – in 1935, which totally reversed the former policy of seeing Social Democracy as the main enemy. The new line was put forward in two powerful and visibly heartfelt reports by the new General Secretary of the International, George Dimitrov, and his assistant – also new as a spokesman for the International – Palmiro Togliatti, or, as he was then known 'Ercoli'.

The point I wish to make here is that the popular front strategy then adopted was more than a temporary defensive tactic, or even a strategy for eventually turning retreat into offensive. It was also a carefully considered strategy of advancing to socialism. It was, in my view, the first, and so far, still the only such strategy evolved for countries in which the classical insurrectionary situations of the type of the October Revolution or

of other types were not to be expected, though not necessarily impossible. This does not mean that it was bound to succeed. No strategy is
bound to succeed, though some are bound to fail. The search for the
magic pill, certified by white-coated or red-flagged scientists, and
absolutely guaranteed to cure cancer, cholera, rheumatism, and the
common cold or their political equivalents, belongs to the field of self-
delusion and advertisement rather than to the field or politics.

Unity the Core

Just to remind ourselves: the core of the popular front strategy was
unity. It was a set of concentric circles of unity: at its centre the united
front of the working-class movement, which in turn formed the basis of
an even broader anti-fascist people's front, which in turn provided in the
relevant countries the base for a national front of all those determined to
resist fascism in the form of the danger from Hitler, Mussolini, and the
Japanese, and finally – even more loosely – an international front of
governments and peoples – including the USSR – against fascism and
war. Each of these circles had, as it were, a different degree of unity.

The object of the united front was the reunification of labour movements split mainly between Social Democrats and Communists. This was
quite clear in the trade union field, where the merger of separate socialist and Communist (or other) unions into a single comprehensive trade
union federation was envisaged – and sometimes, as in France,
achieved. Mergers of socialist and Communist parties into a single
working-class party were not seriously envisaged in practice, since the
conditions for such unity laid down by Dimitrov amounted to asking
Social Democratic parties to become Communist ones by committing
themselves to 'the dictatorship of the proletariat in the form of Soviets'
and 'democratic centralism' of the Bolshevik type. Nevertheless the
question of the political reunification of the labour movement, 'of a
single political mass party of the working class' was formally declared to
be urgent, and in the form of a merger of existing parties rather than of
attracting the masses away from Social Democracy to the Communists.

The peoples' fronts and the broader national fronts were to have a
rather looser unity – they were in fact alliances – though, in the course of
the anti-fascist struggle, a more permanent unity came to be envisaged,
in the form of Peoples' Democracies or the western governments based
on the unity of all anti-fascist resistance forces. The international unity
was more *ad hoc* still; though once again, at the peak of the wartime
alliance – but this was after the abolition of the Comintern – the
Russians envisaged something like its permanent or semi-permanent

prolongation into peacetime.

Dimitrov argued that, strategically, the basic principle of the new policy was to:

> find a *common language* with the broadest masses for the purposes of strug-
> gling against the class enemy, to find ways of finally overcoming *the isolation
> of the revolutionary vanguard* from the masses of the proletariat and all other
> toilers, as well as overcoming the fatal *isolation of the working class itself* from
> its natural allies in the struggle against the bourgoisie, against fascism.

In short, the working class had been defeated because it had allowed itself to be isolated; it would win by isolating its main enemies.

Defensive and Offensive

The novelty of this strategy was to use the same weapons for defensive and offensive purposes. For the people's front was, from the start, envisaged not simply as a necessary short-term alliance of desperation against an enemy who threatened forces which had nothing in common except the fear of this threat. This might be so, as it were, on the extreme outskirts of anti-fascist unity. Thus the British Communist Party shocked its allies in 1938 by proposing to extend its support to Churchill, just as Churchill in 1941 shocked his supporters by unhesitatingly extending it to Stalin – both on the same grounds, namely that even the devil was a good enough ally against Hitler, if he was prepared to fight him. However, governments of the anti-fascist people's front, based on working-class unity, which were the logical outcome of the policy, were from the outset also envisaged as possible elements in the transition from capitalism to socialism. The Comintern was extremely cautious and qualified in its formulations of this question, but clear enough to state that: 'It may be that in a number of countries the *united front government* will prove to be one of the most important transitional forms.' More generally, it was clearly stated that the fight against fascism was the main way forward in the struggle for socialism. To defeat it would also be to strike a major blow at capitalism.

The arguments for this, though not often stated with great clarity in public, were as follows. Fascism was the logical expression of monopoly capitalism, which had reduced the effective control of the economy to a handful of ultra-powerful corporations or groups – the 'two hundred families', as the French put it. These crucial groups of concentrated capitalist power, in a period of revolution and intensifying class struggle, saw their main salvation in fascism at home and abroad. As the French

reactionaries put it, frankly, when faced with a popular front government in their own country: 'Better Hitler than Léon Blum.' In fact, the
bulk of French big business took the logical step of collaborating with
the Germans, and much of private industry after the war was expro-
priated, not on the grounds that it was private, but on the grounds that it
had so collaborated, for example, the Renault works. Under these
circumstances the call for anti-fascist struggle was, in effect, also the call
for struggle against the most powerful, dangerous, and decisive sectors
of monopoly capital. It was not a struggle against the bourgeoisie as
such, as Manuilsky argued in his survey of the Congress (*Inprecorr*, 17
December 1935):

> Whilst we are undermining the power of these elements, we are at the same
> time undermining the power of the bourgeoisie as a whole, because . . . [it] is
> indissolubly connected with the most reactionary, most chauvinist and most
> imperialist elements of finance capital.

This was excessively optimistic, for two reasons. First, because not *all*
bourgeoisies, and not even all groups of monopoly capitalists, joined the
fascists and thus made themselves vulnerable to attack on this ground.
The Americans and the British eventually fought fascism. Second, and
more seriously, because it assumed that fascism was a lasting phase of
capitalist development, that bourgeois democracy had been permanently
abandoned as no longer compatible with capitalism, and that as a result
the defence of liberal democracy had become objectively anti-capitalist.
In the 1930s this was not implausible. Most of us believed it. But, as it
turned out, fascism was a temporary and regional phase of world
capitalism, which after 1945 returned to a modified and bureaucratized
version of liberal democracy.

Period of Anti-fascist Unity

However, in the 1930s and 1940s the front line between fascism and
anti-fascism was indeed that of the class struggle, and the popular front
strategy enabled the left to fight it with the maximum number of allies,
all the more so as it was evidently defending itself, its allies, and its
nations, against fascist attack. What is more, in so far as this defence was
necessarily armed – as in Spain and later in the Second World War – it
turned into a revolutionary struggle in which the Communists were able
to increase their influence, sometimes decisively, by virtue of their
obvious effectiveness and leadership. Let us not forget that the period of
the strategy of anti-fascist unity eventually led not only to something

that had been hardly conceivable in western Europe, namely guerilla warfare – on a much larger scale than anything in, say, Latin America since the war – but also, and more important, to the extension of social- ist power to large parts of eastern Europe. Much of this was due to the Red Army, but by no means all. Yugoslavia, Albania, probably in a large degree Bulgaria, and – until it was suppressed by British inter- vention – Greece, all had genuinely home-grown liberation movements.

Moreover, from the narrower point of view of the success of Communist parties, the period of anti-fascist unity was as brilliantly successful as the 1920s had been disappointing. There was no Commun- ist party, however insignificant, which did not gain relatively enormous ground. I have mentioned the disastrous situation of these parties in 1933. Twelve years later, at the end of the war, the European parties were at their all-time peak, except for the KPD which (in West Germany) never recovered from Hitler, and the Spanish Communist Party (PCE) which shared the defeat of the Republic by Franco.

In France and Italy the party was, or was on the way to becoming, the majority party of the working class for the first time. Even in countries where it had never established any support comparable to that of the socialists, its vote rose dramatically: 13 per cent in Belgium (or more than double its best previous performance), 12.5 per cent in Denmark (or more than five times its previous best), 23.5 per cent in Finland (or almost double its previous best), 10 per cent in Holland (or about three times its previous best), 12 per cent in Norway (or double its previous best), 10 per cent in Sweden (or almost double). Even in Britain, you may recall, the two Communist MPs elected in 1945 mark the high point of the party's modest electoral achievement.

In one sense the period of anti-fascist unity was therefore an undoubted success. It reversed the global trend towards fascism, defeated fascism, and furthermore got the Communist parties out of their sectarian isolation. If the CPF and PCI replaced the socialist party as the major party of the working class in their countries, it was due to the experiences of the anti-fascist period. On the other hand the possible contribution of people's front governments to a transition to socialism is much more debatable.

Debate in the International Movement

There was indeed a deep, if not always acknowledged, division on this question within the Communist movement. The USSR was primarily interested in its own security – mainly against German aggression – and in diplomatic alliances to safeguard it. I think it is safe to say that it was seriously interested in people's fronts chiefly from this point of view, and not from the immediate point of view of making revolutions or the prospects of a transition to socialism in other countries. Since the defeat and destruction of the USSR would have been a fatal setback to the movement everywhere, Communist parties were also prepared to subordinate everything to the defence of the USSR, though this did not prevent them having plans for advancing to socialism in their own countries.

But what plans? There was a leftwing view which still believed that a return to the classical revolutionary perspective was essential. If a broad front was necessary at all – and within the Comintern Bela Kun, Lozovsky, and some others were far from convinced – it should simply, as it were, get the golf-ball of revolution out of the bunker into which it had got itself by 1933, after which the game would go on as before. The people's front slogan led to an enormous revitalization and strengthening of the left, in both France and Spain. The victory of popular front governments produced a spontaneous radicalization in the masses in both countries, which – some people argue – ought to have been used to make a bid for power in France, and which actually produced a social revolution in Spain, when Franco made his insurrection. I do not want to discuss the criticisms of Communist policy which have been made about these episodes, beyond saying that I do not believe there was a revolutionary situation in France in 1936, and that in Spain the need to defeat Franco inevitably dominated the policy of the popular front government.

Policy of the Long Haul

But within the Comintern there was another perspective. It was only hinted at, however, because those who had previously put forward such views had been damned or expelled as right-wing deviationists, for example Georg Lukács, who between 1928 and 1956 was forced out of politics and into literary criticism for this reason. Antonio Gramsci (whose friend Togliatti was now one of the chief spokesmen of the International) had elaborated a policy based on the assumption that the lost opportunity of 1917–20 would not recur, and that Communist parties must envisage not a short front offensive but a lengthy war of position – a policy of the long haul. In effect, they must win the leadership of a broad alliance of social forces, and *maintain* this leadership during a prolonged period of transition, in which the actual transfer of power was only one episode.

In the west Communists were not confronted with a state which had only to collapse for the working class to seize power. The state was only the first line of the bourgeoisie's defence. Behind it there was a whole system of bunkers and fortresses – the institutions of civil society which established the legitimacy of bourgeois rule. To quote Karl Radek in 1922:

> in the West the working masses are not so amorphous. . . . They are members of parties and they stick to their parties. In the East, in Russia, it was easier to bring them into the fold of communism after the outbreak of the revolutionary storm. In your countries it is much more difficult.

Or, as Dimitrov put it in 1935:

> It is a common mistake of a leftist character to imagine that, as soon as a political (or revolutionary) crisis arises, it is enough for the Communist leaders to throw out the slogan of revolutionary insurrection, and the masses will follow.

The struggle for hegemony over a long period implied two things: first, that even in the west the slogan of an immediate transition to the 'dictatorship of the proletariat' was correct only in exceptional circumstances, and second, that it was wrong for the Communists to refuse to take any interest in government until after they had made their own revolution. On the contrary, the more they did so, the more they left hegemony in the hands of the bourgeoisie, and condemned themselves to subalternity.

Now in so far as the popular front governments were seen as possible regimes of transition to socialism, they therefore implied that the dictatorship of the proletariat was not the immediate programme of the Communists, and that there would be an intermediate phase between the rule of the bourgeoisie and socialism. (I am here discussing the meaning of the term 'dictatorship of the proletariat', which has now such associations that many western Communist parties are abandoning it.) But as I have tried to show above, there was a major weakness in this analysis. It made sense on the assumption that capitalism was fatally weakened by the defeat of fascism. As we have seen, this was not so. After the war it still made sense – though a bit less – on the assumption that capitalism would not recover. But as we know, it did. It made sense on the assumption that the popular front government was decisively tilted to the left, so that it could not drift back into a bourgeois coalition with a socialist or Communist appendix. But, outside eastern Europe after the war, this was not so. On the contrary, the governments of antifascist unity in western Europe could get rid of their Communists whenever they wished, and in any case kept them in subordinate positions, where they could take the blame for unpopular government policies, for example as ministers of labour.

It is true that in eastern Europe after the war there were genuine alliance governments, which were not merely Communist regimes in fancy dress, although the leftwing in the Communist movement – led at the time by the Yugoslavs – regarded this as undesirable. Thus Dimitrov in 1946 said: 'Our immediate task is not the realisation of socialism, but the consolidation of the democratic and parliamentary system.' 'People's Democracy' had not yet become a synonym for the dictatorship of the Communist party, nor was a single way of development – patterned on the USSR – imposed on the east European states. But with the coming of the cold war this ended, and little was left of the perspective of a gradual transition to socialism in accordance with conditions in each country, except the name 'People's Democracy' which had become meaningless.

The Situation in which Peoples' Fronts Arise

The criticism of peoples' fronts and broad alliances by the western ultra-left envisages a similar development. Such governments are rejected unless they are the immediate precursors of socialist power, that is unless they stop being peoples' fronts and turn themselves into 'dictatorships of the proletariat'. Here the present ultra-left echoes, among others, the opinions of Leon Trotsky, who dismissed the Comintern's policies in the wildest and most sectarian manner, though he had earlier made some very sound criticisms of the Comintern's disastrous sectarianism before 1934. He actually seems to have believed that peoples' fronts 'doom the working class to impotence *and clear the road for fascism*' (my emphasis). Trotsky and other ultra-radicals at the time rejected the very idea of the broad anti-fascist alliance, and when it became clear that it stimulated a striking revival and growth of the movement, rejected it for not immediately proceeding to make a classical revolution. In the 1970s ultra-leftist attitudes towards Chile have been along the same lines.

This was and is to misunderstand the situation in which peoples' fronts arise. Broad alliances of groups and parties, including peoples' fronts, are necessary only when the working-class party is not strong enough to win on its own: it rarely is. But when such alliances or fronts are necessary, they therefore consist of a variety of groups and organizations with very different opinions, some of them not even socialist. They are united only against a common enemy, or for a common programme, which represents only the first step for some participants, whereas for others it marks the furthest point to which they are at the moment prepared to go. This follows from the fact that they are neither socially nor politically homogeneous. In short, if they are to be more than brief political interludes, the socialists within such alliances must convince and carry along their allies, or at least neutralize them. If they fail to do so, they simply revert to being a relatively impotent minority group. Indeed, they might even be worse off, if their policy had antagonized formerly allied, neutral, or indifferent strata, allowing these to be mobilized by the class enemy.

Some Criticisms

The Italian Communist leader Berlinguer quite rightly pointed out that this is so in countries such as his, whether there are peoples' fronts or not. Even if the PCI were to get 51 per cent of the votes – or even a lot more – and establish a pure Communist government, it would still have to carry most of the other 49 per cent with it. The Italian analysis of the tragic Chilean experience is that Allende failed not simply because his Popular Unity was unable technically to defeat the military, but because it alienated large sectors of the population which it ought to have carried with it, or at least not allowed or stimulated to become bitterly antagonistic. It thus isolated itself at the very moment of danger, and provided the military plotters with both an excuse for their coup and at least a temporary mass base of social support for it. In short, socialists must not allow themselves to forget strategy and politics – isolating the adversary, winning friends, and influencing people – by falling into the trap of arithmetic, whether in the Social Democratic manner by counting votes or the ultra-radical manner by counting guns; which is not to say that either can be neglected.

Furthermore, the problem of winning political support does not disappear even when the revolutionaries are actually in effective possession of power. Portugal is a sad example of a country in which they lost a historic opportunity, partly by relying too exclusively on the backing of a military state power whose revolutionary maturity and homogeneity they overestimated, partly by the old leftist error of supposing that even in a revolutionary situation *all* the masses will automaticaly rally to the revolutionary slogans. They neglected the real distribution of political forces in their country – the fact that the workers and landless peasants were only a minority, the Church's influence, and the ease with which the small and middle peasants of the north could be mobilized by anti-Communist slogans.

This is not to say that popular front governments ought not to be criticized. They may not try to advance towards socialism at all, and may therefore be no more than ordinary temporary coalitions. I think the French Popular Front of 1936 is open to this criticism. They may rely too much on being, as it were, carried in the right direction by inevitable historical forces. As suggested above, this was the weakness of the argument that the defeat of fascism must entail the decline of capitalism, or that capitalism after the war would not be able to recover its initiative and dynamism. This meant that Communists who entered such governments did not do enough to change the political structures of their countries. For instance, it may be argued that the PCI in 1945, when it had the weight of anti-fascist insurrection behind it, neglected to destroy the structure of the old fascist bureaucracy and the political power of the Church, relying too much on a new and admittedly very progressive Constitution which they helped to draft. Again, peoples' fronts may be criticized for failing to appreciate the very serious problems of transforming heterogeneous and mutually suspicious coalitions or electoral alliances into effective reforming governments. This criticism can certainly be made of the Chilean Popular Unity. They may, finally, sometimes be criticized for not sufficiently appreciating the basic fact that government in itself is not power; that reforming governments which go too far for the ruling class may be overthrown by it, its allies, or its foreign supporters.

The Strategy which Reaction Fears

Still, when all these criticisms have been made, the peoples' fronts remain to this day the socialist strategy which most frightens the enemy. They are not scared of barricades going up in Milan or Paris but have always regarded unity as the main danger. Why in the 1950s did the Americans spend so much energy and money on splitting the national and international trade union movements and also any progressive or socialist party (such as the Italian) willing to co-operate with Communists? Why did ideologists invent the myth that nobody could ever co-operate with Communists without being swallowed by them – unless to discourage such co-operation? (In fact, such alliances have, as often as not, benefited the non-Communists, who got rid of the Communists when they had served their purpose. Communists have never regarded this as a reason for condemning all alliances on principle.) Why that other myth according to which no people has ever freely voted a red government into office?

Why, from time to time in the 1970s, did the US government through its ambassadors warn European socialist parties against having anything to do with Communists? Why did they – and do they – repeat daily that the entry of Communists into any government, whether Italian or Nicaraguan, is intolerable? Why did the Italian reaction, as we now know, conspire secretly to make coups against governments willing to include the Communist Party, and cheer – perhaps even assist – the ultra-left assassination of the Christian-Democratic statesman most favourable to this policy? Because they are afraid of the strategy of the broad alliance. They would much prefer the revolutionaries to isolate themselves, the more sectarian in spirit, the better. They know that in most countries where socialism has come, it has been brought about by broad fronts led by Communists – whether in the form of people's fronts or not – rather than through the isolated action of revolutionary Marxists. No war of liberation could have been won on any other terms.

It is sometimes a good thing to remind ourselves of what the enemy fears most. Today, in spite of two generations of criticism from the left, what he fears most – especially in the developed countries of Europe – is still the sort of strategy first systematically adopted by the international Communist movement in the 1930s.

10

Socialism and Nationalism: Some Reflections on 'The Break-up of Britain' (1977)

Nationalism has been a great puzzle to (non-nationalist) politicians and theorists ever since its invention, not only because it is both powerful and devoid of any discernible rational theory, but also because its shape and function are constantly changing. Like the cloud with which Hamlet taunted Polonius, it can be interpreted according to taste as a camel, a weasel, or a whale, though it is none of these. Perhaps the error is to apply zoological criteria instead of meteorological analysis. We are – to continue the metaphor – at present living through some sort of climatic change visibly affecting this type of meteorological phenomenon. Let us begin, unlike Tom Nairn, whose recent book *The Break-up of Britain* suggests these reflections, by charting this change.[1] The political crux of modern nationalism is the demand for 'self-determination', to constitute something like a 'nation state' as it is understood today: a sovereign and ideally homogeneous territorial unit inhabited as 'citizens' by the members of a 'nation', as defined in a variety of conventional ways (ethnic, linguistic, cultural, historical, etc.). Conversely, the citizens of modern territorial states are believed normally to constitute such a 'nation', and those who do not fit the bill are classified as 'minorities' or other 'nations' which ought logically to have their own state. The point has been reached where the terms 'state' and 'nation' are today inter-changeable ('United Nations'). Whatever our definition of peoples, nations, nationalities, etc., it is clear that this identification is historically quite recent, especially in the standardized form which has become fash-ionable and which misleads incautious observers, including Nairn.[2] In the first place, modern territorial states of the kind now taken to be normal were rather unusual until well into the nineteenth century, whether or not they claimed to be national. In the second place, the enormous difficulties and cruelties to which the attempt to divide

Europe into homogeneous nation states has led in this century (including separatism, partition, mass expulsion, and genocide) demonstrates its historic novelty.

The Nation State in the Nineteenth Century

Nevertheless, a strong case can be and was made in the nineteenth century for a certain type of 'nation state', though it has little to do with nationalism in the current sense, except in so far as this also means a convenient form of emotional cement or civic religion to weld together the citizens of such states, divided by class and in other ways ('patriotism'). Such nation states were the main building blocks of world capitalism during a lengthy period of its development, and with it of bourgeois society in the 'developed' world; as Marx recognized when he described that society in the *Communist Manifesto* as both a global unity and 'an interdependence of nations'. They represented that crucial element – the creation of the internal conditions (e.g. a 'national market') and the external conditions for the development of the 'national economy' through state organization and action. Probably, as recent Marxists like Perry Anderson and Immanuel Wallerstein have argued, the existence of an international complex of separate states was also essential to the global growth of capitalism. World capitalism consisted primarily of a set of economic flows to, from, and between such developed national economies. Marx, though in other respects not a nationalist, accepted the historic role of a certain number of such nation-state economies, which was indeed generally assumed in the nineteenth century.

The case for such nation states was not nationalist in the current sense, inasmuch as it did not envisage a world of nation states irrespective of size and resources, but only one of 'viable' states of medium to large size, which consequently (a) excluded a large number of 'national' groups from statehood, and (b) *de facto* abandoned the national homogeneity of most accepted 'nation states'. The classic statement of this programme was the outline of the 'Europe of Nations' produced in 1858 by Mazzini, who incidentally (like Cavour) found it difficult to fit into his scheme one of the few undeniable national mass movements of the time, the Irish. He envisaged a Europe composed of eleven states or federations, *all* of which (with the significant but apparent exception of Italy) were multi-national not only by current standards but also by the essentially nineteenth-century Wilsonian ones of the post-1918 peace settlements.[3] The evidence is overwhelming that at this stage the crux of nationalist movements was not so much state independence as such, but rather the construction of 'viable' states, in short 'unification' rather than 'separatism' – though this was concealed by the fact that most national movements also tended to break up one or more of the surviving obsolete empires of Austria, Turkey, and Russia. Not only did the German and Italian movements aim at unification, but so also did the Poles, the Romanians, the Yugoslavs (for whose eventual composite state there was no historic precedent), the Bulgarians (with Macedonia), very notably the Greeks, and even, through their (unhistorical) aspiration to unity with the Slovaks, the Czechs. Conversely, movements for the actual state independence of small nations, however defined, were exceedingly rare, as distinct from aspirations for various degrees of autonomy or lesser recognition within larger states. Nairn is quite wrong in regarding the nineteenth-century Scots as a striking anomaly ('the country's nineteenth-century lack of nationhood, its near-total absence from the great and varied stage of European nationalism').[4] They were a nation all right and knew it, but, unlike several other small European nations, did not need to demand what they – or rather their ruling class – already enjoyed. It is pure anachronism to expect them to have demanded an independent state at this time.

For the same reason, the prejudice (even among nationalists) against the pulverization of states (i.e. against mini-nations and mini-states) was deeply ingrained, at least in Europe. Petty German principalities or Central American republics were jokes, 'Balkanization' a term of abuse. The Austrians after 1918 could not be convinced of the viability of their small state, though this has been demonstrated since 1945. Danzig was regarded as an abortion, unlike Singapore today. The main significance of such international recognition as was given to most of the surviving pre-bourgeois mini-states was for the purposes of philately and company registration. And indeed, by contemporary standards, they were at best tolerated freaks.

The Separatist Nationalisms of the Present

The present situation is totally different. First, the characteristic nationalist movement of our time is separatist, aiming at the break-up of existing states including – the fact is novel – the oldest established 'nation states', such as Britain, France, Spain, and even – the case of Jura separatism is significant – Switzerland. It is perfectly possible to find *ad hoc* explanations for each of these cases of fission, as Nairn does for the possible break-up of Britain; but these, as he agrees, are beside the point so long as the *generality* of the phenomenon is not recognized and explained. The problem as such is not British; merely its specific circumstances and political implications.

Second, there has been a complete transformation of the concept of state viability, as is evident from the fact that the majority of the members of the United Nations is soon likely to consist of the late-twentieth-century (republican) equivalents of Saxe-Coburg-Gotha and Schwarzburg-Sondershausen. This is no doubt due, in the first instance, mainly to the process of decolonization, which left a half-globe full of small territories (or large territories with small populations) which could not or would not be combined into larger units or federations. It is also due, in the second instance, to an international situation which, with some exceptions, protects even the very feeble mini-states – once their independent status is ratified – from conquest by larger ones, if only through fear of war between the powers. The international situation also, though to a lesser extent, protects large states against disintegration, since few new states are anxious to encourage the sort of movement which might threaten their own fragile unity.[6]

Nevertheless, this Balkanization of the world of states (or rather, this transformation of the United Nations into something like the later stages of the Holy Roman Empire), also reflects a change in world capitalism which Marxists have not hitherto brought seriously into the discussion of nationalism: namely, the relative decline of the medium-to-large nation state and 'national economy' as the main building-block of the world economy. Quite apart from the fact that in the era of nuclear super-power even a fairly high potential of production, men, and resources is no longer sufficient for the military status which was formerly the criterion of a 'great power'[7] the rise of the transnational corporation and international economic management have transformed both the international division of labour and its mechanism, and changed the criterion of a state's 'economic viability'. This is no longer believed to be an economy sufficiently large to provide an adequate 'national market' and sufficiently varied to produce most of the range of goods from foodstuffs to capital equipment, but a strategic position somewhere along the complex circuits of an integrated world economy, which can be exploited to secure an adequate national income. While size was essential to the old criterion, it appears largely irrelevant to the new; as it was in the pre-industrial stage of capitalist development, when Genoa or Hamburg saw no reason to measure their viability as states by the criteria of Spain or Britain. By these new standards, Singapore is as viable and much more prosperous than Indonesia, Abu Dhabi superior to Egypt, and any speck in the Pacific can look forward to independence and a good time for its president, if it happens to possess a location for a naval base for which more solvent states will compete, a lucky gift of nature such as manganese, or merely enough beaches and pretty girls to become a tourist paradise. Of course, in military terms most mini-states are negligible; but so are most large states today. The difference between Britain and Barbados in this respect is no longer one of kind, but only one of degree.

This combination of a new phase in the international economy and the past generation's peculiar international balance of nuclear fear, has not *created* the fissiparous nationalisms of our time, but it has taken the brakes off their dreams. If the Seychelles can have a vote in the UN as good as Japan's, and Kuwaitis can, by dint of oil power, be treated like the English milords of old, then surely only the sky is the limit for the Isle of Man or the Channel Islands (to name two candidates whose case for independence is, by current standards, better than most) or the Canaries and Corsica (whose separatist movements are, no doubt, being supported somewhere or other on grounds of Marxist theory). And, of course, the new situation has transformed the prospects of mini-independence for the time being. Without discussing their merits, such proposals as statehood for a part of Northern Ireland or a vast Saharan republic resting on 60,000 nomads can no longer be excluded a priori from serious consideration on practical grounds. Moreover, the small 'developed' state is indeed today potentially much more prosperous and viable, and is taken more seriously than for some centuries. If Iceland and Luxemburg, why not Brittany and Biscay? For nationalists, who are by definition unconcerned with anything except their private collective, and given to the wilder flights of optimism, such arguments are entirely positive.[8] At most they may find their night's rest occasionally disturbed by what one might call the 'Shetland effect', namely the thought that you do not have to be an old or large state to be vulnerable to fission. Others must see the emergence of the new divisive nationalism in a wider context.

Sovereignty as Dependence

Their first observation will be that the multiplication of independent sovereign states substantially changed the sense of the term 'independence' for most of them into a synonym for 'dependence' – as anticipated by that historic ancestor of modern neo-colonialism, nineteenth-century Latin America. We may leave aside the obvious fact that many of them exist as independent states only on sufferance or under protection. (Cyprus, ex-Portuguese Timor, and Lebanon show what may happen when neither is available.) They are economically dependent in two ways: generally, on an international economy they cannot normally hope to influence as individuals;[9] and specifically – in inverse proportion to their size – on the greater powers and transnational corporations. The fact that these today prefer – or find indispensable – a neo-colonial relationship rather than something like a formalized dependence, should not mislead us. On the contrary. The optimal strategy for a neo-colonial transnational economy is precisely one in which the number of officially sovereign states is maximized and their average size and strength – that is, their power effectively to impose the conditions under which foreign powers and foreign capital will have to operate – is minimized. Even in the 1920s, the real banana republics were small – say, Nicaragua rather than Colombia. And today it is pretty evident that the USA or Japan and their corporations would prefer to deal with Alberta rather than Canada, Western Australia rather than the Australian Commonwealth, when it came to making economic terms. (There are indeed autonomist aspirations in both provinces.) This aspect of the new state system is not to be overlooked, though it cannot, of course, be used as a blanket a priori argument for large states against smaller ones, and even less for unitary states against devolved or federal ones.

A second observation is that, irrespective of the merits of any particular national cause, the present situation encourages – and not only among nationalists – the assumption that state independence, or what amounts to it, is the normal mode of satisfying the demands of any group with some claims to a territorial base (a 'country'), that is, a potential nation.[10] This is mistaken on three grounds. In the first place, there is no warrant for this assumption in theory, history, or even current practice. In the second place, it implicitly or explicitly discards the numerous and (with all their problems) far from unworkable formulae for combining national unity and devolution, decentralization, or federation. To name but a few: the USA, Canada, Australia, Federal Germany, Italy, Yugoslavia, Switzerland, and Austria. In other words, it tends to overlook those problems of the 'revolt against big states' and 'demands for regional self-government'[11] which cannot be assimilated to nationalist ones which can in turn be expressed as separatism: Britanny is visible, Normandy is not.

In the third place, and perhaps most seriously, the problem is sidestepped of how to organize the actual coexistence of different ethnic, racial, linguistic, and other groups in areas which are practically indivisible. These are, of course, the norm.[12] It is no reflection on the merits of, say, Flemish nationalism to say that to anyone except passionate Flemings the discontents of that nation seem objectively much easier to deal with than the problem of, say, the blacks in the USA or settled immigrant workers anywhere in Europe.

Marxism and Nationalism

Does the present phase of nationalism require any change in the attitude of Marxists to this phenomenon? If Nairn's book is anything to go by, it certainly appears to require, rather than the by now ritual breast-beating about theoretical deficiencies in this field, a reminder of the basic fact that Marxists as such are not nationalists. They cannot be so as theorists, given the nature of what passes for nationalist theory. (They certainly cannot be as historians, given Ernest Renan's ancient and true observation that getting their history wrong is an essential characteristic of nations.) They cannot be so in practice, since nationalism by definition subordinates all other interests to those of its specific 'nation'. We need not take the Luxemburgist position to state categorically that any Marxists who are not, at least in theory, prepared to see the 'interests' of their own country or people subordinated to wider interests, had best reconsider their ideological loyalties. This applies not only to Marxists. Israelis and Palestinians may think the maintenance or establishment of their respective states worth a global war, or act as if they did, but the rest of the world's 4,000-odd million can hardly agree with them. The test, of course, must be the Marxist's *own* country or people, for obvious psychological and other reasons. The test of a Jewish Marxist, even one who wishes to preserve what is now an established Jewish people in Israel, is that he or she is *not* a Zionist. This also applies to Scots.

In practice, naturally, the test is not so clear-cut as in theory. This is not so much because most Marxists, starting with Marx and Engels, were and are proud of the nations, and ethnic, cultural, or other communities to which they belong, but because for obvious reasons (which Nairn underlines) most actual Marxist socialist movements operate within the confines of some state or people – indeed, in most successful cases as mobilizers and representatives of nations as well as of their oppressed – and the interests of such national entities are often clearly neither congruent nor convergent. This leaves a lot of scope for Marxist rationalizations and justifications of national policies. The problem lies in distinguishing those which are merely rationalizations. Once again, this is easier for outsiders. Few non-Chinese Marxists are impressed by the Chinese defence in Marxist terms of a foreign policy which in recent years has not looked as if it is designed to advance the cause of non-Chinese socialism. At this moment, Eritreans and the Somali Republic (the latter claiming to be Marxist) are doubtless justifying the break-up of the Ethiopian state with quotations from Lenin, just as the (Marxist) Ethiopian government is justifying the maintenance of its country's unity. Outsiders can readily see that their actions (but not their arguments) would be much the same if none of them claimed to be Marxist.

If Marxists, though believers in national development and mostly devoted to their own nations, are not nationalists, they still have to come to terms with the political fact of nationalism and to define their attitudes towards its specific manifestations. Ever since Marx, this has for the most part, and necessarily, been a matter not of theoretical principle (except perhaps for the Luxemburgian minority which tends to suspect nations *en bloc*) but of pragmatic judgement in changing circumstances. In principle, Marxists are neither for nor against independent statehood for any nation (which is not the same as Lenin's 'right to self-determination'), even assuming that there can be other than pragmatic agreement on what constitutes 'the nation' in any particular case. Neither, of course, is anyone else, including nationalists – except for their own nation. If they have any historical image of the international ordering of a future world socialism, it is certainly not a mosaic of homogeneous sovereign nation states, large or – as we can now see – mainly small, but as some form of association or organizational union of nations, possibly proceeding, though this note has been rarely struck with confidence since the *Manifesto*, to the eventual dissolution of national into global or generally human culture. Since they rightly see nations in the modern sense as historical phenomena rather than a priori eternal data of human society, their policy cannot regard them as absolute. How indeed could it in, say, the Middle East, where the question of war or peace hinges on two 'nations' which, as territorial state nations, had hardly, if at all, been conceived in 1918. In short, the Marxist attitude towards nationalism as a programme is similar in many respects to Marx's attitude towards other a priori abstractions of what in his day was petty-bourgeois radicalism, for example, the 'democratic republic'. It is not unsympathetic, but contingent and not absolute. The fundamental criterion of Marxist pragmatic judgement has always been whether nationalism as such, or any specific case of it, advances the cause of socialism; or conversely, how to prevent it from inhibiting its progress; or alternatively, how to mobilize it as a force to assist its progress. Few Marxists have argued that *no* nationalist movement can be supported, none that *all* automatically serve this purpose and are therefore always to be supported. No Marxist (outside the nation concerned) will regard with other than suspicion Marxist parties which put the independence of their nations above all other objectives regardless of context.

Lenin and National Liberation

Nevertheless, since Lenin Marxists have developed a national policy

powerful enough to associate Marxism and national liberation movements over large parts of the world, and sometimes to build national
movements under Marxist leadership. This policy rested essentially on
three pillars. First, it widened the category of 'national movements'
regarded as essentially 'progressive' in their impact much beyond Marx's
and Engels's own. It could now include the great majority of twentieth-
century national movements, especially when, as during the anti-fascist
period, it was extended to embrace any national resistance to the most
dangerous reactionary powers. Though Nairn appears not to be aware of
this, 'progressive' nationalism was therefore not confined only to the
category of movements directed against imperialist exploitation and
representing something like the 'bourgeois-democratic phase' in the
development of backward countries. Second, it therefore made possible
and desirable revolutionary Marxist movements which acted not simply
as class movements of the exploited and oppressed, but also as leaders in
the fight of entire nations for emancipation: in short, movements such as
those of the Chinese, Vietnamese, Yugoslavs, etc. – but also of Gram-
scian Communism. Third, it recognized the social forces which gave
national movements reality, and the political power of such movements,
by accepting as a matter of principle the right of self-determination
including secession – though Lenin, in fact, did not recommend socialists in the countries concerned to favour secession except in specific, and
pragmatically identifiable, circumstances.

In spite of its remarkable successes, this Leninist policy should not go
uncriticized. Thus there is no denying the fact that only in a few cases
have Marxists succeeded in establishing or maintaining themselves as the
leading force in their national movement. In most cases, especially when
such movements were already in existence as serious political forces or
under the auspices of state governments, they have either become subordinate to, or been absorbed by, or pushed aside by non-Marxist or
anti-Marxist nationalism. To this extent, the Luxemburgist case is not
entirely unrealistic. Looking back on the Irish movement, for instance, it
may well be argued that an Irish workers' party would today be more
politically significant and promising if Connolly had not, by his rebellion
and death identified its cause with Catholic–nationalist Fenianism, thus
effectively making impossible a united labour movement of North and
South. So far from transforming it, the Marxist element in Irish nationalism has produced little more than another nationalist saint and martyr,
and a social-revolutionary tinge on the radical fringes of the IRA which,
as Ulster since 1968 demonstrates, has not been anything like strong
enough to overcome the tradition so readily mobilized by and for the
Provos. Irish Communism is insignificant and the Irish Labour Party
weaker than anywhere else in the British Isles. I am not arguing, even if

such an exercise in counter-factual (i.e. fictional) history were possible, that the Irish socialist movement would have done better to concentrate on the class interests of its proletarian and agrarian constituency, leaving national insurrection to others. I merely point out that, in its own Marxist terms, the Connolly Marxist–nationalist policy must be regarded as a failure. There is no reason to suppose a priori that Scots or Welsh revolutionary Marxists have a good chance of transforming the SNP or Plaid Cymru into some kind of Vietcong merely by offering their services and leadership to the nationalist cause.

Whatever the pros and cons of Lenin's national policy in the abstract, the present situation differs from the one envisaged in his day in four main respects. First, as we have seen, the relation between national states and global capitalist development, internally and internationally, is no longer what it was. Second, the virtual disappearance of formal empires ('colonialism') has snapped the main link between anti-imperialism and the slogan of national self-determination. However real the dependence of neo-colonialism, the struggle against it simply cannot any longer be crystallized round the slogan of establishing independent political statehood, because most territories concerned already have it. Third, the emergence of a large socialist sector of the globe has intro-duced problems of national friction and potential separatism which plainly cannot have the same relation to the overthrow of capitalism as in colonies and capitalist metropoles, and this may also be true of national problems in non-socialist third world countries. Finally, as we have seen, the visible problem of nationalism today is largely that of the fission of 'developed' capitalist states. In short, the relationship between nationalism and both capitalism and socialism (present or future) is profoundly changed.

This is of no significance to nationalists, who do not care what this relationship is, so long as Ruritanians (or whoever) acquire sovereign statehood as a nation, or indeed what happens thereafter. Their utopia – by now at least as shop-soiled by practice as some others – consists precisely in the achievement of Ruritanian (and if possible Greater Ruri-tanian) independence and rule, if need be over the non-Ruritanians in their midst. On the other hand, it raises considerable intellectual hurdles for nationalists wishing to disguise themselves as Marxists, for Marxists who want to be on the winning side for a change, or for anyone else seeking to score the call of the nationalist bugle for the full historical-materialist orchestra. For the problem does not lie in admitting the fact – reluctant though many Marxists have been to do so – that for most purposes or at most times class exists effectively within the confines of a community, territory, culture, racial, or linguistic group or state – i.e. within those of a potential or actual 'nation'. In short, and though Nairn suggests otherwise,[13] the main debate among Marxists on the 'national question' has not been between Leninists and Luxemburgians.[14]

The Contradictions of 'Nationalist Marxism'

The real problem for nationalist Marxists is twofold. First, it lies in the fact that there is no way of turning the formation of 'national communities' (i.e. the multiplication of nation-states *as such*) into a historic engine for generating socialism either to replace or to supplement the Marxian historic mechanism. (This, as we have seen, includes the formation of *some* nation states as an essential part of capitalist development, and a crucial strategic role for *some* national movements; but not what nationalism requires, namely a charter for *any* such state or movement.) Indeed, Nairn's own admittedly rather improvized theory of nationalism[15] does not set out to provide such a mechanism, but merely to establish that the continuing multiplication of independent states ('socio-political fragmentation') up to an undefined completion[16] is an ineluctable by-product of the uneven development of capitalism, and therefore must be accepted as the 'settled and inescapable' setting of socialist aspirations. This may or may not be so, but it can only become a force which socialists welcome as socialists on the entirely unargued assumption that separatism is in itself a step to revolution.

Second, and crucially for nationalists though not for Marxists, there is no way of using the general argument of growing Balkanization as a specific argument for the independence of any one putative 'nation'. To assume that the multiplication of independent states has an end is to assume that the world can be subdivided into a finite number of homogeneous potential 'nation states' immune to further subdivision, and that these can be specified in advance. This is plainly not the case, and even if it were, the result would not necessarily be a world of nation states. British imperialism was certainly biased in using the multiplicity of linguistic groups on the Indian subcontinent as an argument against Indian nationalism; but – if we do not actually deny their 'right to self-determination' – it is far from obvious that the division of the Indo–Burmese–Chinese frontier region into twenty separate 'nation states' would be either practicable or desirable.[17] We need not here discuss the assumption that all 'nations' must, or are destined to, form separate sovereign states, beyond pointing out that any finite number of such states must exclude some potential candidates from statehood. In short, whatever the assessment of the general historical tendency, the argument for the formation of any independent nation state must always be an *ad hoc* argument, which undermines the case for *universal* self-determination by separatism. The irony of nationalism is that the argument for the separation of Scotland from England is exactly analogous to the argument for the separation of the Shetlands from Scotland; and so are the arguments against both separations.

It would, of course, be absurd to deny that the relation between nationalism and socialism also raises enormous difficulties for non-nationalist socialists. There is the subjective dilemma of, say, the US Marxists, whose country is the major pillar of international capitalism (and reaction), who cannot realistically look forward to its socialist transformation in the foreseeable future, and whose nationalism is largely defined by excluding people like them as 'un-American'. Like the German anti-fascists under the Nazis, they could (but with less conviction) console themselves with the thought that they represented the 'true' as against the falsified 'nation'; but in reality they cannot avoid swimming dead against the stream of local 'patriotism'. There is the more general, and alas objective, fact that Marxist movements and states have failed to find a solution to 'the national question'. Neither Austro-Marxism nor (without state power) Leninist Marxism has been able to prevent the break-up of comprehensive parties into national sections when national pressure was sufficiently great; and Leninism has certainly not been able to prevent the break-up of its international movement on largely national lines. Multi-national socialist states have what appears to the naked eye to be much the same problems of local nationalisms as non-socialist ones. Alternatively, Marxist movements and states have tended to become national not only in form but in substance, i.e. nationalist. There is nothing to suggest that this trend will not continue.

If this is so, the already evident gap between Marxism as the analysis of what is, or is coming into being, and Marxism as the formulation of what we want to happen, will grow wider. A little more of utopia will have to be dismantled, or packed off to a future beyond prediction. The socialist world will, if it comes into being in the present historic constellation – but who will bet much on that? – not be the world of international peace, fraternity, and friendship of which philosophers and revolutionaries have dreamed. Not all of us will be as quick as Nairn to write off this 'grand universalizing tradition' (which as he says goes back far beyond Marx) as a mere aberration of Eurocentrism, a 'metropolitan fantasy' – fortunately his theory of nationalism is too unconvincing to tempt us to do so.[18] However, we have had enough time since 1914 to get used to an international socialism – as movements or states – which falls short of the old dreams and hopes. The real danger for Marxists is the temptation to welcome nationalism as ideology and programme rather than realistically to accept it as a fact, a condition of their struggle as socialists. (We do not, after all, welcome the fact that capitalism has proved considerably more resistant and economically viable than Marx or Lenin expected, even though we are obliged to accept it.) Quite apart from implying the abandonment of the values of the Enlightenment, of reason and science, such a conversion also implies a withdrawal from a realistic analysis of the world situation, Marxist or otherwise. That is why books like Nairn's ought to be criticized, in spite of, perhaps because of, the author's talent and frequent insights. Karl Kraus's phrase about psychoanalysis (whether it was right or wrong about Freud) also applies to them: they are at least a symptom of the sickness of which they purport to be the cure.

On 'The Break-up of Britain'

It is not my object here to discuss Nairn's book in detail. This consists essentially of two sets of arguments: a specific case for 'the break-up of Britain' and a general case for the inadequacy of Marxism on the grounds – the author will perhaps pardon a little polemical over simpli-fication – that it does not recognize that the splitting of big states into smaller states is a sort of historical law. The former contains interesting, acute, sometimes remarkable, observations about English and Irish, though not so much about Scottish and Welsh history, but suffers from a tendency to anti-English invective. The latter suffers from the usual disadvantages of special pleading disguised as grand theory. As an inter-pretation of Marxism it is debatable. As a theory of nationalism, in spite of neo-Marxist terminology ('uneven development', references to Anderson and Wallerstein), it is not much different from others now current among academics.[19]

It is more tempting to discuss Nairn's lengthy, impassioned, and often brilliant enquiry into the 'crisis of England', for it really is important to trace back to the peculiarities and compromises of the English revolu-tion, the triumph of British bourgeois society, in some respects unusually complete, in others unusually incomplete. Moreover, Nairn breaks genuinely new Marxist ground here, particularly in linking British capitalism's inadaptability to the conditions of the second half of this century to the cultural–political and state structures which are the result of these peculiarities of 'bourgeois revolution'. One must pay tribute in passing to Nairn's contributions. However, his arguments are double-edged. A century ago they could have been used to explain the triumphs and successes of British capitalism, just as analogous ones can today be used to explain the unusual success of German and Japanese capitalism, and not inconceivably the economic success of German socialism. More-over, in one way or another such considerations apply to any bourgeois country, not excluding, in Nairn's own formulation, to eighteenth- and nineteenth-century Scotland. This is so because by Nairn's own argu-ment 'uneven development' excludes the reality of a 'standard' version of a 100 per cent 'pure' bourgeois society. In any case, since no 'developed country' has so far produced a socialist revolution, some variant of the argument from history can be used to explain its non-occurrence anywhere. Conversely, since a growing number of the old 'nation states' show tendencies to fission, the British analysis that it is due to economic shipwreck is unconvincing as an explanation of the more general phenomenon.

Nairn's book is by no means the only attempt to fudge the differences between Marxists and nationalism. What makes such books as his so melancholy a symptom of our times is precisely that he is *neither* the sort of nationalist who today sports a Marxist badge as before the war he might have looked to the ultra-right, *nor* the sort of Marxist who, in the crunch, discovers that he/she is a Jew or Arab *rather than* a Marxist. His strength has always been to see the auto-mystifications of those who talk of 'demystification', the intellectual cotton wool behind political phrases masquerading as political analysis, the refusal to recognize realities because they are disagreeable. Where neither his nor most of the world's emotions are strongly committed, as on Ulster (about which, as he rightly observes, few people outside Northern Ireland really *care*), this lends his analysis an admirable muscular ruthlessness. Even his Scottish nationalism – not the same thing as his Scottishness – seems not so much a basis and objective of his politics as a last retreat.

For anybody can be a realist when prospects look good. The difficulty begins when, as today, analysis suggests to realistic observers like Nairn conclusions of deep pessimism. In spite of his disclaimer, his attitude is strongly marked by Walter Benjamin's image, which he quotes, of 'progress' as the pile of debris which we, advancing backwards into the future, see accumulating in the storms of history; by the fear that perhaps the future will not be as we wish, or even as we would find tolerable. The various mechanisms on which Marxists, more or less loosely basing themselves on Marx's analysis, have relied for the replacement of capitalism by socialism are not working: neither in the developed countries, nor in most of the 'third world' – itself a concept whose looseness is now obvious. As for the actual socialist states, their internal problems and the uncertainties of their own future are not to be denied. Moreover, even for those of us who refuse to diminish their extraordinary historic achievements, they are in their present form diffi-cult to accept as models of a desirable socialist future. Capitalist society is at present in global crisis, but few can believe that its probable, or even in the short term its possible, outcome in any country will be socialism. On what then, other than blind will or an act of faith in historical inevitability, are we to base our hopes? But Marxists have never been blind voluntarists, nor have they ever based themselves on historical inevitability or philosophical generalization in the abstract. They have always sought to identify specific social and political forces, specific conjunctures and situations, which would dig capitalism's grave.

The Temptations of Separatism

Here lies the temptation of separatist nationalism, an unquestionably active, growing, and powerful socio-political force, capable, on its own limited ground, of imposing terms not only on the workers, but also on the bourgeoisie and on capitalist states. Moreover, it visibly grows with the crisis of both. Nairn rightly stresses that Scots and Welsh national separatism as serious forces arise out of the crisis of British capitalism; he sees it as 'escape from the final stages of a shipwreck'. It is equally and more concretely true, though he does not say so, that they acquired such mass support as they have, especially among workers, as a direct result of the failure of the British Labour Party in the sixties. So long as the Scots and Welsh put their hopes in whatever was the all-national party of 'progress and the people' – first liberalism, later Labour – the mass basis for separatist nationalism was (unlike Ireland) negligible; and conversely, as in some other developed bourgeois states – notably the USA – the 'people's party' could acquire added strength (and the capacity to serve its supporters) by broadening into an alliance of workers, intellectuals, national, racial, and religious minorities, and disadvantaged regions.[20] There is no reason to suppose that the discovery by the Scottish middle class of the oil bonanza – which in any case post-dated the rise of a nationalist mass basis – would have made the mass of Scots workers automatically more inclined to follow the SNP; or indeed that the argument that a flourishing and dynamic Scottish economy is stifled by the connection with backward England would have sounded more convincing in Strathclyde than it does anyway outside Scots nationalist circles.

Cannot this undoubted and formidable force, inseparable from capitalist (or perhaps any) 'development', constantly generated by it, growing and becoming more universal with its inequalities, tensions, and contradictions, be in some way the grave-digger of capitalism? Can it not, with all its admitted ambiguity ('The Modern Janus') be seen as not only inevitable but also desirable – for example, as helping to restore 'the real values of smaller, more recognizable communities'? Must not, as for Sherlock Holmes, the elimination of all other hypotheses produce the true solution, however implausible? It can perhaps only produce 'a detour on the way to revolution', but where the main road has been blocked or destroyed, have we any other option? The temptation to discover that it can or must is great, but so also is the danger that the detour will become the journey. If separatist nationalism (in the form of the 'break-up of Britain' or in any other country) turns out *not* to be 'a progressive action – a step forward not only for their own peoples, but for England and the wider state-order as well', 'then neo-nationalism needs no further justification at all'. 'Who, in that case, can deny (the Scots, Welsh, etc.) effective self-determination, not as a moral piety, but as an urgently necessary, practical step?'[21] We have insensibly got to the point where creating another nation state becomes its own purpose, and the leftwing argument becomes indistinguishable from that of all the Ruritanias of the past whose spokesmen were anxious to assure us all, and doubtless to believe, that what was good for Ruritania was good for the world, but if it was not, they would go ahead nevertheless.

Nationalism and Socialism in Britain

Yet whatever the general theoretical or historical argument, the crucial questions must be whether the 'break-up of Britain' or other large nation states will help socialism, and indeed whether it is as inevitable as Nairn states or implies. But these are not questions of general theory but of concrete reality and probability. To the uncommitted eye, the positive socialist effects of a break-up of the United Kingdom, however inevitable, are not at present visible. It may be true that 'forces capable of unhinging the state finally appear . . . as harbingers of a new time', if, with Nairn, we regard the prior destruction of the old state as a necessary precondition of, or even 'the principal factor making for a political revolution of some sort'. It is a matter of pure faith to suppose that this will help the left. To Nairn's rhetorical question 'why should this not be true in the British case also?' the only answer is: 'Please give reasons why it should.' Even if we leave aside as too 'electoralist' the probability that the Labour Party in a rump-England would be an almost permament minority party, by far the most likely effect of a secession of Scotland and Wales would be an enormous reinforcement of English nationalism, that is to say, under present circumstances, of a xenophobic, vicious and – one must use the term in spite of its deviation by the mindless ultra-left – a semi-fascist radical right. It is easy to make fun of the fact that English nationalism has not been quite like so many others and to foresee that, after enough of a beating, it 'will become a nation like all the rest' (!).[22] Nairn, whose generation has been lucky enough not to live through the time when Germany went through such a process, may well regret such politicians' bromides as: 'In time the rest of us will learn to live with the result, which will have some compensations as well as its bitterness and ultra-nationalist follies.'[23] It is easier to anatomize the eccentric Enoch Powell who did *not* become the leader of English nationalism than the first English Nationalist movement 'like all the rest' which has actually achieved a degree of mass support, not least among workers. Is it really possible to discuss the future of English nationalism in 1977 without, so far as I can recall, a single reference to the National Front or movements of its kind?

Unless one is a Welshman or a Scot, the prospect that the break-up of the United Kingdom is more likely than not to precipitate forty-six out of its fifty-four million into reaction (the million and a half in Ulster may be left aside as *sui generis*) is not offset by the possible advance of socialism among the remaining eight. But, in fact, there is no very convincing reason to expect such an advance. The best that can be said about independent Wales is that it will probably not be all that much different politically from the present Wales. It will quite evidently be *less* close to socialist revolution than in the great days of the South Wales Miners' Federation; but it is perhaps not impossible that, faced with some real competition from a Plaid Cymru fortunately also imbued with the basic political traditions of the country, which are those of the historic left, Labour will try to recover some of its ancient spirit. The triumph of the SNP, a classical petty-bourgeois nationalist party of the provincial right suddenly precipitated into government, can only be achieved on the ruins of the Labour Party, from which – alas – the Communist Party, whose record as a champion of the *people* of Scotland is much the best, is far from likely to benefit much. Anyone who thinks the SNP would readily let itself be transformed into something like a socialist party is whistling in the dark. It might or might not break up. Labour might or might not recover. What the Scots Tories and Liberals might or might not do is anyone's guess. The safest prophecy is that Scottish politics would be complex and unpredictable, and might be rather savage if the hope of universal prosperity as the Kuwait of the North, or as an industrial economy whose problems will miraculously disappear with independence (unlike those of, say, the English northeast), proves unreal. What is pretty certain is that it will be nothing like another Norway.

Is Separation Inevitable?

By any short-term calculation, the break-up of the United Kingdom is, therefore, a prospect to which the left may have to resign itself, but which calls for no enthusiasm and some foreboding. This is not an argument in favour of maintaining the unity of this or any other state on principle. But are such break-ups of multi-national or other large states inevitable? It is obviously to the interest of separatists to argue that nothing can stop their cause, but experience does not suggest that they are. Let us leave aside the counter-tendencies which have, in the past fifty years, made, for example, the federations of Brazil, Mexico, and the USA probably more unitary or centrally controlled than before. Let us omit the – so far – successful examples of postwar devolution as opposed to break-up in West Germany and Italy. Nairn, who acknowledges them, suggests that it may be too late for others, but that is a matter of argument. In fact, the great bulk of the new states since 1945 have not arisen by the division of existing states, but by the formal separation of already separate dependent territories, within pre-established frontiers, from their metropoles.[24] There are examples of successful secessions – notably that of Bangladesh from Pakistan – but perhaps rather more of failed ones (Biafra, Katanga, Azerbaijan, Kurdistan, etc.). Concretely, the question is one of power, including military power; of the determination of governments; of help or opposition by foreign states; of the international situation in general – and no a priori generalizations about it are possible. Concretely, the argument that state independence for Scotland and Wales is 'inevitable' assumes that, if the local pressure for it were to prove overwhelming, England would behave like Sweden towards Norway in 1905 or Denmark towards Iceland after 1944 – which may be a reasonable assumption, but has nothing to do with historical inevitability.

But is the pressure for separation overwhelming? Does neo-nationalism imply the aim of state independence? Is the present – and undeniable – reaction against centralized bureaucracy felt as such by the individual, and against entities (not only states) on a scale beyond human relations, necessarily 'nationalist' in origin or character? Once again, it is to the interest of nationalists to argue that it is – at least in so far as states are concerned, these being the only entities they normally consider. But to accept this assumption is to beg questions not only of analysis but also of policy in a manner which Marxists cannot do. It is to accept nationalism at its own valuation, or rather at that of the ideologists and politicians who claim to be its spokesmen; to recognize not problems and facts, but manifestoes. It is to recognize the problems of declining industrial areas (or even to deny them) when they are formulated in 'national' terms (Walloon nationalism for the Belgian ones, Scots nationalism for Strathclyde), but not when they are not (northeast England); to see the crisis of rural life when the influx of second-homers or commuters is 'foreign', as in north Wales, but not when it is 'native', as in Suffolk. It is to recognize as 'nations' those who shout and not those who do not; to risk identifying the problems of the Jews as a people (most of whom, including 10 per cent of the population of Israel, continue to live in the diaspora, and are likely to go on doing so) with the problems of the state which includes one fifth of them. It is to forget – as Nairn does – the distinction between unquestionable 'nations' and movements with undoubted political weight, such as Scotland, Wales, the Catalans, Basques, and Flemings, and what – at present anyway – are little more than doubtful and fuzzy ideological constructs like 'Occitania'.[25]

Even if we do not choose to query the existence of nationalism or (more unwisely) the claims of this or that political party or ideological group to give us its only true version, the number of questions this assumption begs is immense. What actually changed in the aspirations of Welsh-speaking Welshmen in Merioneth and Caernarfon when they finally decided to elect a Plaid Cymru MP instead of a Liberal or Labour one? Certainly not that they suddenly acquired a nationalism which they previously lacked. (Conversely, why did more than half the Ladinsh speakers in South Tyrol vote to emigrate into Hitler Germany in the plebiscite of 1939? Hardly because they considered themselves ethnic Germans or German nationalists.) Were the Catholic Irish somehow less nationalist when they overwhelmingly supported Parnell and his successors who did not demand anything like independence, than when they later voted for Sinn Fein which did? Are the Welsh less nationalist than the Scots because Paid Cymru is electorally weaker than the SNP? An uncommitted observer might conclude the opposite, both from history and from inspection. Would even the Plaid prove to be less nationalist than the SNP if, as is not improbable, it proved to be less rigidly committed to breaking all state links with England? Is it enough to state the obvious, namely that the strong pro-Catalan and pro-Basque votes in those parts of Spain are evidence of nationalist predominance, without investigating how far they are votes for secession, for some other form of autonomous association, and if so which?

Nations and Historical Change

But there is, for Marxists and others, a broader set of questions which such nationalist assumptions beg. It is or ought to be obvious that the specific character of regions or groups does not point invariably in one direction, both for reasons of political calculation and because they themselves do not remain historically unchanged. Nairn admits the first consideration, when he insists that the specific interests of Protestant Ulstermen led them, logically enough, to insist on union with Britain, and that even today 'independence is seen here as a Biblical last strait . . . the awesome threat at the end of the line'.[26] Political independence is one option out of several. Tyrol has in the course of the twentieth century attempted to maintain its rather strong 'identity' and special interests by ultra-loyalty to the multi-national Habsburg empire, by seeking various degrees of autonomy in Austria, by integration into a pan-German Reich, and once, though only for a moment, by playing with the idea of a separate Tyrolean republic.

The second consideration is equally relevant. Economically, the trend to transform and integrate regional interests in larger unities is undeniable. In the USA 'where the pull of the old southern sectionalism was to remain apart from the rest of the country, the South's sectional interests today are impelling it to move into the national mainstream.'[27] It may be, for reasons discussed earlier, that it is today fairly practicable to combine integration with small-state independence, so long as the operations of the multi-nationals are not made impossibly inconvenient. Nevertheless, the point is not whether, if need be, Frisia could be independent of the Netherlands and West Germany, or Salzburg once again from Austria, but whether 'centuries of world history' are in fact leading in this direction and in no other.

I do not make these points to question the reality and force of nationalism today, or even to query Nairn's empirical observation that, once a nationalist movement has entered the politics of a country as a mass force, it is likely to stay there permanently in one form or another. Nor do they imply any attitude in principle towards big or small, unitary or any variety of federal states, separatism in general or in any particular case, in Britain or elsewhere. What they do imply is that Marxists ought not to swallow the story that the process of 'socio-political fragmentation' or the development of nationalism into 'a kind of world norm', even if we were to accept it without further analysis (which we should not), allows us to make any prediction of moment about the future of any particular state, region, people, linguistic or other group, or nationalist organization; and still less that history has been working exclusively up to the particular set of political arrangements advocated by, say, the SNP. It implies recognizing the character of nationalism as a dependent as well as an independent variable in historical change. In short, it implies making a Marxist analysis of the phenomenon in general, whether or not we decide to cheer or to oppose it in any particular version or instance. That this implies a continued rethinking and development of the Marxist *analysis* is self-evident. Not only because – in spite of a much larger and more valuable body of past work than critics are prepared to recognize – Marxist views on 'the national question' are not satisfactory; but above all because the very development of world history changes the context, the nature and the implications of 'nations' and 'nationlism'. However, I cannot see that Nairn has made a useful or convincing contribution to this.

Marxists and Nationalism Today

Meanwhile, the practical *attitude* of Marxists to the concrete political problems raised by 'the national question' hardly requires serious modification. They will, no doubt, continue to be as conscious of nationality and nationalism as they have been for most of the twentieth century: they can hardly not be. Subject only to the built-in fuzziness and changeability of the concept, they will continue to favour the fullest development for any nation, its right of self-determination including secession; which as always, will not mean that they will regard secession as desirable in every case. They will no doubt continue, in most cases, both to be profoundly attached to their own nations, and to champion these: their record in the European resistance movements of the Hitler period speaks for itself. However, unlike nationalists, they will also continue to recognize – generally before others – the multi-nationality behind the facade of states, large or small. Their very non-nationalism and their refusal to identify 'the nations', its 'interests', 'destiny', etc. with this or that nationalist programme at any given moment will continue to make them effective champions of nations, racial groups, etc. *other than their own* (as English Communists have consistently been of Scots and Welsh nationhood), whether or not they actually demand state separation. Marxists will, therefore, continue to be not merely enemies of 'great-nation chauvinism', but also of 'little-nation chauvinism', which is not a negligible force in a world largely composed of little nations. They will not always get it right, though one may guess that they are more likely to get it wrong when they find themselves swallowing some nationalist assumption whole, as so many Marxists have done for so long in the matter of Ulster. They will, alas, sometimes – especially when in government – fail to live up to their own principles. When they do, one hopes that some of them will have the courage to say so, as Lenin did when, in his 'Testament', he criticized the 'chauvinist' behaviour of Stalin, Dzerzhinsky, and Ordzhonikidze.

Nobody has given good reasons why this attitude, which is essentially shared (in spite of Nairn's combats with the ghost of Luxemburg) by most Marxists, should not provide adequate guidance in principle to the political problems Marxists are likely to encounter in this field. Including the 'break-up of the United Kingdom', which, in the form of Scottish and Welsh secession, most of them would today not regard as a desirable solution, unlike the secession of an independent Ulster, which many of them might welcome. Which does not mean that they would not accept it as a fact or even in other circumstances, welcome it. This attitude provides no guarantee of success, but neither does Nairn's. The difference between the two is that one deludes itself less than the other. In so far as Nairn remains within the established, and historically or politically far from unrealistic, range of Marxist debate on the attitude to nationalism, his assessments are arguable, though some of us may think them mistaken. In so far as he tries to change the terms of that debate, the main drift of his arguments seems to be not, as he claims, to make Marxism 'for the first time an authentic world theory', or 'to separate out the durable – the "scientific" . . . from the ideology in our *Weltanschauung*', but to change the ideology and undermine the 'science'.

It puts Marxism at the mercy of nationalism. In this, unfortunately, Nairn is not alone nowadays, particularly in countries in which national issues dominate political debate. As Maxime Rodinson has put it, writing about the Arab Middle East:

> On the one hand, pure nationalism utilized justifications of a Marxist kind and recruited apologists formed by Marxism. . . . On the other international leftism . . . vigorously denounced the pure nationalist regimes. . . . But it did not give any less priority to the national struggle. The sophistical device for justifying this consisted in the thesis that 'the masses' were the ones to show unqualified loyalty to the nationalist cause in its most extremist form. . . . Social revolution was therefore seen in what was in the final analysis a nationalist perspective. Thereby it runs the risk of subordination to nationalism.[28]

One does not have to be a Luxemburgist to recognize the dangers of a Marxism which loses itself in nationalism. Lenin was not talking about the Flemings or the Bretons, but about what he saw as the clearest case of 'progressive' and 'revolutionary' anti-imperialist nationalism, when he warned Zinoviev and his colleagues who wanted to preach 'holy war' at the Baku Congress of 1920. 'Do not paint nationalism red', he said.[29] The warning still stands.

Notes

1. Tom Nairn, *The Break-up of Britain* (BB), Verso, London 1977.
2. England is no less a nation than Scotland because Nairn does not think that it is yet

'a nation like the rest' (ibid., p. 301), that is, having a nationalist ideology and party of the now standard model like the Scots.

3. Even on the assumption (doubtful in those days) that the Italians formed a single homogeneous nation, post-1945 devolution has rightly recognized the need for a special status for Sicily, Sardinia, the bi- or tri-national South Tyrol, and the Val d'Aosta.

4. BB, p. 144.

5. The major exceptions to this trend in Europe, the German Federal Republic and Italy, have almost certainly avoided separatist tendencies so far – for example, by Bavaria, Sicily, and Sardinia – by virtue of adopting or being forced to adopt a far-reaching devolution after the war, as part of the reaction against fascism which pushed nineteenth-century tendencies of national unification to their logical conclusion.

6. Paradoxically, this means that separatist movements with genuine 'national' or ethnic mass support, are today apt to be discouraged by the bulk of other states, irrespective of ideology; compare the attitude of most African governments to the Biafran and Katangan secessions. The safest way to win support for independency is to be a dependence of a decolonizing power, that is, to be already marked on the map as a separate territory – the current equivalent of being a 'historical nation'.

7. This is probably the first period in the history of the modern state system when two states generally admitted to be *economic* 'great powers' in the old sense – Germany and Japan – have made only the most nominal attempts so far to acquire corresponding military status.

8. However, some small peoples or states have probably learned by long experience to scale down their hopes to more modest size, for example perhaps the Welsh (as distinct from the Scots), the Slovenes (as distinct from the Croats). The reasons for such differences may be worth investigating.

9. The temporary stranglehold of some oil-producing states over the world energy market is exceptional. No other primary commodity, however uneven its geographic distribution, has given small states possessing it comparable resources or leverage.

10. Cf. Nairn's remark that 'self-government' is 'the boringly normal answer to nationality-conflicts' (BB, p. 241). As so often, the tendency to use rhetorical epithets ('boring') is a warning to readers and should have been to the writer.

11. BB, p. 253.

12. Quebec nationalism, being essentially linguistic, is an excellent example of setting out to solve one language question by putting substantial minorities – of anglophones, immigrants, Eskimos, and Indians – into precisely the same situation from which it wishes to emancipate francophones.

13. BB, p. 82.

14. In Lenin's period it was a four-cornered debate between: (a) those who placed the 'national' fact first (like the Polish Socialist Party and Nairn, cf. pp. 350-2); (b) those who placed it nowhere (like Luxemburg and the SDKPL); and those who recognized its political reality but wanted to prevent it from weakening the socialist movement, (c) under the conditions of Tsarist Russia, and (d) under those of the Habsburg Empire. It so happened that, for historical reasons, (c) and (d) tended to imply different theories of what a nation was – i.e. stressing respectively (to simplify matters) its *territorial* character and its nature as a '*cultural community*'. It also happened that the Bolsheviks, who favoured self-determination (including the right to secession), were revolutionaries; whereas the Austrian Social Democratic leaders, who favoured the maintenance of their state's unity in some federal form, were not. And that the Russian party, which had no mass base, maintained its all-Russian unity; whereas the Austrian party failed to. Finally, the Austrians paid no attention to the Russian discussions, whereas the Russians felt obliged to refute the Austrian solution – if only because it was favoured by the (non-territorial) Jewish *Bund*, and might encourage other tendencies to weaken RSDLP unity by national fission, Cf. Perez Merhav, 'Klassenkampf und Nationale Frage zur Zeit der II Internationale' in *Annali Fondazione G. Feltrinelli*, 1976, pp. 165–87.

15. BB, pp. 334–50.

16. Ibid., p. 356.

17. I use the data given by the late R.P. Dutt in *Modern India* (1940 edn), pp. 264–5,

omitting languages (or as Dutt claimed 'very minor dialects') spoken by less than 50,000 people. Six were spoken by more than 200,000. The argument does not depend on the validity of the data.

18. BB, pp. 336–7. For one thing, the argument that it derives essentially from the reaction of 'peripheral' elites against metropolitan progress and penetration neglects its historic origin and role in the core countries of capitalist development, which provided the conceptual model for the nationalism of the rest: England, France, the USA, Germany. In fact Nairn's argument can be easily turned around, and the modern world of nation states, territorial 'relatively mono-cultural, homogeneous, unilinguistic entities that have become the UNO standard pattern' (ibid., p. 317), can be presented as essentially a – one hopes temporary – product of Eurocentric fashion. This would, of course, be no better as political rhetoric than Nairn's version.

19. Cf. pp. 96–105. and chapter 9. Except, possibly, in the doubtful contention that nineteenth-century nationalism was essentially a reaction against 'indubitably archaic state forms' such as the old multi-national or rather multi-communal empires (ibid. pp. 86–7, 317–18). It was this evidently and necessarily, but it does not follow that archaic state forms 'were doomed to *disintegrate* into nation states on the western model . . . by the nature of capitalism' (emphasis added). As argued above, they were at least as likely, indeed in the core areas of capitalist development *more* likely, to sink 'particularism' in large and more unified nation states such as the UK, France, Germany, and Italy.

20. In an essay written in 1965 I argued this for the United Kingdom, but asked: 'Whether with the erosion of the traditional labour movement, nationalist slogans may in future have a greater appeal to the Scottish or Welsh working class, is a question to which only the future can give an answer.' By the time the essay was in proof (1968), it was already possible to say: 'Since 1966 disillusion with a Labour government has turned both Scottish and Welsh nationalism into an electoral force for the first time in history.' (*Mouvements nationaux d'indépendances et classes populaires aux XIX et XX siècles*, Paris 1971, vol. 1, p. 42). Nairn quotes the essay, but not the argument.

21. BB, pp. 89–91.

22. Ibid., pp. 291–305.

23. Ibid., p. 301.

24. I omit (a) cases of constitutional fiction, in which overseas territories were officially classed as metropolitan provinces (France, Portugal); and (b) divisions of states as a result of power conflicts (Germany, Korea, China/Taiwan, temporarily Vietnam).

25. 'Occitanism' is the attempt to argue the 'nationhood' of an area of uncertain size, covering, in extreme versions, most or all of southern France, united by the fact of speaking or having spoken dialects and languages – doubtfully classifiable as one – which did not become the basis of modern standard French (roughly analogous to the 'Low German' of the northern plains which did not become the standard German language). 'Except for the truly pan-Occitanian world of the troubadours, there has never been historically a unified Occitanian consciousness. The consciousness has always been on the level of Auvergne, Languedoc, Limousin, Guyenne, etc.' (E. Le Roy Ladurie, 'Occitania in Historical Perspective', *Review* I, 1, 1977, p. 23). There is no good reason to suppose that its common characeristics outweigh its internal heterogeneity; no evidence that it has ever considered itself a 'nation' or indeed envisaged independence as 'Occitania' before the present Occitanist movement – which, up to now, plainly lacks anything like the regional mass support of the Basques and Catalans (who, incidentally, overlap the territory claimed by some Occitanists).

26. BB p. 241. He is wrong to see this as 'absurd' and self-government as 'the boringly normal answer to nationality conflicts: a now standard product of centuries of world history' (ibid.). In the unfortunately usual situations like Ulster, where the neat territorial separation of communities is impossible, 'self government' in itself is irrelevant to nationality conflicts. Partition either fails, or succeeds only by the mass expulsion or forcible subjugation of whoever happens to be the weaker group or minority.

27. Lubell, *The Future of American Politics*, New York 1956, p. 135.

28. *Marxism et monde musulman*, Paris 1972, pp. 564–5.

29. M.N. Roy, *Memoirs*, Bombay 1964, p. 395.

11

Labour in the
Great City (1987)

The giant city was a new phenomenon in western capitalism, and a type of human settlement virtually unprecedented in the non-Oriental world before the eighteenth century: that is to say, the city whose population was measured in several hundreds of thousands, and very soon in millions. Until the nineteenth century cities of more than 100,000 were regarded as extremely large in Europe, and probably no city except an international port could have been larger than 500–600,000, because its food-supplying hinterland could not have been adequate. In fact, we know that there was no city of a million in the west from the end of the Roman Empire to the eighteenth century, when London reached this figure, and probably no cities of even half that size except Paris and Naples. But on the eve of the First World War Europe contained *seven* cities ranging from one to eight million inhabitants, plus another twenty-two between half a million and a million. What is more, such cities were expected to grow and expand without a foreseeable limit, and this also was quite new. This article considers the problem of labour movements in such giant urban areas. When social historians of labour have focused on particular locations, it has naturally been on the characteristic settlements of the industrial working classes, the centres of factory and forge, mill and mine. But these, in the nineteenth century, were smallish by our standards, though they were, of course, growing rapidly in size. In 1849 the union of Operative Stonemasons recognized only four towns in Britain where tramping journeymen were allowed to stay for more than one day to look for work: London, Birmingham, Liverpool and Manchester. In 1887 there were forty-eight such towns. Nevertheless, the average working-class settlement was not large. Paterson, New Jersey had 33,000 inhabitants in 1870, at a time when the major cotton-mill towns of Britain, the world's workshop at the peak of its glory, contained between 30,000 and 80,000. Mining settlements were, notoriously, more like villages than towns. Even the centres of heavy industry were, in themselves, not enormous. Clydebank, which contained major shipyards, chemical works, distilleries and the Singer Sewing Machine factory, had 22,000 inhabitants in 1901; Barrow-in-Furness, a purpose-built engineering and shipbuilding boom town, had 58,000. In short, we are talking about communities in the literal sense of the word: of *Gemeinschaft* rather than *Gesellschaft*, of places in which people could walk to and from work, and sometimes go home in the dinner-hour, of places where work, home, leisure, industrial relations, local government and home-town consciousness were inextricably mixed together.

It was in exactly this sort of location that labour movements established their strongholds. In 1906, the year of Labour's first major parliamentary breakthrough, out of the thirty MPs elected by the British Labour Representation Committee five came from cities of over half a million, four from cities of between 200,000 and 500,000, and the rest from smaller places, including districts whose main township was of the order of 20–25,000 or even 10–15,000. Or, to take another index of proletarian consciousness, the places whose teams were in the First Division of the British League in the early 1890s – a time when cup finals were already attended by 65,000 (Manchester 1893). Out of the sixteen leading teams of England, eleven came from towns ranging from 60,000 to 200,000, another two from cities of the order of 200–300,000 (Nottingham, Sheffield), and only three from parts of giant cities (Manchester, Liverpool, Birmingham): all three, characteristically, were named not after the city but after the neighbourhood or borough within it (Aston, Everton, Newton Heath). At that time London was not yet a major force in football.

The phenomenon was by no means only British. The municipalities first captured by the Parti Ouvrier in France in the 1880s and 1890s were not large by European, even by French standards. They were places like Commentry, Montluçon, Roanne, Roubaix, Calais, Narbonne. The first strongholds of the German SPD in the 1870s were in rural industrial zones of central Germany which never generated more than one city which we would today call even medium-sized (Chemnitz, now Karl Marx Stadt). We may suppose that this was for the reasons suggested by that admirable historian of American labour, the late Herbert Gutman. 'The size of the industrial city,' he wrote, 'and the particular composition of its population made the industrialist's innovations more visible and his power more vulnerable there than in the larger and more complex metropolis.'

The Organization of Labour

But what was the situation of labour in the larger metropolis? For there, precisely, the conditions favouring its organization were notoriously absent. Its population was far too large to make virtually unavoidable (to quote Gutman again) that 'close contact with the large factory, the corporation, and the propertyless wage-earners', and made it difficult or impossible to 'judge the industrial city's social dislocations by personal experience.' More than this, it even made the basic task of organizing and mobilizing the working class difficult. For the giant city had enormous and unprecedented physical dimensions, and it kept on expanding. Paris incorporated a suburban belt in the 1860s, as did Berlin. Vienna more than trebled its area in 1892 and increased it yet again by 20 per cent in 1902. New York trebled it in the 1890s. We should not read too much into scores or even hundreds of square miles of what might often be just open space, although for all nineteenth-century cities we must allow far more than earlier for spaces not occupied by housing: for wider streets and squares, vast belts reserved for transport, open spaces, parks, as well as, of course, public, commercial and industrial building. Haussmann's Paris contained 300 inhabitants per hectare, compared with 500 to 700 in eighteenth-century Paris, let alone the 900 in pre-industrial Genoa. Twentieth-century New York and London were even more thinly spread (apart from isolated patches). Hence, as the century advanced, the city area for a given size of population would have increased in any case.

However, even if we do not take the official area of cities as our measurement, the actual built-up area of London in the early twentieth century stretched twenty miles from east to west, and the same distance from north to south; Chicago stretched twenty-six miles along the lake front. And until the construction of rapid urban transport systems, which began in London and New York in the third quarter of the century but elsewhere not until near its end – for example, the Paris Metro in 1898 – for practical purposes working people walked. As many union working rules tell us, they were expected to walk at the rate of three miles per hour and, if they had a job more than four miles from the starting-point, they expected to be paid a lodging allowance for an overnight stay. Four miles, in fact, seems to have been the limit for what might be called 'spontaneous' urban cohesion. The London Tailors in 1834 defined their 'London District' by means of a radius of four miles from Charing Cross, and the bricklayers of Newcastle and Gateshead in 1893 did so by means of a radius of four and a half miles from the Central Station.

This was almost certainly too large an area for neighbourhood visiting

– a London Friendly Society in 1860 thought three miles was the limit here. But it was not too large for city-wide mobilization if the city was compact enough, although even in the 1840s London – Radical and Chartist London – must have been at the very limits of pedestrian mobilization, stretching as it did some seven miles from east to west and four miles from north to south, all the more so since the main locations for mass meetings tended to be on the outskirts, where large open spaces were to be found (Spa Fields, Stepney Green, Kennington Common). It would not be too large for easy mobilization in the era of mass transit, but by that time the built-up city area would itself have grown enormously.

Sheer numbers and area, however important, are not the only factors to have affected the fortunes of labour in the giant city. They would be so only if we could regard the megalopolis simply as a 'conurbation', an otherwise unstructured continuous built-up zone of large size and population. But such conurbations, which could develop out of the gradual growing together and eventual fusion of expanding townships, cities and suburbs, may be merely mosaics of urban areas, without any of the institutional and political characteristics of cities. Southeast Lancashire became such a conurbation, as did Tyneside, though both had central and dominant cities. But neither can simply be seen as Manchester or Newcastle writ large. For that matter today the three-state triangle with New York at its apex is not seen by its inhabitants as a single unit. Nobody thinks of Newark, New Jersey as part of New York, even though it contains one of the metropolis's airports.

Such zones must be distinguished from the real giant cities. These involved the fusion of neighbouring cities, or of growing cities with those 'suburbs' which, ever since the eighteenth century, had come to be regarded as forming a single urban unit with their town. Sometimes these components maintained an increasingly unreal separate institutional existence while physically forming a single city: Hamburg and Altona, Manchester and Salford, Berlin and several of its components did so. More commonly the great city absorbed its suburbs and neighbours as it expanded, as New York absorbed Brooklyn. But such fusions were not spontaneous and automatic developments but *political acts*. They determined whether the social protests in a particular built-up area would be seen as movements within one city or not. Labour movements in megalopolises were (and are) functions not just of geography and economic development, but of politics. Thus Paris stopped its administrative expansion in 1860, so that it is still confined to the twenty arrondissements then established. The so-called 'red belt' surrounding the city never formed part of it, but remained a collection of separate municipalities – Ivry, Aubervilliers, Villejuif, Saint-Denis, and the rest. Vienna, on the other hand, absorbed its outer suburbs between 1892 and 1905. 'Red Vienna' therefore became possible, whereas 'Red Paris' ceased to be possible, at all events in the period of the Socialist and Communist movements. Administrative boundaries in cities, like national frontiers in states, determine the targets of labour mobilization.

As it happens, most giant cities grew up round a relatively old-established urban nucleus, even though over a third of the world's large cities of 100,000 plus existing in 1910 had not existed at all in the mid-eighteenth century, or had existed only as villages. They were therefore mostly settlements with established urban institutions and traditions, and sometimes (as capitals) with national institutions, and this facilitated the political mobilization of their inhabitants. They were (with some exceptions such as Berlin and St Petersburg) centres of administration, politics, transport, or commercial activities rather than of industry. However, the general trend of nineteenth-century urbanization raised the proportion of secondary activities within them compared to tertiary or service activities, so that, even without a specific bent for industry, such cities in the early twentieth century contained perhaps 50 to 60 per cent of workers – probably a higher proportion than ever before or since. The giant city was, among other things, a giant concentration of workers.

All this provided labour movements with some potential cohesion. Even within London, which possessed no institutional identity at all until 1888, apart from its medieval 'square mile', people could see themselves as Londoners or 'cockneys', and were seen as such, because the eighteenth- and nineteenth-century giant was the lineal extension of the medieval city, because it was the capital of kingdom and empire. Labour unions conceived of the whole of London as a single district, whereas in, say, Tyneside, which was no larger than the metropolis and economically far more homogeneous, they did not.

I do not want to dwell on the fact that some giant cities were also capitals. It made governments rather more sensitive to labour demonstrations under their noses than they would otherwise have been, but whether this strengthened or weakened such metropolitan movements is an open question. Of course, in extreme cases social protest in the capital could make revolutions, and social protest which failed to reach the capital would not, but the problem of labour movements in giant cities cannot be confined to their – in the best of cases – rather rare chances of successful insurrection. In any case, in the more developed nations, the role of capital cities in national politics, insurrectional or peaceful, has tended to diminish quite substantially since the classic era of west European revolution (say 1789–1848).

An Inhospitable Environment

While labour thus had some potential assets in the megalopolis, the giant city was so vast and disarticulated that, on balance, it ought to have been an inhospitable environment for labour movements. Except in port cities (which tended to grow to great size in the nineteenth century) it was industrially too heterogeneous to have a unity based on work, as mining villages or mill-towns or shipyard towns had. Even single industries within it were often too disintegrated for unity: the south side of the port of London had a different union from the north side, while the south end of Liverpool docks was organized at a time when the rest of the port was without unions. Almost everyone in 'Kentish London' – the southeast corner of the metropolis – systematically worked different hours and had lower wage rates than people who were only a tramride away. Such examples could be multiplied.

The great city was far too large to form a real community. Professor Higgins, in Shaw's *Pygmalion,* claimed that he could tell which part of London a speaker came from by their accent, and whether this was true or not, it must have seemed quite plausible to Edwardian Londoners. Citizens of the megalopolis, after all, spent most of their time not in the big city as such, but in some part of it – it was this which could be a real community. Even in 1960 few areas in London did not find jobs for at least 50 per cent of the population within their boundaries, and most contained no more than a 20–30 per cent night-time population who commuted to work by day.

Two London examples of such inner-city community potential may be given here. The first is theatres, or rather vaudevilles and music-halls. While a central show-business area unquestionably developed in the West End and Holborn, consisting in 1900 of eleven theatres with a total capacity of about 15,000 seats, the main regular entertainment was patently to be found in the thirty-three neighbourhood theatres with a total capacity of 37,000 seats. These were distributed over twenty-four districts, eight south of the Thames, six in the northwest, and eight in the East. It is perfectly evident that while inhabitants of Hackney might occasionally consider going to the West End's Hippodrome or Alhambra, they would no more think of going to the Duchess at Balham or the Shepherd's Bush Empire than to a performance in Middles-brough. The second example, as already suggested above, is football. There is not and has never, I think, been a football team bearing the name of London. *All* the celebrated teams of the capital are named after neighbourhoods, except Arsenal, which moved to north London from its original location as a works club in Woolwich. They belonged to Queens Park, the hills round Crystal Palace, to Charlton, Leyton, and

Tottenham, or to West Ham – another team which began as a works club.

Now, this way of defining communities is directly relevant to labour movements. Out of the twenty-three metropolitan branches of the Amalgamated Carpenters and Joiners in the 1870s, eighteen actually had the same locality names as either music halls or football teams or both. And if we take an area like Woolwich, it was by general consent a town within a city, a defined community whose working class was based on the great Arsenal, which generated both the football club and the Royal Arsenal Co-operative Society which eventually colonized other parts of London. (The other metropolitan co-operative society of importance, the London, was originally based on the railway workshops in Stratford.) And if we take West Ham, whose Thames Ironworks generated the famous 'Hammers' team, its character as a separate proletarian community was so marked that it was the first district in Greater London to elect a Labour majority on its council, having already, in 1892, elected the socialist Keir Hardie to parliament by means of a coalition of the Irish with the local left.

It would therefore be tempting to argue that the real strength of labour in the megalopolis lay entirely in those urban villages which actually constituted so much of giant cities, and around which Abercrombie tried to structure his London development plan of 1944: places like Poplar or Clerkenwell. The famous 'red belt' of Paris certainly consisted entirely of such communities, which could be of quite modest size. Bobigny became a socialist stronghold in 1912 when it had barely 4,000 inhabitants, and it had less than 20,000 during the period when it became and remained a legendary stronghold of the Communist Party. Any historian of big-city labour movements comes across these townships within cities: Floridsdorf in Vienna, Sans in Barcelona, Wedding in Berlin, Sesto San Giovanni in Milan, etc. – sometimes, but not always, clustering round some major factory or complex of industrial works. And, for obvious reasons, large plants tended to draw on and to generate a largely local labour force. Thus, shortly after the Second World War, one large factory (of over 5,000 workers) on the southern outskirts of Paris drew 50 per cent of its workforce from the immediately adjoining arrondissements and communes (the 14th, Malakoff, Montrouge), only 7 to 8 per cent of its manual workers and office staff from north of the Seine, and virtually nobody from the northern Paris suburbs. However, the strength of such necklaces of proletarian communities as the 'red belt' should not allow us to forget their weaknesses. Apart from providing safe seats for generations of Communist parliamentarians, and admirable 'progressive' municipalities which, incidentally, created the municipal theatres on which the reputation of

Parisian theatre today rests, their political significance was small.

Yet it would be a mistake to think of the giant city entirely as an aggregate of urban villages. For one thing, such cities tended to be disproportionately proletarian and, other things being equal, disproportionately red. In pre-1914 Germany cities over 100,000 were 60 per cent proletarian as against a national urban average of 41 per cent, and the situation of Stockholm in Sweden was similar. German big cities contained 18 per cent of all voters but 45 per cent of the members of the Free (socialist) trade unions. Berlin and Hamburg, with about 60 per cent each, had the highest SPD vote in the country. Even London became and remained a Labour stronghold after 1923, when it elected 20 per cent of the national total of Labour MPs, or twice its percentage of the British population. Moreover, such cities might stand out dramatically against their political surroundings by their very uniqueness: as red Vienna did against rural Austria, Democratic New York against a long-time Republican New York state, Berlin against the wide open spaces of northeastern Germany, and as London did in southern England. To the extent that Labour or the left acquired hegemony in such lonely giants, it might even be argued that it became more established there, and attracted political support beyond what it might otherwise have done, becoming a sort of symbol of metropolitan identity. This may account for the failure of British Conservatives, from the 1890s into the 1980s, to break the political domination of the left in inner London by creating rival metropolitan authorities, or constructing and then destroying 'Greater London'. It may also help to explain why, even in the millionaire areas of Manhattan, in 1984 and 1986 Republicans could not get an actual majority of votes. However, more research into such speculative hypotheses is needed.

Transport and Housing

A second point to note is that megalopolises developed certain kinds of issues which, if not absolutely specific to them, were far more explosive there. The first and most obvious was (and is) transport. Giant cities depend on mass transit. Probably the safest way to provoke political trouble in them was and is to monkey with bus, tram, subway, or commuter railway, as Brazil still demonstrates at regular intervals. Indeed, in that country mass transit was one of the few issues capable of producing urban riot and rebellion even under the military regime, and it has produced riots and general strikes from time to time in cities as different as Barcelona and Calcutta; assisted by the fortunate fact that burned-out streetcars are harder to shift than burned-out automobiles. It is no accident that in the 1980s urban transport services and fares were seized on by the leftwing leaders of the Greater London Council as major issues on which to fight the Conservative government. Conversely, urban transport tends to be a stronghold of trade unionism, because it is overwhelmingly owned and run or controlled by public authorities, and because the public's sensitivity to interruption gives unions considerable leverage. The RATP (Paris municipal transport) is one of the few strongholds of the CGT among manual labour in that city, while the London busmen between the wars constituted one of the two pillars in the capital of strength and militancy of the Transport and General Workers Union, which became the biggest union in the country.

The second such issue is rented housing. This is politically radical in a double sense: because control of rents and tenancy agreements consti-tutes a flagrant intervention in the free market, and because it implies the development of public housing on a substantial scale. In both these respects the giant city was prominent. During the First World War tenants' movements, leading via strikes to rent control legislation, developed in Britain's second city, Glasgow. The other publicized rent agitations of that time were, with one exception, also in cities of the largest size: London, Birmingham, Merseyside, Belfast. New York, one gathers, was the only American city in which the tenants were able to win control in 1920. As for public and municipal housing, it is perhaps enough to say that of the relatively few units built by municipalities in Britain before 1914, half were in the two giant cities of London and Glasgow, and that when council building became massive (1.3 million units between 1920 and 1940) the great city administrations made the running, London in the lead.

The reasons are not far to seek. Until the municipality took it up, there was in the giant city – unlike the smaller settlements – no real alternative to the private rental market for housing the poor. In the nineteenth century the rental market worked well enough in building dwellings, but at the cost of providing extremely bad accommodation for the poor, and generating constant friction and tension between landlord and tenant. For workers in the giant city house-owning was not a realistic option, and conversely, company or quasi-company housing, which was common in industrial centres developing from green-field sites, was not – and did not have to be – significant. Rent and wages were therefore the two basic parameters of the big-city workers' life. My own introduction as a small boy to the political consciousness of 'red Vienna' was that I learned at school from other boys that landlords supported the Christian-Social party and tenants were Social Democrats. Of course, while this was a general experience in all giant cities, actual social movements were particularly likely to flare up in the 'towns within cities', where wages, rent, community feeling, and class organization coincided. Govan, a shipbuilding area annexed to Glasgow in 1912, was the core of the Glasgow rent-strike movement, as Woolwich was of the London movement. Both had local traditions of independent labour politics and co-operation.

Tenants' movements flicker up and down. But the aspect of big-city housing which proved to be permanently relevant to labour was the potential for community-building of the large housing projects, public or private. This was so by virtue not only of their size but also (in the case of public housing) of the political investment which they represented. Any vast complex could, indeed, provide labour movements with golden opportunities for organizing. Thus the Berlin district of Neukölln in 1912–13 had a population of about a quarter of a million, an electorate of about 65,000 adult males of whom 83 per cent voted for the SPD; a party membership of 15,000 or one in four of the electoral roll, who were in turn shepherded by almost 1,000 functionaries, each responsible for about four tenement blocs. Clearly, without the existence of class-specific residential concentrations such organizational triumphs would have been more difficult, or even impossible.

At the same time special housing projects aimed at workers – in practice mainly the regular, reliably rent-paying kind of workers – automatically generated concentrations of activists. The Shaftesbury Estate in Battersea (London), observed Charles Booth, was the centre of socialistic activity in that working-class borough which was the first to elect a Labour MP (John Burns) in the County of London. Between the wars a safe ward for Labour in the borough of Paddington was based on the Queens Park estate, built in 1875–81 by the Artisans and General Dwellings Company for respectable artisans. (The author's uncle, who was to become the first Labour mayor of his borough, was its councillor for many years.) When eventually Labour or otherwise progressive municipalities built their own estates or apartment complexes they became, deliberately or not, labour strongholds. Red Vienna is a clear case in point. The strength of the party, including its armed strength, rested on the network of the great public housing projects it constructed in the 1920s, named after Marx and Goethe, Jaurès and Washington. And finally, public housing tended to unify the politics of the munici-pality which organized it by creating a bloc of voters whose choices were largely determined by their status as public tenants. This, and municipal employment in general, were to be the major patronage assets of labour city political machines.

However, at this point we must note a major change in the nature of the occupants of public housing. With suburbanization, the exodus of industry and workers and the crisis of inner cities, inner-city public housing projects were to be transformed from settlements where the skilled and regularly employed lived, to places where the economically disadvantaged lived. And the social and political character of such buildings and settlements has consequently changed.

The Changing Face of the Megalopolis

This brings us to the fundamental transformations which have affected the giant city in the past two or three generations, at all events in the west. First, it has been decentralized by migration to suburbs and satellite communities. Second, it has been de-industrialized, not only by the general decline of secondary occupations, but by the class-specific emigration of formerly city-based manufacturing industry and the more skilled workforce. Often this was the actual result of progressive city policy, as when the London County Council between the wars decanted 100,000 workers into a new semi-rural estate at Becontree, where they became the labour force for the Ford Motor Company's works which were set up at Dagenham for this reason.

Two further by-products of this movement may be suggested. For an increasing number of workers it has snapped the links between day and night, or between the places where people live and those where they work, with substantial effects on the potential of labour organization which is always strongest where work and residence belong together. It may also be that the change in the city working-class economy has led to a breakdown of those highly segmented labour markets which, paradoxically, made labour solidarity easier to achieve. For so long as different groups and strata of labour, and especially ethnic groups, in practice did not often compete for the *same* jobs but filled their own niche or niches, intra-proletarian rivalries and jealousies could be more easily kept down.

Third, in general the administrative expansion of the giant city has ceased or been halted, as prosperous suburbs (or, as in the UK, reactionary governments) wage battle against political domination by the inner-city poor and against higher local taxes. Fourth, the 'inner city' has increasingly seemed to be dominated by the specific population which we associate with it today: the miscellaneous poor, the unskilled, the socially marginal and problematic, the ethnic and other minorities of whatever kind. It is not that the older kinds of workers have all gone, but that the others now dominate the image we have of inner cities. These newly typical inner-city populations are not only those left behind, but sometimes consist of those attracted to the giant city precisely because it contains, and has always contained, as it were sociologically open spaces designed for the socially indeterminate. It was always *par excellence* a place of transients, visitors, tourists, and temporary residents and was in some ways designed as a no-man's-land, or rather an any-man's-land. Its 'anomie' and anonymity are not a myth.

Finally, while its structure and population were changing in these ways, urban development, public and private, was destroying the very bases which had allowed the formation of the 'urban villages' on which so much of labour strength had rested. This was notably so in the 1960s, that most disastrous decade in the long and distinguished history of city life on this globe. The urban scene in what used to be working-class areas is today often one of featureless towers surrounded by open spaces and the shells of former warehouses and factories waiting to be turned into leisure complexes or up-market luxury flats. The sheer demoralization of poor people in these scarred and spray-painted deserts is not a negligible factor. As against this there is gentrification, generally a minority phenomenon, except in Paris, where the city has been kept to its 1860 area. Gentrification in effect turns workers into a purely daytime population which withdraws into its lairs somewhere outside, as in Paris where corner *bistros* are locked after office hours. There may, of course, be some community-building among new ethnic immigrants, but probably not on the old scale. And there may be new, potentially radical populations in inner cities such as students, but they will not be of the old working-class type.

The effect of all this on labour movements in the great city has been to deprive them of their former cohesion – except for what continues to be provided by the focus and framework and patronage of city politics. If the city itself is politically abolished or does not exist (as in London), nothing remains except the cement of *national* politics, provided the urban area retains sufficient social cohesion. In short, big city labour movements are living on the accumulated capital of the past. They are Labour or Socialist or Communist, or even, in the USA, Democratic, because that was the basis of poor men's mobilization in the past, and the parties concerned are still identified as 'parties for us' by the poor. But if such cities grew on the basis of new populations – as perhaps in Miami or Los Angeles – they would have no necessary affinity for the parties once automatically identified with political mobilization in such environments.

What labour movements are losing, or have lost, is much of that class identification of working people as such which used to give them force, and a sense of collective power. If the entire conurbation were to form the unit of urban politics, the workers or the poor might not even any longer have the sense of being, in some way, the norm or majority of city dwellers. However, within the inner city they often still do. For, paradoxically, the disintegration of the megalopolis has tended to leave the inner city as a natural centre of concentrated discontent. But what discontent? Whose? In one sense the labouring population of the great city is returning from the status and consciousness of a 'proletariat' to that of the pre-industrial and miscellaneous 'labouring poor', or just 'the poor'; or, what is worse, from workers or 'common people' to 'underclass'. And, in most European giant cities these 'labouring poor' are, at least ethnically, much more disunited and internally fragmented than before, not having had as long as in US cities to adapt themselves to that national, linguistic, and racial mosaic which is now common everywhere.

The characteristic form of action of these new 'poor' or 'labouring poor' is no longer the strike, or giant demonstration or public meeting, but once again, as in the past, violence. The great city has once again become riotous, not to mention dangerous, in a way in which it had ceased to be since the middle of the nineteenth century. Yet in another sense the political assumptions which gave reality to Edward Thompson's 'moral economy' and political effectiveness to George Rudé's 'crowd' are no longer there. Neither are the grassroots social structures for mobilizing it. The divisions within a heterogeneous and often socially disorganized population of the new 'labouring poor' mean that its actions are directed inwards and sideways rather than upwards. The typical riot or outburst today is not political in any realistic sense, and not so much unfocused – often it is only too clearly directed against some other racial or territorial or lifestyle contingent – as lacking in aim and purpose. It has no demands which might be met. And it has no structured organization or, in effect, cadres in the old labour movement sense. Ghetto politics is not working-class politics.

All this is a serious handicap for labour movements. For in the big city 'labour' was at the best of times never as cohesive as in the smaller industrial communities, even when these were not single-industry settlements. It was always a much more miscellaneous and heterogeneous stratum, held together by a common style of working life – the life of manual work – and by a common consciousness of class, of relative poverty and low status. It was this which allowed labour parties to become containers simultaneously for class and other minority interests. They were, like the Democratic Party in the USA, alliances of minority interests, but they were not *only* such alliances, since the concept of a 'working class' provided a common denominator for otherwise different and even divergent groups. This was so even when labour movements did not stress their special appeal to minorities such as, say, the Irish or the Jews. Protestants and Catholics in Glasgow, whose mutual hatreds are evident on the football field, could both join together in a single camp for purposes of city politics.

Divisions within the Big City

But today the labouring or non-labouring poor of the rump big city are divided: ethnically, by socio-economic status, between those who work and those who live on relief, between residents and commuters, between proletarians and lumpen proletarians or marginals, and, not least, at any moment between mutually uncomprehending and hostile age groups. The old are divided from the young, whom they fear. Such a population is, or may seem to be, *only* an assembly of minorities, or an aggregate of people lacking any political effective common denominator. The risk of this situation is that labour politics in the great city adapts itself by functioning only as a coalition of minorities or outgroups. This is very visible in London in the 1980s.

There are two problems about this strategy. The first is that, adding up nothing but minorities, especially of outgroups (rebaptized, for publicity purposes, as 'new social movements') does not, politically speaking, produce majorities. Even the British Liberal Party in the 1890s, when it won – and only just – purely by mobilizing the lesser nationalities and religio-ideological minorities, could not have hoped to return to the triumphs of 1906 if it had not rested on a broad base as an accepted 'people's party' for the majority. The minorities strategy, moreover, is more than likely to alienate more than it mobilizes. Its victories may be illusory. In most big cities of the USA the blacks now elect mayors, but they do so because their votes are concentrated in such locations, not because nationally, or even within great cities, they are any less a minority than before. Furthermore, appealing to one minority, or even a 'rainbow coalition' of minorities, risks leaving the rest open to the appeals of the demagogic right which speaks the old language of community and morality, the basis of Labour's appeal, but in the vocabulary of racism and the police state. That, after all, is what has been destroying the old big-city red belts in France, and most of us know, even if fewer of us are ready to admit, that Labour's main losses among workers have been not to the Thatcherite appeal to prosperous selfishness but to the Thatcherite appeal to race and 'law and order'.

It seems clear that the old-fashioned class appeal which was the force of labour no longer works in profoundly divided big cities. Now that we are in some ways reverting to a version of the 'city crowd' politics of the pre-industrial days of the 'lower orders' and the 'labouring poor', would it not be logical also to revert to the populist politics of those days? For there is still scope for an ideology, and a mobilizing principle, based on what all inhabitants of a city have in common: not least pride in the city and its superiority – which can be a very powerful sentiment in great cities – and concern with its problems; no doubt with a special edge of concern for its poor and exploited? This is entirely within the range of strong and properly rooted labour movements. In the 1970s, for instance, such implausible centres of proletarian consciousness and organization as Rome and Naples found themselves administered, for the first time, by Communist mayors. In Britain, London pride was a major element in metropolitan labour politics during the years of struggle against the dissolution of the Greater London Council. Given the potential strength of labour in what remains of western mega-lopolises, and given the tradition of municipal leadership by the parties of the left in such cities, why not?

Of course such a strategy is possible. Indeed it is essential for labour movements to adopt it, if they wish to avoid the fatal mistake of turning themselves into sectional pressure groups on behalf of special interests which do not coincide with – and are often at odds with – those of the rest of the citizens, including the rest of the urban working class. Moreover in present circumstances, at least in Britain, the defence of the city's interests and autonomy against a government which sets out to destroy it, fits in readily enough with even the short-term interests of the left. Only one thing is wrong with such a perspective of an 'urban people's policy'. It can be applied by labour movements, but it is not specific to them. Others can practise it just as effectively, and for less desirable purposes. We do not have to look far round the world for examples of city-boosting politicians with a sharp sense of political and financial realities, but with no concern for social justice.

12

Farewell to the Classic Labour
Movement?

A hundred and twenty-five years after Lassalle, and a hundred years after the founding of the Second International, the socialist and labour parties are at a loss as to where they are going. Wherever socialists meet they ask one another gloomily about the future of our movements. I think it is perfectly justified to ask such questions, but – and I think this should be emphasized – they are not confined to the socialist parties. All the other parties are in the same position.

Who really knows what the future will bring? Who even thinks they know, apart from the Muslim, Christian, Jewish, and other irrationalist fanatics whose numbers are again on the increase precisely because blind faith alone appears to be reliable in a world in which all have lost their way. Do they know their future in the United States, where they are haunted by the ghost of economic and political decline? Do they know in Rome, where, despite every effort, the Catholic Church is falling apart? Do they know in Jerusalem, where the dream of the national liberation of Judaism is collapsing under the batons of Israeli soldiers? That they do not know in Moscow, and do not even profess to know, is obvious. But what is happening in the Gorbachev era, developments which had been declared a priori impossible by generations of cold warriors on the basis of theories of totalitarianism, proves that even the intellectuals and ideologues of the cold war have come to the end of their cul-de-sac. And the economists – the theologians of our time, disguised as technical experts – do they know? Evidently they do not. How little talk there is about monetarism these days, considering that even at the beginning of the eighties it still dominated the thinking of Conservative governments. When was the last time even Mrs Thatcher mentioned the names Friedman or Hayek, although it was just ten years ago that they were parading their new Nobel prizes? Do businessmen know? Who really believes that? Certainly we in the socialist movement are only scratching our heads as we face the future, for we appear to be entering a land for which our guidebooks ill equip us. But the others no longer have relevant guidebooks either.

That, of course, is not surprising, though, even without taking into account the fact that movements born in the last century bring a great deal with them from their period of origin which can only be transposed very indirectly from the era of Krupp's howitzer to the modern age of laser technology. However, the main point is this: in the thirty years following the Second World War the world was transformed globally, fundamentally, radically, and with such unprecedented speed, that all previous analyses, even when they remained quite correct in principle, simply had to be modified and brought up to date in practice. There is no need to demonstrate this in detail. To put it in a single sentence, one might say that, taking the world as a whole, the Middle Ages ended between 1950 and 1970. And I would go further and assert that as far as Europe is concerned, those twenty years saw the end of the modern era too. Let us only consider what happened to the peasantry in those two decades, not only in central and western Europe but also in large parts of the third world. This unique acceleration of historical development alone would have demanded a fundamental revision of previous inter-pretations. In my opinion this will present the main problem for historians of the late twentieth and early twenty-first centuries.

However, for a generation after 1950, it was possible, or at least tempting, to try to conceive this macro-historical revolution in a linear fashion, or to over-simplify it by, for example, describing it as 'economic–technological growth' or something along those lines. But this epoch of global boom – not only in capitalist economies, but also, in a very different setting, in socialist economies – these 'thirty golden years', as a French commentator has described them, led to a world-wide, long-term economic crisis, which has already lasted at least fifteen years. I do not think we can expect a new long-term era of 'economic Sturm und Drang', as Parvus once called it, before the 1990s. I know of no more optimistic forecast that we could really take seriously.

But it is in this time of crisis (which strangely enough began exactly 100 years after the beginning of the analogous 'great depression' of the Bismarck era), that the internal and external contradictions of the post-war period have moved to the front of the world stage. What has become clear is how frail or untenable old analyses or political remedies are, and how hard it is to replace them with new ones. For example, the de-industrialization of the old industrial economies has clearly emerged for the first time as a possible future for our countries. I mean *not* a shift away from the old industries to technically superior ones, or the transfer of industry from the Ruhr to the Neckar, but the movement of industry away from the west altogether. For the so-called 'new industrial nations' of the third world are a phenomenon of the current era of crisis. May I merely remind you that at the beginning of the seventies South Korea was still classed as a 'developing country', and her industry was described as follows: 'foodstuffs, textiles, plywood, rubber and steel works under construction.' The real crisis of the left today is not that we do not understand the new world situation as well as the others, but that we do not seem to have much to say on the matter. Capitalism does not need to say much, as long as a sudden collapse of the type which occurred in 1931 is avoided – and, after all, that much has been learned from the thirties. Capitalism can retreat to the logic of the market, for as a millionaire in New York explained to me a few days after the stock exchange crash: 'Sooner or later the market finds an appropriate level again, so long as we avoid revolution in the meantime.' We, however, are expected to say much more.

The crisis of the old ideas, and the need for new thinking, were imposed on socialists by reality itself and its effect on political praxis. The world has changed and we must change with it.

I would almost go so far as to say: we more than anyone else. For as parties and as movements we are very much trapped in history. We became mass movements, very suddenly, a hundred years ago. In 1880 there was no socialist or other workers' party with mass support, with the partial exception of Germany. Twenty-five years later Sombart considered the worldwide rise of such mass parties so natural that he tried to explain why the United States, which had no socialism, was an exception.

I should like to make five points about those new movements, which have by now grown to be very old movements. First, they were formed on the basis of a proletarian class consciousness among manual and wage workers, in spite of the striking heterogeneity – the inner and outer fragmentation – of the workers. One cannot even say that those workers who joined the new parties formed a particularly homogeneous group. Nevertheless, it is clear that for workers at that time, what they had in common far outweighed any differences, with the exception sometimes, but not always, of religious or national differences. Without this consciousness, mass parties whose only programme in practice was their name could never have emerged. Their appeal – 'You are workers. You are a class. As such you must join the workers' party' – could not have been heard. What we find today is not that there is no longer any working class, but that class consciousness no longer has this power to unite.

Second, despite the fact that both their theory and practice were tailored specifically to the proletariat, these parties were not purely workers' parties. This is probably not so apparent in the highly proletarian SPD but it can be seen clearly in Scandinavia. Given the level of development of the Finnish economy at the time, only an insignificant proportion of the 47 per cent of Finns who voted for Social Democracy in the free elections of 1916 could have been proletarian. Like other Social Democratic parties, the Finnish party was a people's party built around a proletarian core. Of course, no one disputes that, normally speaking, Social Democratic parties hardly expected to win over more than a minority of voters from other social classes.

Third, the mass organization of the class-conscious proletariat appeared to be bound, organically or logically, to the specific ideology of socialism, and typically a Marxian brand of socialism. Parties organized along class lines but without socialist ideas could either be seen as transitional forms on the road to the socialist labour party or as unimportant peripheral phenomena.

Fourth, the sudden rise of the socialist mass parties reinforced the preconceived view of Marxists that only the industrial proletariat, organized and conscious of itself as a class, could act as the bearer of the future state. For, unlike in Marx's own lifetime, the proletariat appeared everywhere to be on the way to forming the majority of the population. The labour-intensive growth of the economy typical of the time reinforced the confidence in democracy, whose standard-bearers the socialists became everywhere. The question who was to bring about socialism seemed to answer itself.

Fifth, these movements originally formed purely oppositional forces which only moved into the area of potential or actual government after the First World War – as founders of revolutionary new systems in the case of the communists, or, in the case of the Social Democrats, as state-sustaining pillars of a reformist capitalism. For the socialist labour movements both alternatives signified a fundamental change of their previous role.

It is now clear that all these characteristics were historically determined, especially their convergence in the international phenomenon of the socialist labour movement. I would go even further. All socialist and Communist parties of significance, without exception, emerged before the Second World War and, apart from a very few exceptions – China, Vietnam, or West Bengal, for example – had done so even before the First World War. Since the Second World War, in the dozens of new states in an economically transformed world, no movements comparable with the socialist mass parties have emerged. Even where new proletarian mass movements have appeared and are structurally comparable with those of the early twentieth century, in practice, politically, and ideologically, they turn out to be quite different, as in Brazil and Poland. The umbilical cord once connecting the labour movement and social revolution with the ideology of socialism has been cut. The greatest social revolution in the current world crisis is the Iranian revolution. It is easier to explain why the European labour parties originally emerged before 1917 – and also, incidentally, their spread to the third world, which, thanks to the October revolution and the Communist movement, took place principally between the two World Wars – than it is to explain the non-emergence of such parties and hegemonies since. One can even observe a decline in some existing parties, which at one time were far from uninfluential, for instance in the Middle East. I mention this set of problems here only because as an historian I have long been puzzled by such questions as why a mass labour movement in Argentina, for example, first became possible not on a socialist, but eventually on a Peronist basis. This case simply underlines the fact that our movements, the classic socialist or Communist labour parties, were born in a specific, historical epoch which has now passed.

This patently does not mean that these movements have now ceased to be viable within their original heartlands. Quite the reverse. Such parties are still what they were in the past, workers' parties, but not exclusively so. In the non-socialist part of Europe these parties form either the governing or the chief opposition parties in *all* states except – if I am not mistaken – for Ireland and Turkey. In socialist Europe they are the parties which constitute the system, but this is not comparable. In the course of the past century the socialist labour parties have shown a significant capability for revival and adaptation, though probably more in their Social Democratic than in their Communist form. Again and again they have risen from the ashes of their ruined or destroyed predecessors to become politically important centres of power, like the SPD in Germany after fascism or, in the last decade or so, the PSOE in Spain or the French Socialist Party under Mitterrand. The question 'farewell to the classic labour movement?' does not mean 'is there a future for the SPD or the Labour Party?', but rather 'what kind of future do they have?' However, we must not forget that we can no longer simply *rely* on historical continuity. Other movements are not obliged to meet the same fate as the PCF, which recently seemed to be disappearing as an effective mass party: even the gods are powerless in the face of political stupidity. But this case does prove how conditional the loyalty of members is these days.

Of the five original characteristics of the movement outlined above, only two still apply fully: the classical party is still a party of the people, and it is still a potential governing party. The old assumption that the transition to socialism would ensue from the development of the industrial proletariat is no longer tenable. The connection between party, socialist ideology, and a vision of the future still seems to be alive, thank goodness, despite the fact that from the 1950s onwards all party leaders, even those of some western Communist parties, have waved socialism goodbye, and, if they continue to speak of it at all, have tried to make it appear that socialism simply means having a bit more sympathy than the others. Nevertheless, if there is still a place in western politics for socialists today, then it is within the old mass parties, despite the agreement among leftwing sects that these parties now do nothing more than shore up the system. Moreover, in contrast to the United States, where almost all American socialists have no choice but to work within the Democratic Party, in Europe the classic parties remain true, at least theoretically, to the idea of a better and transformed society. This, however, reflects the fortunate strength of our historical tradition rather than the necessary connection between the existing parties of this tradition, the working class and socialism.

It is class consciousness, the condition on which our parties were originally built, that is facing the most serious crisis. The problem is not so much objective de-proletarianization which has been brought about by the decline of old-style industrial labour, but is rather the subjective decline of class solidarity. This segmentation of the working class has received a good deal of attention recently, but I would like to mention only the case of the British Labour Party, where the traditional proletarian vote has fallen far more sharply than the size of the proletariat. In 1987 almost two-thirds of skilled workers, 60 per cent of trade union members, and more than half the unskilled and semi-skilled workers voted for other parties, and the Labour Party mustered the support of barely more than half of the unemployed. Conversely, almost 50 per cent of Conservative voters were workers. A similar shift can be detected in the support for the PCF. Yet once both parties could rely upon the blind class loyalty of their proletariat.

There is no point in simply mourning this lost class consciousness (although as an old Marxist I still do) nor in retreating into the few remaining nature reserves where the good old proletariat can still be observed. The great and heroic British miners' strike evoked a great deal of honest romanticism, but there is a difference between 200,000 pitworkers and a country of 55 million. What is more, half of the pitworkers have disappeared since 1985 anyway. And as for the argument of the romantic left – the strike proved the exact opposite assumptions to be true: even among miners one must expect mass strike-breaking today. It is comforting, of course, that class consciousness is also crumbling in other classes. In 1987, for example, 40 per cent of the upper classes in Britain voted against Mrs Thatcher, and among the university-educated classes this figure was as high as two-thirds. But the possibility of new political combinations does not compensate for the fact that workers are crumbling into groups with diverging and contradictory interests.

And yet, in the face of all this, the fact remains that the parties which emerged historically as the defenders and representatives of workers and the poor cannot lose this function as long as such defence is necessary. And this is the case, for today there is no longer any 'common recognition of social principles' – at least not in Great Britain. Fortunately, too, our parties are not *purely* workers' parties and never were; as they have lost neither the capability of forming broad people's parties or coalitions of classes and social groups, nor the potential to become ruling parties of government. Today it is not class consciousness which holds our parties together, but the national existence of these parties which unites groups and classes which would otherwise probably crumble.

And this is no small thing. Our movement, the whole of democracy, is once again under threat. We have become so used to the re-democratization – or rather the liberalization – of the bourgeois system since 1945, and the fact that such words as fascism and neo-fascism have been fully emptied of their content, that it is now difficult to remember that in periods of crisis, capitalism could again resort to the solution of the political right. In my country the radical right is in power and, thanks to our mistakes, has been given the opportunity to eliminate the labour movement, the Labour Party, and the entire left as a serious factor in politics. This is the quite blatant aim of the regime. It could happen again in your country too. And the only resistance we can raise against this danger is a coalition of all democrats around those mass parties of the left which still exist in Europe. That much, thank goodness, still remains of the classic labour movement.

Translated by Hilary Pilkington (Material Word)

PART III

Making a New Start

13

Past Imperfect, Future Tense
(1986)

Three years ago the prospects of another Labour government were not worth talking about concretely. Today, with all precautions, they can again be envisaged. What this article tries to do is not to discuss Labour's programme, and still less various speculative electoral outcomes, but what, if anything, we can learn about the prospects of another Labour government from the historical record of earlier ones. I shall consider mainly home policy, even though this is unrealistic, because today international constraints impose the most effective limits on what national governments can do. This is because (with rare exceptions) nothing positive is to be said about the foreign policy of past Labour governments. They have rarely if ever had a Labour or socialist foreign policy as distinct from a Liberal, Tory, or ruling-class consensus one. That is the first lesson to be drawn from the past.

There have been five periods of Labour government (1924, 1929–31, 1945–51, 1964–70, and 1974–79) as well as the years of wartime coalition (1940–45). What was their record?

The first government was a minority administration, since the Labour Party was not even the largest party in parliament, polling little better than the Liberals, who ran a good way behind the Tories. In fact, Labour was put in by both the Liberals and intelligent Conservatives because, as Neville Chamberlain put it, a ruling-class coalition to keep it out would strengthen the working-class party for the future, while in office 'it would be too weak to do much harm but not too weak to get discredited.'

The first Labour government certainly did not do the British ruling classes much harm, although the secret service which, then as later, had Communism on the brain, regarded it as a sinister subversive conspiracy and did its best to sabotage it, for example with the Zinoviev Letter. On the other hand neither was it discredited. After a short-lived Labour government, the Labour vote went up 25 per cent. But what, if anything, did it do in its nine months?

It certainly did not try to install socialism, not only because it was in no position to, but because this was the last thing that its leader, Ramsay MacDonald, wanted. He wanted Labour to be accepted as a party thought suitable for government by respectable people. Or even by Labour people themselves, for the party took a very long time to overcome the feeling that it was more normal for the upper classes to be in government than for representatives of labour. Even Harold Wilson was irrationally pleased when he had been premier long enough to claim – quite mistakenly – that Labour was now 'the natural party of government'.

Nevertheless, the first Labour government actually had some achievements to its credit, apart from recognizing the legal existence of the USSR. Even though it disappointed both moderate and leftwing supporters, it did not do badly by the standards of Wilson in the 1960s or Callaghan in the 1970s. It improved unemployment benefits and education, and its Housing Act, which subsidized council building for tenants on controlled rents, was a major landmark in the history of the welfare state. More than half a million houses were built under this 'Wheatley Act', named after the leftwinger who pushed it through as Minister for Health before the National government of 1933 abolished the subsidy. Wheatley did not have time before the government fell to push through an act controlling rackets in building costs, but a rather tentative programme of public works to reduce unemployment was introduced which left behind it a project to establish a national electricity supply system, subsequently carried out by the Conservatives. By and large, the record was not bad unless one expected Labour to make a revolution.

The second Labour government of 1929–31 is one old Labour loyalists would want to forget. Fortunately it was possible, though mistaken, to load the blame for its failure on to its premier Ramsay MacDonald, its Chancellor of the Exchequer, Philip Snowden, and the ex-trade-union rightwinger J.H. Thomas, who joined the Conservatives and some Liberals to form a 'National government' in 1931 when the Labour government fell. The 1929 government did not have a Labour majority, though by then Labour was – but only just – the largest party in parliament, on a slightly smaller number of votes than the Tories. It depended on Liberal support. But since the Liberals had fought the election on a rather more ambitious social and economic programme than Labour, this was hardly much of a handicap. The Liberal programme very much anticipated the sort of Keynesianism that Labour was later to make its own. In fact, J.M. Keynes was the Liberals' economic advisor.

The second Labour government was not entirely without some reformist achievement, but it had two major weaknesses. The first was that the leadership was rapidly moving to the right, but was not sure that it had the situation in the party under adequate control. It had therefore saddled the party in 1928 with a programme which was strong on the rhetoric of socialist aspiration (it was drafted by R.H. Tawney), but very foggy on just what a Labour government proposed to do. Furthermore, unlike 1924, the Labour left was systematically excluded from the government. The second weakness was that this clueless administration found itself plunged into the world depression of 1929–33. It had not the faintest idea what to do about it, especially since it rejected any policies to deal with unemployment, put forward within the party or outside, which conflicted with the current economic orthodoxy of Treasury advisors.

It was by no means the only government in the world which found itself reeling under the blows of the world slump, but it was almost certainly (with President Hoover's USA, but in a very different manner) the government whose reactions to the slump were the most pitifully inadequate. In fact, Scandinavian social democracy was immediately inspired by the awful example of British Labour to work out better anti-slump policies.

The spectacular failure of this government is indicated by the collapse of the Labour vote in the general election of 1931 – it dropped by about 25 per cent – and by the visible disintegration within the Party. Mac-Donald, Snowden and Thomas went over to the Tories. Sir Oswald Mosley, then a radically minded minister, headed a revolt supported by substantial figures on the left such as A.J. Cook and the young Aneurin Bevan, until it was clear that he was headed in the direction of fascism via the so-called 'New Party' he founded on the way. Those pillars of rightwing Fabianism, the Webbs (Sydney had been a government minister) henceforth wrote off the Labour Party and looked to the Soviet Union. The most important organization of socialists within the party, the ILP, drew away and shortly thereafter committed suicide by disaffiliating from Labour.

In 1931 the cause of Labour was in greater disarray than at any other time except 1981–1983. Unfortunately the fact that the Communist International was passing through its most sectarian period at the time meant that no section of the left benefitted. Any way that we look at it, the second Labour government was a disaster.

The third period of Labour government (1945–51) is the only one so far which was not patently disappointing and as a result it has acquired a

mythical halo in retrospect. 'The Attlee administration', according to
K.O. Morgan, 'is in grave danger of retreating from reality into the half-
world of legend and fantasy.' True enough, but the legend is based on
massive achievements at home, in spite of a much more negative record
internationally.

It has been argued that these achievements only represented the
middle-of-the-road consensus which had developed during the war, and
which stretched from moderate Tories to centre-left Labour politicians,
with two Liberals as its central ideologists: Beveridge and Keynes. This
is misleading. Of course, in the main, the Attlee government carried out
what wartime committees had planned; and at least one of the major
pillars of postwar Britain, the Butler Education Act of 1944, was actually passed under the Churchill coalition. It was also undeniable that
the Conservative governments after 1951 accepted most of the Labour
programme, until the Thatcher governments which were the first to try
to dismantle the Britain of Butler, Beveridge, Keynes and Attlee.

But this does not mean that Britain would have been much the same
if Labour had not swept into power in 1945. It is one thing to accounce
great plans for the postwar future in the middle of a war, especially
when the citizens are known to be fighting for a better future. It is quite
another thing, as the years after the First World War proved, to carry
them out when the pressure is off. Postwar Tory governments might had
done something, but it is inconceivable that they would have thrown
themselves into the job of reforming the country with as much genuine
enthusiasm as the Labour government did, its left and right for once
working together. Labour can legitimately claim the credit, and take the
blame, for 1945–51.

Its actual achievements are impressive in sheer quantity. They include
the nationalization of the Bank of England, coal and civil aviation
(1946), of electricity (1947), gas, railways and some other forms of
transport (1948), iron and steel (1949); the complete reconstruction of
the social service and welfare system (family allowances, national in-
surance, national assistance, changed in 1966 to supplementary benefit,
and the National Health Service); major changes in planning (new towns
and a major Town and Country Planning Act); most of the modern
system of appeals machinery (rent tribunals and the rest), and a great
deal more. In short, no government of twentieth-century Britain has
changed the framework of British social and economic institutions
more dramatically in five years than the Labour government did in
1945–50.

Nationalization was undoubtedly at the heart of this programme,
together with the welfare state. But here there was a crucial vagueness in
Labour's policy. Everybody in the government backed the national-

ization programme (except on iron and steel), either on grounds of
efficiency, or because public control was needed to integrate them into
national economic policy, or because the removal of capitalist bosses
would transform industrial relations (as everyone thought), or as a
symbol of Labour's determination to end the old order, or for a mixture
of all these motives and a few others. But there was actually very little
thought about how nationalization fitted into the general economic and
social strategy of Labour, and practically no thought about how 'common ownership' should be organized.

The form of nationalization adopted, virtually without debate, was
that introduced by Herbert Morrison for London Transport in 1933. It
was more or less based on the earlier models of the BBC and the Central
Electricity Board, namely the autonomous public corporation which
replaced a board of irresponsible private capitalists by an equally auto-
cratic board of public bureaucrats, with whom the unions now negotiated. Unfortunately the union leadership of the time actually seems to
have preferred a system where workers did not participate in, or have
responsibility for, management.

There was no pressure for any kind of workers' control – even the left
showed little interest in it before the 1960s – and, unlike Germany or
France, neither government nor unions nor private enterprise showed
any interest in formally associating workers with industrial management.
Of course such arrangements have not proved very satisfactory, but it is
curious nevertheless that French nationalization after 1945 was influ-
enced by British thinking on workers' control – G.D.H. Cole via the
Austro-Marxist Otto Bauer – whereas British nationalization by a Labour
government was not. There was also no real thinking about other forms of
public and cooperative ownership and management.

As for the management of the economy, it is an extraordinary fact
that the Labour government showed no interest in planning the economy, unlike the French government which, in the very same years, systematically developed devices for planning a mixed economy. Labour
appeared uninterested in planning, and the mechanisms inherited for
this purpose from the war were dismantled. The government was not
even particularly Keynesian in its first years. But while this should warn
us against reading too much socialism, or even economic competence,
into the 1945 government, its economic achievements were impressive.
In 1951 Labour left the British economy in good shape; largely because
the government, especially during the so-called period of 'austerity', put
national recovery before consumer advertising, and ensured fair distribution. The rich were still too nervous to flaunt their wealth. Meanwhile
the welfare and social security system installed by Labour was certainly
the best and most human existing anywhere at that time. Hence the

government retained the loyalty of its mainly working-class voters. Labour's support rose after 1945. When the Tories, on a slightly smaller vote, defeated it in 1951, due to the vagaries of the British electoral system, Labour actually polled its highest ever number and share of votes: about 14 million and 49 per cent.

But by this time, in fact by sometime in 1947, the Attlee government had plainly run out of steam. Once it had carried out the programme it had acquired by 1945, it had no further ideas. The major internal criticism of the Attlee government is that it lacked any long-term strategy for the future, whether of social transformation or economic growth. Further advance, even for the Labour left, henceforth became a matter of drawing up shopping lists of further nationalization, and since it was evident that the economy would be 'mixed' (partly private) for the foreseeable future, the length of the list was a symbol of socialist intent rather than part of socialist strategy. As the right argued that not much more nationalization, if any, was needed 'to give the community power over the commanding heights of the economy' (Gaitskell's phrase), the left called for more of it.

The truth is that the right really believed that the British productive system was now working well enough with a bit of macro-economic Keynesian steering, either because it still thought of Britain as one of the world's great and permanent industrial economies which couldn't possibly decline, or because it thought enough had been done to put a mixed system on the right road. Almost certainly the left also underestimated the long-term economic crisis of the country. Labour's victory was the internal aspect of Britain's heroic wartime stand and victory over fascism. Was it conceivable that Britain's finest hour should have left us potentially worse off than the ruined countries we had beaten? Actually, it was.

Very little needs to be said about the disastrous international record (with exceptions like India) of the Attlee years, which turned Britain into an American satellite. This failure was partly due to the same inability to grasp that Britain was no longer a great power of the first rank; partly to the discovery that economic weakness – believed to be temporary – made us dependent on American good will and pressure (for example, Labour reforms depended on an American loan in 1945); and partly on ideological anti-Communism. It ought to be said that the record of the Labour left in resisting these tendencies, in so far as they knew about them in time, was better than its feeble record in economic matters. Still, once again, the absence of any specifically Labour foreign policy must be sadly noted.

The fourth period of Labour government, 1964–70, was in its way as disastrous as the second. Labour entered it without a discernible programme of perspective except that of advertising slogans ('Let's Go With Labour' in 1964, 'You *know* Labour government works' in 1966) and an appeal to gleaming technological modernity which Harold Wilson, who dominated this government, had copied from that well-known socialist, President Kennedy of the USA: 'We are redefining and we are restating our socialism in terms of the *scientific revolution*', Wilson said.

In fact, there was some calculation behind this empty rhetoric. Tactically, by avoiding policy commitments, it tried to bypass the bitter feuding which had divided right and left since the end of the Attlee years. Unfortunately this meant that the government had no particular policy on matters of urgent concern to the British people. Thus it was fairly clear by the mid 1960s that the social security system, no longer so outstanding by world standards, was ripe for some systematic updating and rethinking, but there was no major reform in this field (though at the tail-end of the decade Crossman played with plans for pensions reform, which got nowhere). The nearest thing to a coherent policy in the Wilson era was the systematic liberalization pursued by Roy Jenkins at the Home Office in the matters like homosexuality, abortion, and divorce, but welcome though this was, it did not require Labour governments and it was not a sufficient substitute for a Labour policy in this area or more generally.

But the rhetoric also implied a policy. It assumed the country was on the right road, but, in Wilson's words was held back by 'restrictive practices or outdated methods on either side of industry'. In one way this recognition that something was seriously wrong with the British economy was an advance on the 'revisionism' of the Labour right in the 1950s which had assumed that production was no longer a problem, and that socialism was therefore no longer about planning and social control, but about 'equality'. In another way it was not an improvement. For Wilson talked as though Britain would forge ahead without any other major changes, once restrictions and outdated methods were removed by one great and inspiring heave.

The civil service would thus be shaken up by forming new ministries, renaming or breaking up old ones, and by other bureaucratic games which have since been taken up by the Thatcherites. There was to be a major push into science-based technology, for which distinguished scientists were mobilized. Concorde was one result, but the chief content of Wilsonian industrial policy was an enthusiastic support for the capitalist concentration which advanced rapidly in those years with the government's blessing. There was even, under the mercurial George Brown, a 'National Plan' setting out aims for the British economy, but not much was actually planned. Compared to the six years of Attlee, the six years of Wilson, in spite of useful legislation here and there, appear empty and rudderless.

Governments like to excuse their failures by claiming they have been 'blown off course' by uncontrollable storms. But the Wilson governments were not steering a course. They spent most of their time coping with symptoms of the weakness and vulnerability of the British economy which, as usual, they grossly underestimated. For the great world boom, in which Britain modestly participated, was at its height, and the British people really had 'never had it so good'. But for the first signs of the global golden age ending, and of the dramatic acceleration of Britain's relative decline, the Wilsonians could perhaps have got by as moderately reforming administrators of the marriage between capitalism and the welfare state. This was about all they had hoped for. As it was they stumbled internationally and came up against the contradiction between welfare costs and trade union strength on one side and the sluggishness of the economy on the other.

Thrashing about, the Wilson government found itself desperately trying to impose legal controls on unions and strikes. This was a triple mistake. Set against a policy which trade unionists recognize as being in the workers' interests, as in 1945–51, union restraint is possible, though it goes against the natural instincts of any union leader, right or left (Bevin hadn't liked it). In 1948 the TUC actually voted for a permanent wage freeze to help along Stafford Cripps' 'austerity'. But the Wilson government did not look and act like a working-class government. It seemed like a slightly more liberal and humanized version of the usual consensus Keynesian Tory government, and (unlike Cripps in 1948) it did not even try to trade off union restraint against some other reform to equalize income or wealth. In the 1970s, when it was too late, this was actually tried in the 'Social Contract' developed by Jack Jones, the leader of the Transport Workers. Second, *legal* compulsion was quite certain to divide the party and the left. In fact, its opponents included politicians far from the left (Callaghan, Crosland, Crossman, Marsh), but who could recognize a suicide mission when they saw one. Wilson was defeated because he showed no sense of what the movement was like. But third and finally, his failure to impose legal restraint on the unions, once he had himself put it on the agenda, guaranteed that legal control would inevitably become the slogan of the Tories.

Add the totally negative record of these years in foreign policy, and the Wilsonian 1960s come out as badly, in their way, as the 1929–31 Labour government; worse, in some ways, since Wilson succeeded in dividing the party profoundly, but without himself leaving it. After 1931, the co-operation of right, centre, and left, which made possible the 1945 government, was as difficult and troubled as it always seems to have been in the Labour Party; but it was at least made possible by the fact that all could agree in damning the traitors who had gone over to the other side. But after 1970 the 'guilty men and women' (whoever one thought they were) were still inside the party. It moved to the left as its leading rightwingers moved to the right.

The less said about the fifth period of Labour government, the second Wilson and Callaghan years (1974–79), the better. Having lost 11 per cent of its vote or almost one and a half million voters since Wilson's peak, the minority Labour governments of the 1970s were in any case too weak to do much. They lived on by the kind permission of Liberals and a few others, from hand to mouth, beset by problems on all sides, increasingly unable to control anything, and were eventually overthrown by a wave of strikes. The most that can be said about them is that they kept the loyalty of the eleven and a half million basic Labour voters who went on supporting their party steadily through the four elections of that miserable decade. It took the lunacies of secession and infighting after 1979 to lose another million Labour votes (or 27 per cent of the remaining Labour electorate) in four years.

What can we learn from this not very inspiring record? First, that Labour governments persistently underestimated the seriousness of the crisis of the British economy and the reality of Britain's decline as an international power. So, of course, did most people in Britain until the middle 1970s, but that is no excuse. Is this still the case? If not – and I think it is not – there is reason for optimism. For if both the British people and the Labour Party and movement are, at last, convinced that our problem is like that of a country defeated and half-destroyed in war, then both can concentrate, without foolish illusions, on the task of national recovery, and envisage the sacrifices it must certainly entail. And this may once again give Labour something like the dynamism and, in spite of all, the temporary unity it had in 1945; and the rest of the British people the readiness to give a Labour government support, or at least toleration.

The Thatcher years have made this easier in three respects. First, they have so visibly reduced much of Britain to the equivalent of a bomb-site that it is much easier to recognize the life-or-death issue Britain faces. After all, as Tony Benn has said, Thatcher has destroyed much more British industry than Hitler did. Second, they have utterly discredited, in the minds of most people, the privatizing 'free market' ideology of the suburban crusaders who dressed up the right of the rich to get richer among ruins as a way of solving the world's and Britain's problems. They have had their chance and we can see what has happened. It may even be that in her decline Thatcher will lose her grip on those traditional assets of ancient Toryism, crown and empire, flag and patriotic reflexes. Third, the defeats and set-backs of Labour have been so massive and undeniable (even by many once blind sectarians) that probably conditions for all parts of the movement working together are better than at any time since the 1930s. And it is another lesson of the past that Labour governments divided, or paralysed by fear of division, get nowhere.

On the other hand, it will be more difficult in two respects. The distance – even the geographical distance – between the sectors of the British people who are doing well and those who are not has grown so great that the prosperous may be reluctant to make their share of the necessary sacrifices. And what is lacking today, more than ever, is what gave Labour in 1945 so much impetus: the hunger (not only among workers and socialists) for a new and better kind of society, as distinct from revulsion at what has been done to an old society. Also, it must be said honestly, there is not (yet) a lot of confidence in the Labour Party as the engine of national recovery and salvation.

Nevertheless, Labour's best and perhaps only chance is to convince the people that recovery from a major national catastrophe is overwhelmingly the primary task before us. The economy will obviously stay mixed. It was always likely to, and not even the most radical version of the left's Labour Party programme ever said otherwise. But it is equally clear that, after Thatcherism, there must again be a substantial turn to social control and management in economic and social affairs, not for ideology but for practical reasons. And on the other hand it ought to be clear to workers, as it was to most of them after 1945, that an economy in ruins cannot be regarded as a going concern from which unions can demand rises regardless, even if this or that group could still get a favourable deal for themselves. In short, a genuine and justified sense of crisis can push the ideological evangelists back to the fringe of real politics.

Whether, and how, we advance further towards socialism, and indeed what we actually mean by a socialist Britain (given that even among the socialist states actually in being there are different varieties, not one of them – perhaps excepting Albania – any longer commited to a totally state-run centrally planned economy without market elements) are questions for the future. Without the rebuilding of Britain, we shall hardly get to confronting them. Still, much can and ought to be achieved. 1945 did not give us a socialist Britain, but it changed the face of the nation, profoundly and for the better, and it was Labour's achievement. We can be proud if the next Labour government achieves half as much.

However, 1945 suggests two final lessons. The first is that a major reforming Labour government should waste no time. Practically the entire programme of change was carried out in the first three years of the Attlee government. Delay multiplies obstacles. No doubt this speed was made possible by the substantial unity of right, centre, and left, but it would also have been impossible without a clear programme. This Labour had in 1945. It didn't have anything like it in the 1960s and 1970s. And the awful example of the Wilson era shows what happens when a Labour government has nothing in mind except how to get back into office and bypass internal dog-fights.

The second lesson is that you must know what to do. The temptation to avoid trouble – and bad publicity – by saying as little as possible about future plans is enormous, and, given the internal history of the movement since 1979, more than understandable. But someone must work out what a Labour government would do. If this is done by committees or advisers to shadow ministers, someone has to fit the pieces together. And then these plans have to be identified with the party. Not, as one kind of Labour left thinks, to hold a Labour leadership consisting of potential traitors to promises extorted from it by conference, but because a Labour government must have an idea of where it is going, what its main problems are, and how to tackle them. This is because a Labour government will *not* be, like Wilson, in the kind of politics in which 'a week is a long time', and therefore it cannot just play it by ear or by poll. This kind of planning does need discussion and formulation. It can't be replaced by rhetoric – socialist, as in 1929, or technological, as in 1964 – designed to sidestep trouble.

Is Labour today in the position of late 1944 – long before an election could be anticipated and several months before it happened – when the national executive had 'precise policy documents . . . to cover full employment, housing, social security, a national health service, education, control of the banks, public ownership and world peace'? It *ought* to be.

This is the last lesson of the past, and is again from the Wilson era. It is not enough, after a period of Labour retreat in the wilderness, to rely on the Tories beating themselves. They may do. They did in 1964. It was enough to give Labour its chance. Which the governments of the 1960s threw away.

14

Snatching Victory from Defeat
(1987)

The time for the general election is coming, and so is the time for people on the left to face the truth about it, before it is entirely drowned in electoral rhetoric and forecasters' algebra.

Three things have been manifest since 1983, if not before. First, that the defeat of the Thatcher government is the essential task in British politics, and should have absolute priority over any other aim and political calculation. There is no need to argue the case. *Marxism Today* has done so for years, and anybody who does not believe that this appalling government, by far the most dangerous and disastrous in twentieth-century British history, ought not to be allowed to do even more irreversible damage to Britain, had better stop reading here. But before stopping, they might just remind themselves that this is the only government this century which has made the actual destruction of the labour movement and the Labour Party its declared aim.

Second, it is clear that the Thatcher government is and was, even in 1983, elected as a *minority* government, against the wishes of 58 per cent of those who voted. At present, to judge by the polls, it has about two-thirds of the people against it. There has never been a Thatcherite wave of public opinion like the Reaganite wave in the USA. Most Britons have never bought the Thatcher line of products, in spite of the packaging and hard sell. On paper, there is no basis for a Thatcher victory.

Third, we know that the Thatcher government could not have been elected but for the divisions among the opposition, namely between Labour and the Alliance. And if Thatcher has any chance of being re-elected, it is *entirely* due to the continuance of these divisions. After the election of 1983 I wrote in 'Labour's Lost Millions':

Given the approximately even split between the two parts of the anti-Tory vote, the Conservatives could drop about a quarter of their total vote and still come first past the post. It is vital to keep this point in mind for the next five years, because the prospect of defeating Thatcher hinges on it, whatever else the labour movement does to recover.

If, at the next election, Thatcherism is everywhere opposed by two or more candidates competing for each other's votes, the Tories can look forward to being in power well into the 1990s. Some way of uniting the majority of the British people, which is opposed to Thatcherism, must be found.

This is as true today as it was then. Only in October 1983 there were almost four years left to do something about it, and today we have only weeks or at best months.

A fourth fact, unfortunately, has now also become established beyond serious argument. The Labour Party is extremely unlikely to win the election on its own and to form a single-handed government, although this does not mean that Labour may not emerge as the largest single party or provide a prime minister and cabinet. Labour bounced back from the 1983 disaster with remarkable speed under Neil Kinnock's new leadership. But since then it has never really risen above the quickly recovered level of 37 per cent or so, and it has never seriously looked as if it might. What is more, in the polls, it has usually lagged a little behind the Tories, and has rarely been ahead of them as we might expect the major party of opposition and alternative government to be. This is not the time to try to explain why Labour has failed to extend its support since 1983, thus making extremely unlikely what would have been by far the best solution: a Labour government elected by a good majority of voters. The crucial point is that it has failed to, and that it is mere whistling in the dark to predict that somehow in the course of a few weeks of electoral campaigning, things will somehow come right.

The best Labour can realistically hope for in what, like it or not, has become a three-way system of British politics, is that it will come out of the election as the largest party, or the largest non-Tory party in parliament. That is not an unreasonable hope.

The emergence of what is clearly a permanent tripartite division in British politics is the fifth fact which must determine our political choices. It is not really a three-party system, since the middle camp has only the negative unity of not wanting to belong to the right or to the left. That is why the support for the Alliance has normally been so much more unstable and fragile than that of either the Tories or Labour, responding disproportionately to casual short-term events and media exposure.

But this should not mislead us. Whatever the future of the Alliance, some kind of central mass in politics is here to stay, if only because *both* the major parties are patently continuing their long-term process of decline. (Much of the talk about the decline of Labour served to divert attention from the fact that in 1983, the year of Thatcher's electoral triumph, the Tory Party mobilized a smaller share of the British electorate than at any time since 1923.) The Alliance vote may or may not rise above 30 per cent but it is almost certainly not going to fall below 20 per cent in this election.

There is only one logical conclusion for those of us who put the defeat of Thatcher first. It is, in every constituency, to vote for the candidate who offers the best chance of beating the Tories, whether Labour or Alliance. None of the leaders of the parties of opposition will tell us to do so. In fact, all will tell us the opposite, following the electoral mythology and political folklore which holds that politicans, like boxers before the big fight, must on no account admit that they could not knock the other fellow out of the ring. Thus David Steel, against all probability, looks forward to the Alliance sweeping Scotland, and Neil Kinnock waves away any thought of negotiating with the Alliance even after the election, for fear of discouraging Labour voters. But neither of them believe what they are saying and we also know better.

We know, as well as Steel, Owen, Jenkins, and Kinnock, that if we had a two-stage electoral system like the French, tactical voting would be as normal as breathing. We should all vote for our own party in the first round, and, having seen which candidate was ahead – Labour or Alliance – vote for him or her in the second round to keep the Tory out. Well, we have to do the same without a French system, and without any guidance from our parties. We shall have to take the decision ourselves. I think there are enough citizens to use democracy sensibly and there-fore to defeat Thatcher.

All arguments against tactical voting assume *either* that a single-handed victory of Labour (or the Alliance) over Thatcher is possible, *or* that a defeat of this government is not the overwhelming political priority of the moment. The first possibility is, of course, available in theory, but there is no bookmaker in the country who would not welcome punters who wanted to give away their money by betting on it. Given the split in the non-Tory vote, the odds *must* be stacked in favour of Thatcher, or at least against the single-handed victory of either opposition force. Some kind of unity is the only effective hope for beating the government. Anyone who opposes it, does not really mind whether the government is beaten or not, or else he or she is simply not using their head.

This applies even to the rare arguments against tactical voting which have any merit at all. On the Labour side there is only one, though it is not usually publicly acknowledged. It is that tactical voting, by producing a substantial third party in parliament, will destroy the two-party system and therefore the chance of future single-handed Labour governments. It would permanently put the left (and the right) at the mercy of centre parties and coalition governments.

On the Alliance side (or rather on the SDP side, for the Liberals have been much more reticent in this respect), the argument is frankly that a Thatcher victory is a price well worth paying for the chance to ruin the Labour Party for good in order to come back after another five years of Thatcherism as the major, and hopefully the only, opposition force and alternative government. (This, incidentally, is also the Thatcher scenario for the future of British politics.) Such views have been expressed frankly by SDP utopians like Peter Jenkins and are clearly much discussed in and around the relevant wine bars. As Peter Kellner reports, 'Their strategic dilemma is whether to seek a share in power after the next election, or the destruction of the Labour Party by the one after that.'[1] If they opt for the second, then tactical voting against the Tories has no attraction, since it is likely to produce a Labour-led government or coalition.

But in fact, except for megalomania, personal ambition or the festering wounds of past political feuding, a Labour-led coalition, or even a Labour government depending on Alliance support, are entirely acceptable options for the Alliance. They have to be far preferable to the alternative of a third Thatcherite government. For the Alliance is unquestionably an anti-Thatcherite phenomenon, and in so far as the Tory Party has been hijacked by the self-made suburban stormtroopers of the right, a secession from Conservatism. Dr Owen might prefer a centre–right coalition, though even he cannot publicly say yet that he would be prepared to ally with the Thatchers and the Tebbits, but the only alignment that is being seriously considered in case no single party wins an absolute majority in parliament is one of the centre–left.

The educated middle classes who form the social core of the Alliance are repelled by Thatcherism and what it has done to Britain. Even the ranks of the SDP, which, as the jokes go, is the Professors' Party and (when at prayer) the Church of England, are not likely to welcome paying the price of another five years of Thatcherism for the chance to have a David rather than a Neil as premier in 1992 or 1993. They are certainly not socialists, let alone left-wing socialists. However, voting in union to defeat a Conservative comes a lot more naturally to most Alliance voters than voting separately to let a Conservative in.

Given all this, tactically united voting also suits the Alliance. It would, for the first time, give the centre a substantial block of MPs in

parliament, and thus break the barrier which has virtually disen-
franchized a quarter of the electorate. It would, quite likely, allow that
centre block to hold the balance between the two major parties, and thus
give it disproportionate political leverage. It would negotiate electoral
reform from strength. Sensible Alliance strategists would happily pay
the price of putting in a moderate government headed by Labour. No
doubt they would prefer an Alliance government, but, in spite of
campaign rhetoric, this is not on at present, barring a conjunction of
miracles.

For Labour this is not a brilliant prospect. One way or another it
means making room for a permanent middle party, and probably a long-
term prospect of tripartite politics and governments by coalition such as
have operated in West Germany, Austria and the Irish Republic for a
long time. It does not necessarily remove the possibility of a single-party
government in the future (think of Austria), but undoubtedly this
becomes more difficult. And under normal circumstances, it would give
the centre a good deal of control over what a Labour-led government
could do or not do. It will undoubtedly be a set-back for British socialist
hopes. Nobody will open champagne bottles in celebration, even though
it would bring about both the defeat of Thatcherism and, more than
likely, a government headed by Neil Kinnock.

But what is the alternative? A third Thatcher government. A union
of centre and left is the best hope we have. The game of the 'ifs', as in 'if
Labour recovers what it lost since 1979', is over. It hasn't, and it
certainly won't by the election. The same applies to 'if the Alliance were
to collapse'. It hasn't, and it certainly won't by the election. Neither will
the Tories. Anyway, what more can we reasonably expect than a Tory
Party which, on the present polls, will have a lower percentage of voters
than it had in Labour's triumphal election of 1945? There is today only
one way to get rid of Thatcher, to get a Labour-led government, and to
keep open the road to a real Labour revival in the future.

It will, at best, offer Labour the chance of a half victory or a victory in
shackles. But the alternative prospect is far darker and less acceptable.
Defeat in the election means not only another five years of Thatcherism,
which will thus gain the chance to make its rightwing revolution irreversible. It will also, as the SDP calculations make clear, put the future of
the Labour Party at risk (not to mention the leadership of Neil
Kinnock). What is at issue for Labour supporters is both the future of
the British people and of their party.

There is, of course, no need to listen to apocalyptic predictions about
its demise from people whose only purpose is to demoralize Labour
voters and to prepare more Labour politicians for secession. But two
things cannot be denied. First, that the body of *unconditional* support

on which the party can count today is no larger than it was in 1983, and may by now have crumbled a bit more. We can no longer safely count on more than a quarter of the electorate unless there is a genuine Labour revival. (The supporters who came back to Labour after Neil Kinnock became leader were precisely *conditional* supporters, ready to give the party another try – but also ready to reconsider their options.) And second, that a Labour defeat will pretty certainly produce troubles in the party, perhaps with the renewal of the public infighting and civil wars which are the safest known way of alienating supporters.

That is exactly what Labour's opponents, and especially Mrs Thatcher's Tories, are counting on: a party demoralized by a third successive defeat, a party tearing itself to pieces in public, a party which does not look as though it has a future.

There is only one way to give Labour a further chance. It is to secure the defeat of the Thatcher government. There is only one way of defeating the Thatcher government. It is by *voting for the candidate who is best placed to keep out the Tory*. Anyone who tells us anything else, however sincerely, is betraying the British people, not to mention democracy and the labour movement.

Notes

1. *The Independent*, 30 March 1987.

The Emancipation of Mankind (1987)

Eric Hobsbawm interviewed by Peter Glotz

P.G. Margaret Thatcher has become the first prime minister this century to be elected to office three times. What does this mean for Great Britain?

E.H. A third term of office for the Thatcher government means exactly what Mrs Thatcher said it would in her programme, that is, the systematic undermining of the bases of the Labour Party as a viable party of government and of a labour movement capable of effective action. Thatcher's victory also means the systematic dismantling of the social welfare and educational systems. This itself entails a double offensive: first, against leftwing organizations and bases of support, and second, against workers' solidarity and – how shall I put it? – against people's sense of social responsibility.

The attack will focus primarily on local government where the opposition still has some scope for independent initiative. The real paradox of this government is that its struggle for economic and social individualism is, in practice, being conducted through an increasingly centralized state power. The parliamentary opposition is powerless for the next four or five years.

P.G. During the last election you advocated tactical voting, that is, voting either Labour or Alliance depending on which was tactically the most sensible choice. Why did so few intellectuals adopt this recommendation?

E.H. Unfortunately there is a very simple explanation. A united front against Mrs Thatcher could only have been organized through the political parties, and all three opposition parties had officially rejected any such policy. Within these parties there were actually many people in favour of tactical voting, and in some constituencies, where the leftwing middle-class vote is strong, there is evidence to suggest that, to a certain extent, people did vote tactically. This was not enough, though, and those who advocated it never believed it would be. Perhaps logic will now finally bring the parties to their senses. Unfortunately, they do now have plenty of time to reflect on their crushing defeat.

P.G. I am interested in the position of the European left today and its future. In *Marxism Today* in 1982 you wrote:

> It is not enough to deplore the decline of 'the movement' from the great old days, whenever the militants situate them (General Strike, the time of Maurice Thorez, Togliatti, or Vienna in the 1920s). Nostalgia will not bring them back. They have gone for good. We must build on the foundations of the past; but the building must be new. This situation is common to the Left throughout Europe; and certainly to the socialist Left.[1]

Two questions spring to mind here: what kind of nostalgia were you thinking of when you wrote this, and do you think this nostalgia still exists among the European left?

E.H. The nostalgia I was referring to is the tradition of struggle in the old labour movement. I can't really say to what extent it exists in other countries but it certainly exists here in England, perhaps even more so than elsewhere, because our labour movement was in some ways exceptionally strong. In fact, Britain was the only major country where the proletariat ever formed the real majority of the population. The British movement also had a kind of solidarity and fighting attitude which not only acted as a pointer for the older generation, but directed their whole life. As you yourself have written, there were traces of this in the great miners' strike in 1985, for instance. I am sure these traditions exist elsewhere too – the anti-fascist tradition, for example, which is clearly visible in Italy. The resistance which made it possible for the Italian people, especially the working class, to free themselves from the burden of defeat or guilt inherited from the fascist period remains, and is an important and positive factor. However, as I wrote at the time, this is not enough. Of course one is loth to reject one's own traditions, but somewhere and somehow we have to overcome this.

P.G. And it is now degenerating into nostalgia?

E.H. It degenerates into nostalgia if people do not reflect on the real situation but simply play over the old repertoire. That might be all right in the concert hall, but not in politics.

P.G. Let's move on to the reasons for the crisis in the European left. Perhaps first of all a word about the outline conditions. The first question I should put to you as a Marxist, of course, concerns the 'crisis of world capitalism' and its consequences. The economically strongest Western nation now has a rather disrupted economy, above all a horrendous deficit, producing high interest rates which attract capital from the whole world. This means that we all share in financing the American deficit. We also still have a real debt crisis despite the improvements to the institutions of international crisis management (the IMF and the World Bank). I don't believe there will be a great crash in the personal or borrowed capital market, but I do think the successful commercial banks will drive the less successful out of the market. Nevertheless, the situation looks likely to be fairly bleak (at least for the next four or five years of what we suspect to be a secular recession). Let me ask you in a brief and very general way – what will be the repercussions, in your opinion, of the 'crisis of world capitalism' for the European left today? The times when one could rely on immiseration theory to provide strategic hope are surely gone.

E.H. Yes, you see I don't think that has ever worked for the left. After all, if there was ever a system-threatening economic crisis, it was the 1930s crisis.

P.G. That ended in fascism.

E.H. It ended in fascism. Previously, people had somehow expected that the crisis would automatically lead to a radicalization. But it didn't – in fact quite the opposite. And I think, in a way, one must go back to Marx here. You see, Marx and Engels expected the first world crisis – that of 1857–58 – to produce a radicalization and a revolutionary upturn or about-turn, but it didn't come, and I think that after that we ought to be very cautious about predicting that crises, even serious crises, automatically lead to a crash. But I do think that, like many things, the capitalist system is more likely to crumble at the edges than in the centre. After all, even in the 1970s there were revolutions, for example anti-colonial revolutions, the Portuguese revolution, the end of fascism in Spain and Greece, and then of course, the Ethiopian and Iranian revolutions, and so on. One cannot expect these to bring an automatic shift to the left in the traditional sense, but nor can one say that there is no chance of revolutionary changes capable of weakening world capitalism a little. But on the other hand, I believe that in Europe the left is in fact weaker today, not so much because it has potentially less support (I think its constituency is not that much smaller than it was earlier), but because in the seventies and eighties it could not develop a programme or project for the crisis. It underlined that itself. Somehow the left yielded the economic initiative to the neo-Liberal and neo-Conservative right, and in a way they had to because their own projected programme was not really geared to the crisis.

P.G. I have used the concept of a 'two-thirds society' (*Zweidrittelgesell-schaft*) to try to describe the situation. My theory is that our society is developing in this way. It is basically a modern version of Disraeli's 'two nations' theory. The problem is simply that a minority of society – the unemployed and their families, those surviving on small pensions, single mothers who are forced to live on social security, marginalized workers who can become unemployed again at any time – are all pushed to the bottom of the pile, while the majority (including many skilled workers) hold on to secure positions. The danger is that this part of the workforce will be simply 'co-opted' by, or drawn into, the upper strata. How can the left prevent this?

E.H. Your idea of a 'two-thirds society' seems to fit. It is certainly true that even in Britain, which perhaps has suffered relatively more than other countries, the majority of people, including the majority of the working class, are no worse off than before; they are better off. The minority can be more or less disregarded, except that the geographical distribution of votes in Britain more or less guarantees the Labour Party a disproportionate parliamentary representation in Scotland, the North of England, and so on. But that is not the same thing. One wonders whether there is enough of the old solidarity ethic left, the solidarity which first produced the labour movement and has characterized it ever since.

P.G. It is surely not just the ethic. There has also been a partial change in concrete social conditions, at least in West Germany. Take the disinte-gration of working-class districts, the way people have moved out into the suburbs. All this, of course, encouraged the crumbling of the working-class environment, at least here in West Germany, where only parts of the Ruhrgebiet remain to any extent close-knit working-class districts.

E.H. Yes. You see, I think a whole host of historical developments have contributed to the destruction of working-class solidarity. What you say is certainly true of today. Between 1880 and 1920, and perhaps even between 1880 and the great depression, the opposite was true. Firstly, industrial society was based on a constant influx of working people. These people came in to the towns and formed great armies of workers. Secondly, technological development at that time was based not just on a concentration of capital, but on a concentration of production. Huge factories emerged in which workers in their thousands recognized each other as fellow workers.

And thirdly, with the exception of the United States, the age of the consumer society had not yet dawned, and the whole of the working class, including skilled and better-off workers, were forced into a kind of permanent ghetto-like existence. For this reason they shared a common lifestyle which was fundamentally different from that of the bourgeoisie and the new middle class, as well as the rural classes. In my courses, you see, I have always set people the task of identifying the point at which the workers began to wear the cap which became the international symbol of the proletariat. People recognized themselves as a class, even if it was clear that a highly skilled mechanic, say, was very different from an unskilled shipyard labourer. But they were forced together. At the moment, and especially in the years after the war, the opposite has been true.

P.G. We really had to improve people's standard of living; that was the great achievement of the reformist labour movement, but in so doing it lost its own basis of support.

E.H. That is possible. I don't think the labour movement need have too bad a conscience about this. Slum clearance, for example, was also part of the labour movements between the wars, and people were resettled in new housing areas without necessarily losing their sense of solidarity or class consciousness. The basis of a new proletariat was in fact formed. The Ford Motor Company made use of this resettlement of Londoners by the County Council, and set up its main factory in Dagenham, making these people an industrial working class. What is happening today is that the working class is, so to speak, crumbling, disintegrating – I refer to the fact that people are migrating not only to new housing areas but to new, socially heterogeneous areas.

P.G. Workers are drawing level with more senior office workers, and since by now they often drive the same car, some people are inclined to say they ought also to vote for the same party.

E.H. I think a whole host of other things contribute, for example our consumer-oriented society, which gives people almost equal opportunity for consumption and extensively privatizes it. What I have in mind is the fact that one simply has more things to spend money on, and one has more to spend today, and that collective life, both in and out of the factory, has become much weaker.

P.G. Classes 'in themselves' have remained, while classes 'for themselves' have disappeared. They have all been travelling in the elevator going up. But there are definitely still quite clear class differences; the real difference between the true property-owning classes and the workers has not diminished. Consciousness, though, has been considerably altered by this 'elevator effect', suddenly allowing this 'two-thirds' model of society to develop. Skilled workers in the key sectors, where jobs are secure – in the case of West Germany this includes the car-manufacturing, machine-building or chemical industries – become so secure psychologically that, for some of them, the solidarity ethic you were talking about earlier is no longer something they know.

E.H. Well, I don't really know how one can judge that. I don't have any firm basis of comparison between the thirties and this decade. What you found to be true of the seventies is equally true today: if a whole firm or an entire branch of industry is closed down then the workforce can be mobilized. If only a third of the workers are given the push, though, they are sacrificed.

P.G. What's more they don't sack them as such, but 'let them go' very skilfully. The older ones are made to take early retirement, for example. Only rarely are people really brutally thrown out – in West Germany at least.

E.H. But while you say classes still exist, we must not forget that the working class, in the sense of the old industrial proletariat, is declining in numbers. Some would say that it is only being replaced by 'white collar' workers anyway. But I still think that existentially, so to speak, those who work in offices feel differently from those who . . .

P.G. . . . work on a production line.

E.H. Exactly. I think even Marx somewhat underestimated the difference between manual and intellectual work. He certainly recognized it, but he did not fully appreciate that class consciousness was not built on the wage relationship alone but also came directly from the experience of people who worked with their hands, who got their hands dirty. That is the essential difference between blue-collar and white-collar workers. And I think the proletariat and the industries based on manual labour are still an important component, but as a class they now form a much smaller proportion of the population than they did earlier, and certainly smaller than had been anticipated by the socialist movement. I think the chief problem for those who are reluctant to adapt to the new situation, and prefer to go on mourning the demise of the old proletariat, is the fact that the class on which our movement was built has shrunk.

P.G. Let me try and describe a few of the points which I feel we, either as a labour movement or as a political party, have not really grasped yet. I think what we are faced with is a drive towards individualism. This can be seem more clearly in West Germany than in Britain, but I think it is a common development throughout Europe. The last three decades have seen a considerable rise in income as well as in the educational opportunities available to the lower classes. There has been a movement towards the decentralization of the workplace and more flexibility in working hours. Individuals are stripped of their class loyalties and income from state benefits, but become dependent in different ways – dependent on the labour market or on their consumer existence. My impression is that the left's reaction to this drive towards individualism is to try to deny its existence. What do you think?

E.H. What is being denied are the real and profound changes that have occurred in the social and economic structure of modern society, whether this be in the form of a drive towards individualism or not. These changes have been particularly profound since about 1950. Take for example the fact that the disappearance of the peasantry as a class, predicted by Marx and others a hundred years ago, has now finally become a reality. Up until the 1940s, when I was a student, the survival of a peasantry was still being put forward as an argument against Marx. . . .

P.G. In Western Europe there are more people unemployed than there are working the land.

E.H. Exactly, that is the first point. A second and obvious point is that the working class itself has changed as new technology has developed and old industries have declined. Furthermore, since the 1970s there has been a change in the world division of industry and the entire industry of the nineteenth and early twentieth centuries can no longer function in the same way in its country of origin. This doesn't only apply to the coal and steel industries. I think it is increasingly true of the car manufacturing industry. You are wrong to say that German workers can always depend on people wanting to go on buying Volkswagens.

P.G. Not forever, obviously, but they hope that the next five years . . .

E.H. Of course. But the fact is that it is becoming increasingly essential for advanced industrial countries to switch to other forms of production. Then there are the social differences and social transformations. Once again this concerns the incredible rise of a consumer-oriented society which once seemed inconceivable outside the United States. Until after the war it would have seemed incredible to imagine the majority of workers having cars. I can still remember clearly a comrade who was sent to organize in Coventry in 1941 during the war, saying, 'Guess what, lads – in Coventry the workers have got their own cars!'. That was almost a miracle. And that was only in the forties. So what I am saying is that today's poor live like yesterday's rich. This has enabled the development of youth culture by creating the economic basis for each generation to develop its own distinct culture. This was practically nonexistent before the fifties, because adolescents simply had no money. The transformations taking place within the family and the changes in relations between the sexes and between different generations have only been partly integrated into the policy of the left. This explains the emergence of specific movements not initiated by the left and only partly linked with the left – like the Greens, for example.

P.G. Earlier, I used the term 'individualization'. I get the impression that you are rather sceptical about this term. But your description of what is happening to people makes me think that a process of individualization is indeed taking place, and that people are being 'let go' more. On the one hand, there are more options open to individuals, but on the other, they have new ties; they are chained to the labour market and to their consumer existence in new ways. Nevertheless, I want to come back to this concept of individualization because I think social democracy, or the Labour Party, must adapt itself better to different lifestyles and different income levels than they have done in the past. Is my theory right? What do you think?

E.H. I think your diagnosis is probably the correct one; the labour movement must adapt itself better to a new individualization. How it can do this, in a theoretical way, is not so obvious. It seems to me that there is a great danger here. I see the major problem as being how to reconcile this individualization with the collective tradition of solidarity. Take the American journalist Frances Fitzgerald, who published a study of various new social movements, sects and so forth, in the USA. She found that they were not really collective movements but movements of people who wanted, more or less, to realize their own egos through working together within these groups. The danger is the fact that people do not want to work for others but for themselves, that paradise is conceived as a purely individual paradise.

P.G. Does this just refer to 'movements' protesting against roads being built in their neighbourhood, or are we talking about the peace movement for example?

E.H. I think it does include movements like the peace movement, but also those from the array of right-wing extremist groups. Indeed, in the United States, where this process of individualization . . .

P.G. . . . is even stronger . . .

E.H. . . . has gone further, even those who claim to be social revolutionaries somehow believe that what they will get out of the revolution will really only be something of personal value. I can't explain exactly, but there is a kind of frailty among certain ultra-left movements as people switch from one to another and then in a year or two start looking for something new again. This seems to me to be a sign of a fundamental weakness. The problem, then, as both you and I continually emphasize, is how this can be combined with 'solidarity', or to put it simply, with working for other people.

P.G. How do I convince the economically strong to help the economically weak? How do I manage to get them to put their own interests second? Motivation can no longer come principally from material interests. We must change people's consciousness.

E.H. That cannot be reconstructed today on the basis of material interests. I don't think one ever really could.

P.G. This seems to be evidence that you are not enough of an orthodox Marxist – but I think you are right.

E.H. Of course, any ideal without a material basis is pointless. But man is a conscious being and therefore everything, even material interests, are expressed through human consciousness, through ideas. I don't think people can be analysed in a purely behaviouristic way, as if they react 'automatically', depending on whether real income goes up or down, say. People just aren't like that, thank God, although there is an attempt to turn them into this kind of being. Today's materialist determinists work in publicity.

P.G. Lifestyles no longer vary purely according to income. People may have relatively similar incomes yet thoroughly different lifestyles. For this reason a differentiated strategy is required, a strategy capable of addressing people of different lifestyles and, at the same time, of winning them over to some kind of political action. Parties frequently fail in this. These huge political melting-pots are finding that their powers of integration are becoming weaker and weaker.

E.H. I'm afraid I must disagree with you on this point. You say you are opposed to a sentimentalization of tradition and to looking to the past. Fair enough. Nonetheless, I think that today one of the most important points is that people in Britain are seeking a certain moral security, and part of this moral security is the idea that the world is not simply made up of individuals who are concerned only with 'number one' and are locked in constant struggle with one another. I think one of the left's problems is that it has left the search for the good old times, which in a way is the search for a good society, to the right. One of the strongest features of the communist movement in Italy, for instance, is that it has learnt how to deal with the transition from an old proletarian to a new society. One of the PCI's greatest assets is that all Italians see it as the only upright and honourable party.

P.G. Because it fought against fascism ...

E.H. Partly, but partly because it has not become corrupt. People talk about it being the only uncorrupted party, and in this respect it has somehow understood the need to make a moral appeal. This is not a purely individual appeal. With few exceptions, we have left this to others – we have left patriotism to others.

P.G. ... social patriotism ...

E.H. The left fears it will be outdone somehow. It is afraid. I think a new basis must be found for solidarity. On the other hand, the old 'bases' should not be forgotten.

P.G. That is, there should be no attempt to disregard history. There is a new consciousness of history – in West Germany at least – even, it seems, in the social democratic movement which, when in power during the sixties, had pushed its history completely aside because it wanted to accommodate the bourgeoisie. Now there is a new awareness of history again. But one must be careful not to let it degenerate into nostalgia.

E.H. A consciousness of history is useful. The past contains elements which can be built into the future.

P.G. I am still trying to establish where the left falls short. I get the impression that people are increasingly aware that our programme cannot adequately represent their interests, and cannot satisfy them. I would like to illustrate this with two examples. Firstly, the risks we face are now of global dimensions. Take Chernobyl, for example. It cannot be dealt with on a national scale. Secondly, turning to economic policy, it is sheer illusion to think that classic Keynesian full-employment policies, the basis of socialist economic policy for decades, are capable of combatting today's unemployment in the face of American interest rates, the euro-dollar market and what is happening in international capital trade. There are so many international determinants, that national policy is rendered ineffective. My conclusion from all this is that if we do not arrive at a Europeanization of politics, but continue to foster the illusion that one can overcome problems within the old nation state, credibility will wane increasingly because people will begin to sense that we are all talk and are not properly equipped really to influence politics.

E.H. I couldn't agree with you more. Personally I have no great enthusiasm for Europe itself. But what you say is supported by the fact that today no country, except the United States, can define its economic policy autonomously. For most European countries, indeed for most countries of the world, any national policy is impossible. And in the absence of any world policy the only possibility is to combine on a supra-national level. Given the current situation, this must be on a European level. A standardized currency would be a useful thing. Economically, therefore, it is certainly a necessary and useful thing, and in political terms it could also facilitate an extremely desirable sense of comparative understanding among the various national movements of the left. On the other hand, of course, it could strengthen the European right.

P.G. The British left seems to find it particularly difficult to steer a European course. Can this be put down to the general anti-continental tradition in Britain or is there some other reason for it?

E.H. I think it must come down to historical tradition. I mean that historically our greatness depended on our separation from Europe. European ties only became important for us, in economic terms, in about the mid nineteenth century, when we exported machinery, technology, and so on to mainland Europe in the early phase of its industrialization, until it began to compete with us itself. The basis of the British economy was its focus on overseas trade, and it remained so, and this weighs quite heavily in the tradition. On the other hand, it is also true that the EEC did not appear particularly advantageous for Britain in the first instance. Only if one recognized just how weak Britain's real economic situation was, could one understand the real arguments for the country's integration into the EEC. And until the sixties, perhaps even the seventies, the fundamental weakness of the British economy was denied, or at leastly grossly underestimated.

P.G. But it still seems strange that Edward Heath should have had a better understanding of this problem than the Labour Party, although they shared the same tradition of an isolationist, island mentality with its orientation towards the Commonwealth and its negative attitude towards mainland Europe.

E.H. Yes, one can even say that the Labour Party, with a few exceptions, has always been entrenched in an attitude of subalternity, and has always seen itself as the opposition.

P.G. Even when it was in government?

E.H. Yes, even when it was in power. That is one of the problems of the labour movement. People think someone or other is bound to take charge, that it's not their job. It is something they demand from 'those in government'.

P.G. From 'the bosses' ...

E.H. From the bosses, the rulers. And I think this is a historical problem shared by all labour movements. It means that within social-democratic parties it is very easy for people to criticize even their own leadership, if they do manage to get into government. They simply do not think what the responsibilities are when one takes over government or society oneself.

P.G. ... But, after all, the victory of the British – and of the labour movement too – over Hitler was possible in the end only because they were not so orientated towards mainland Europe.

E.H. I certainly wouldn't wish to underestimate the strength of this rather narrow-minded and blinkered attitude of the British labour movement. I myself can remember my days in the British army, in 1940, when I, the intellectual, said to myself, 'It's looking bad, son'. Each company had, I don't know, say, four machine guns – that was it. And somehow we were supposed to defend Britain's shores. I said, 'How can we go on like this?' But for the other soldiers there was no problem. Their attitude was 'let's just get on with it'. The idea that it could all end in defeat just didn't occur to anyone. That made a great impression on me at the time.

P.G. They couldn't conceive of the idea that Hitler could cross the channel at all.

E.H. That he might be able to cross was perfectly obvious, but it just didn't occur to them that the balance of power in Europe was such that a British victory, in practice, appeared completely out of the question.

P.G. In a study of the British working class you wrote that the direct life experience of workers here in Britain is more local than national. This brings me to a very important problem – in West Germany at least – which is the rapid decline of the Social Democrats in the large cities such as Hamburg, Frankfurt or Munich, effectively that is in those cities where there is a high proportion of service industry and where the old working-class districts have been extensively destroyed. I ask you then, as a historian of class formations – for there are various theories about how to explain this – are the regional Party organizations to blame? Does sociological change play a major role? Is it a mixture of these? Can we discern a general trend? What sense can you make of this in the face of the British experience?

E.H. I don't think it is an exclusively German development, but a quite general one. The cities are being deindustrialized and the number of tertiary, highly paid positions in the 'two-thirds societies' (*Zweidrittel-gesellschaften*) goes on increasing. In New York and London more than anywhere else. You have seen the City for yourself – it's flourishing. My wife teaches in a primary school in a lumpen community. These two opposing classes live within half a kilometre of each other, and hardly know anything about one another.

P.G. Now I'm going to pick up on an idea which I found in something you had written, that is, the isolation of Labour Party activists. You suggest that a minority of full-time and voluntary officials and represen-tatives are isolating themselves and cutting themselves off from society. I think that one of the reasons for the decline of the Social Democrats in the cities is the fact that social democracy is losing contact with the people at large. The activists say now that the correct line has been esta-blished, but it just hasn't registered yet, so we need only stick to it until the people finally grasp that it is the correct line. How has this come about, and what is the position in Britain?

E.H. I think it has come about because the Party is ceasing to be a movement, that is, it is ceasing to have a mass base in everyday life and is therefore becoming an organization in which the initiative passes to the Party functionaries. They are no longer controlled from the base. I think this is a common phenomenon.

P.G. Is this more developed here than elsewhere?

E.H. Yes, it has gone further here because the mass base of the party simply no longer exists, and a number of activists are becoming officials without having much in common socially with the average person. For example, they are much younger, mainly single, generally work in community welfare and are often not necessarily intellectuals but certainly not factory workers. There is nothing to control them, because, as I said earlier, there is no working-class community any more.

P.G. In Germany this is helped by factory committee members, who are not directly comparable to your shop stewards. They have so much close contact with their people on the factory floor that they maintain a grounding in reality.

E.H. In the trade union movement it is a bit different. Union officials have to maintain close contact because if they organize a strike they have to have the workers with them. Otherwise there's no strike.

P.G. I would like to ask you to look at German reality from the outside, from the British point of view. You have lived in Berlin. How do you see the development of the German left as an outsider? I am asking you for an outside opinion what are the prospects for West Germany?

E.H. The future looks brighter for West Germany than for Britain. Brighter, firstly, because people are better off and, secondly, because in spite of everything the SPD is in a stronger position than the Labour Party. This is because it adjusted a long while ago to the fact that it must work in reality and not 'uncompromisingly'. It had to adapt to coalition politics, for example, which it did perhaps unwillingly, but it had to do it. I think the SPD's greatest weakness is that it has lost a good deal of its ideological support, namely those who have gone over to independent movements such as the Greens.

P.G. In Britain the Party split towards the right.

E.H. Yes, towards the right rather than the left. But in both movements the main problem is how the 'split' is 'absorbed'. One cannot simply ignore these people when one is working or thinking. My third point is that, in my opinion, for us as outsiders perhaps the most important thing about Germany is that she acts as a link between East and West and is the crucial factor in reducing tension and improving relations between the socialist movements of East and West in any rebuilding of a united Europe. Fourthly, we all dislike the Kohl era. I cannot predict what the future will bring though.

P.G. Let us end on a personal note. You have always ascribed the concept of freedom an important role in the socialist scenario. In 1956 when Soviet troops marched into Hungary you protested loudly. If I come to Britain today then I see you are taking a very pragmatic stand with your attitude towards tactical voting. Taken together with the fact that that you have constantly remained a member of the Communist Party, this makes one wonder – why are you still a member?

E.H. Your question has two halves. Firstly, why have I advocated a move towards the 'Alliance'? The answer is very simple: I see the Thatcher government as extremely dangerous. After the Turkish government it is the most reactionary in Europe. I don't want to use the word fascism lightly but under the Thatcher government there really is a danger of a powerful right-wing radicalism capable of weakening the whole labour movement and the whole progressive movement. It seemed, and still does, therefore, that the most important political task had to be to bring this government down. Secondly, why have I stayed in the CP? I ask myself that too, sometimes. After 1956 it was certainly very difficult for a while. The British party is small. It was not so dogmatic as others – otherwise it would have thrown me out. But it had become so weak that it couldn't, and didn't want to anyway. But that is not so important. Your question brings us back to Germany, by the way. My political awakening came while I was at secondary school in Berlin from 1931–33. The first organisation I joined was a small group which, at the time, was called the *Sozialistischer Schülerbund* and which was a dependency of the KPD. That was in the worst times of sectarianism. But when one has been involved constantly, from the age of 15, and has gone through the school of anti-fascism in the thirties and forties, one is reluctant to renounce this past. I would even go further. I don't want to disclaim my comrades who wanted to devote their lives to a great cause even when they acted mistakenly. So many people who left the Communist Parties, for example in France, have done an about-face and become anti-communists. I do not want to be in that company. Politically it is perhaps not particularly important to belong to the British Communist Party today, although as a party it has contributed a lot to the British labour movement. It is a small party, but not a sect: a small party which was typical of the best in the British labour movement. Maybe, it is not particularly important any more. My political activities today, such as they are, do not depend on whether I am in the Communist Party or not. Nevertheless, I do not want to disown my generation and the generation before me, who devoted their lives to the emancipation of mankind and were often killed for it, sometimes even by their own side. I think it is important that one accepts that this was – this is – a great cause. Perhaps it won't be accomplished now in the way we thought it would then, when we still believed in the world revolution. But it should not be said of us that we no longer believe in the emancipation of mankind.

Translated by Hilary Pilkington (Material Word)

Notes

1. Eric Hobsbawm, 'The State of the Left in Western Europe', *Marxism Today*, October 1982.

Out of the Wilderness (1987)

As Mrs Thatcher enters her third period of government, the situation of the British left is particularly troubling. The defeat of 1983 was plainly self-inflicted by the Labour Party, and made quite inevitable by the split in the opposition. That split naturally remains a fatal obstacle, and the case for backing single candidates against the Tories at the next general election, against which there were no rational arguments in 1987, is just as unanswerable now. Just as it was possible to say with certainty in 1983 that a divided opposition would keep the Tories in power into the 1990s,[1] so it is equally certain that in the absence of unity at the next election, the Tories will stay in power almost to the end of the twentieth century. There will have to be as many single opposition candidates as possible opposing each Tory. The time to start thinking about how to ensure this is now.

However, in 1987 Labour had abandoned the suicidal follies of 1980–83, and the technically excellent campaign was fought under superior and united leadership. So much so that it actually scared the Tories and Mrs Thatcher. Our defeat therefore suggests that the reasons for Labour's failure are more deep-seated.

Not that the results of the election were entirely negative. It had four positive results. First, there was the rout of the Tories in Wales and Scotland. Second, and confirming the insistence of the left (and not least of *Marxism Today*) on the importance of the women's movement, there was the substantial turn of women away from the Tories – especially of young women, who surged towards Labour with an 11 per cent swing (compared to 1.5 per cent for the men aged 20–24). Having the first British woman prime minister patently did not help the Tories.

Third, and equally striking, was the dramatic Tory loss among the middle classes. Only a little more than a third of electors with a university education voted for them in 1987, compared with 44 per cent in 1983, the rest dividing 29 per cent Labour and 36 per cent Alliance. The middle class today is not a homogeneous political block, but profoundly divided, roughly between the more and the less educated, those involved with the public side of society and those in private business. And fourth, there was the dramatic failure of the Alliance, which entails the prospective disappearance of the Social Democratic Party, at least as a serious factor in politics.

This will have two welcome results. It will eliminate fantasy projections of third-party majorities or other dream-like political scenarios, and it will establish Labour once again as the major force of opposition, and the party which will head any post-Thatcherite government. And the end of the SDP will make the indispensable task of building an anti-Thatcher alliance easier because it will eliminate much of the embittered – and understandable – mutual ill-feeling which stood in the way of collaboration between Labour and anti-Labour seceders from the party. Building bridges will still be hard, but the obstacles will be less.

However, we should resist the natural pleasure most of us felt at the electoral crash of the SDP. A quarter of the electorate supports neither Tories nor Labour. These people are not going to go away, nor will more than a fraction of them pass over or return to Labour in short order. If the Alliance vote had been stronger in 1987 this would have helped *Labour*, because it would have deprived Thatcher of that three-figure majority which now helps to override all the government's possible hesitations.

The election results were so bad because, with or without tactical voting, the Alliance was just too weak to win any of the seats in which its chances were objectively better than Labour's. Without tactical voting, Shirley Williams failed to edge out the Tory in Cambridge. *With* tactical voting, Labour won Oxford East, but (with equivalent tactical support from Labour voters) the Alliance candidate was unable to dislodge the Tory in Oxford West. The defeat of the SDP is a plus, but the minus side of the Alliance failure probably outweighs it.

So much for the positive side. The four negative results of the election are much more serious. First, and by far the most significant, 1987 confirms Labour's loss of majority support among the working class. But for the women's shift to Labour this would be even more striking. Whether or not skilled workers actually moved *away* from Labour in 1983–87, as some data suggests, the fact remains that barely more than one skilled worker in three voted Labour, six out of ten trade unionists refused to support the party the unions had founded, four out of five white-collar workers supported other parties, and less than half the semi-skilled and unskilled voted for the party of the working class.

(Conversely, almost half the Tory vote came from workers.) Only among the unemployed did Labour score more than 50 per cent and then only just. Add to this the fact that two-thirds of voters are now home-owners and 50 per cent of these voted Tory – less than a third of workers owning their homes stuck by Labour – and the scene looks bleak.

The second negative result is that, in spite of all the talk about a deepening rift between the two Britains, the position of Labour in its own heartlands is far weaker than the position of the Tories in theirs. The poor Tory showing in Scotland conceals the fact that Labour's own score in that country (42.2 per cent) is the *same* as the Tories' national score in 1983 and 1987. In both countries, for different reasons, a minority of votes has swept the board in terms of seats. The Tories have absolute majorities in three of Britain's eleven regions (omitting Ulster as a special case), whereas Labour has an absolute majority in none. In two of the five regions where Labour is ahead, the Tories are hard behind – about 3 per cent. In none of the six regions where the Tories are ahead is Labour less than 12 per cent behind. There is no way in which such figures can be made to look encouraging.

Third, there is Labour's poor showing in London, which contrasts with its spectacular success in other big cities, where – outside Birmingham – the Tories were virtually wiped out. If Labour cannot win London again, it cannot win at all.

Fourth, and last, there is Mrs Thatcher's impressive success in reinforcing her own party's position. She has practically stopped the erosion of support which both major parties have been suffering for decades – and which Labour still feels. And she has done so by compensating her losses to the opposition with massive advances everywhere from the Midlands southwards. This means that we can no longer ascribe her victory entirely to the divisions within the opposition. It means that the excuses have run out. In 1983 the folly of the opposition may have thrown away the election, but in 1987 Mrs Thatcher won it almost on her own.

The Thatcher regime now has five more years to complete its reshaping of Britain and make itself irreversible, and there is nothing in Britain to stop it. The outlook is therefore more dangerous than ever. The Tory objective seems to be, and is probably seen by most of them including Mrs Thatcher as, the utopia of economic neo-liberalism: every man an entrepreneur, the triumph of the unrestricted market, and the dismantling of state interference in the economy and the affairs of the private citizen. In short, the anarchism of the lower middle classes. But this objective can only be achieved by an enormous increase of centralized state power, because it implies the destruction of the system of

British institutions and policies which was constructed over the past 150 years by Tory, Liberal and Labour governments with a very different model of capitalist society in mind.

What is more, Mrs Thatcher's political appeal is the opposite to that of the do-nothing politician her programme dreams of. Like a number of other public figures today – for example, Craxi in Italy, or, in a comic-strip Rambo version, Colonel Oliver North – she capitalizes on the longing of puzzled and disoriented voters for leaders who take decisions and bypass talking-shops and legal niceties. It is a fashion which sends a chill down the spines of those of us old enough to remember the last time politicians made their fortunes by exploiting these longings during the last great world depression.

Furthermore, it is extremely doubtful whether the Thatcherite utopia of a totally sovereign free market is fully achievable under conditions of bourgeois (or any other) democracy, even though the British consti-tution gives governments far more power than other parliamentary systems, especially with the help of compliant judges. However, Mrs Thatcher's rightwing revolution may need more restriction of traditional British rights and liberties than even tame judges are ready for.

I do not think the left is fully aware of what is likely to happen in the next five years, and how powerless we shall be to stop it while oppo-sition MPs (and dissident Tories) score debating points in a rubber-stamp Commons, and hard-left activists call, more ineffectively than before 1987, for action in the street and workplace. Already opposition politicians, after a brief exposure to the real world of the election, are once again retreating into the private world of conferences, division-bells, and wishfulness. Business as usual can resume within that world because the actors in the play (plus a few political reporters) are their own audience. It is easy to see how absurd, and politically senseless, the post-election dogfights in the SDP are, but we too risk a return to similar bouts of self-destruction. For speeches, references back, gestures, and postures have four years of clear running before they really have to be tested again. In the meantime all they seem to cost is air and paper.

So it is urgent to remember what the situation actually is. If Thatcher wants to go ahead with any project today, however unpopular, hopeless or absurd, in the short run there is nothing to stop it. This is as true of the poll tax as it was of the GLC. That is no reason for not fighting the government, and it does not exclude the occasional success in battle of an army which, for the time being, is fighting a rearguard action. But the object of such a fight cannot realistically be to 'stop Thatcher now' (or whatever the *Morning Star* or *Socialist Worker* headline will call it). It must be to prepare policies, supporters and allies to reverse the situation in future.

What is more, there is not much that we can do to stop Thatcherism reinforcing its political strength by eroding Labour's base. It will flog more council houses, and sell public industries and property, not only to make a present to big investors, but to make worker-buyers identify with capitalism. (It doesn't help simply to point out that, as the *number* of share-owners has multiplied, the *percentage* of shares controlled by individuals in Thatcher's Britain has gone down sharply, while that controlled by institutional investors has risen.) It will continue to transfer economic activities to regions and activities where Labour is weak or can be weakened. Thatcherism does not mind a Labour Party reduced to representing and speaking for a minority of declining areas and interests, especially those (like coal mining and council housing) which the government itself can cut down further. It will eliminate local government autonomy. It will not mind cries of defiance from Brent, as these have not actually proved massive vote-winners even there. In the mean time, arrangements to muzzle or self-muzzle the media will have been further strengthened making it difficult to give mass circulation to any reports which might be seen as critical of the government. For this government is hard-nosed enough to aim not at journals like *Marxism Today* or *Tribune* but at *Panorama* and the *Ten O'Clock News*. Probably the first successes in building a united front against Thatcherism may be won in the common fight against this government's attack on press freedom.

So what can and ought Labour to do? We have a double task: to rethink our policy and to rethink the question of the social forces which can create a viable basis for a progressive government. Neither is served by cries of betrayal against those who insist on looking at the world the way it is. This double task, by the way, is not peculiar to Britain. The left has taken a beating in most of the developed European countries. The specific problem of Britain is that we are, to a greater and more dramatic extent than other developed countries, an economy in decline and perhaps a people in disarray; that we have, perhaps for this reason, fallen prey to a particularly dangerous bunch of rightwing ideologues, who happen to have laid their hands on what is a political system of theoretically unlimited central power, which lacks any effective counterweights and controls such as those provided elsewhere by written constitutions, supreme courts, various kinds of federalism, and – in some richer countries – alternative resources not under the direct control of the central power. One should not forget that Britain is, in theory, an absolutism for governments with unshakeable majorities. In the past the guarantee of British freedom, including both civil and personal liberties and those of local communities and authorities, rested essentially on politically calculated self-restraint. We no longer have a government that accepts such self-restraint.

The potential majority for a future progressive government, it is now clear, will rest on a social coalition. All the major classes and strata are today politically divided, so that a simple class appeal will not mobilize more than a part of any of them. This applies to the Tories as much as to Labour, for more than 40 per cent of *their* class core – the professional and managerial strata – refused to vote for Thatcher. So far as Labour is concerned, it means that even as a party seeking to win back the working class, or as much of it as can be recovered, Labour has to appeal to a variety of interests and attitudes, and think in terms very similar to those of building an alliance or coalition. Politically, the workers in the ruins of Merseyside do not respond to the same appeals that strike home among the workers in Harlow and Basildon (which have more industry today than Sheffield). In practice 'class politics' can no longer be realistically counterposed to 'people's politics'. In any case an appeal which mobilizes a minority of a class at the cost of pushing a majority elsewhere cannot realistically claim to be class politics.

Granted that our appeal should be to all the 'workers by hand or brain', it does not follow that it must be one-sided, or an appeal to the right. Certainly the workers have to be recaptured. But if it is absurd to claim that they have been lost by watering down the pure milk of socialism, and politically senseless to concentrate on the support of some groups at the cost of alienating other and larger ones, then it is just as wrong to suppose that Labour's problems can be solved simply by moving the party to the right. If Labour, or for that matter any broad anti-Thatcher alliance, wants to win some day, they need to keep the support of the left as well as the right. Losing Merseyside could be as fatal as losing Basildon was.

It is equally mistaken to suppose that Labour must automatically shift its appeal to the right to win the growing white-collar and middle strata, now that the industrial workers are too small a class to provide a majority single-handed. Obviously the left-of-centre and progressive middle classes are not going to queue up to vote for what they understand to be Tony Benn's or Arthur Scargill's line, and even less for the sort of Labour activists who can be labelled 'loony left', but then, neither will a lot of workers. On the other hand, it just is not the case that readers of the *Guardian* or the *Observer* as a social type are put off voting for a socialist Labour Party, or even that (as some on the left feared) Alliance voters would be more reluctant to vote tactically for Labour candidates than the other way round. The key to broadening Labour's appeal outside the working classes is not avoiding the transformation of society but making it more credible as well as attractive.

But social alliances must be more than electioneering combinations trying to attract voters with programmes cobbled together only for this purpose, even though elections do have to be won. Thatcherism won and kept power by offering not immediate benefits, but a break with the past, the end of a long period of national decline and radical action which claimed to secure a modernized Britain. That is still the main Thatcherite appeal, for in terms of self-interest the material pay-offs for most of those who are or feel better off (except for the really rich) are modest – probably they do no more than continue the trend-line of the past thirty years. On the other hand, the social costs of Thatcherism are felt to be shocking – that was the basis of Labour's campaign success – and the set-backs on the road from 1979 to 1987 have been severe and dramatic.

The reason why we have not made headway is that Thatcherism is still the only programme on offer with the object of changing the British economy. In the absence of any other party with a vision of a renewed Britain and the determination to get there, even the absurdities of free marketing look better than nothing, and the ruin of industries, the millions out of work, the bonanzas for the rich at the expense of the helpless, can be sold as the necessary short-term costs of the transformation which will eventually succeed. Labour cares, but – as the election showed – caring doesn't seem to be enough.

What Labour, or rather a Labour-led alliance of forces, must offer from the left is the equivalent of what Thatcher offers from the right – and, incidentally, in spite of all the hype, has not even begun to look like achieving; for there is a difference between a prosperous consumer society in parts of England and the modernization of the British economy. Labour will return to office only as a party which offers such a New Deal: modernization – and in a human and responsible manner. Whatever the long-term prospects for Britain, what the country needs *now* for any kind of future is such a transformation.

There are three guiding principles for such a policy. The first is the hardest to accept: the recognition that the British economy of the 1970s, including the parts dearest to the Labour movement, *needed a kick in the pants*. We must therefore distinguish between those economic changes since 1979 which ought to be reversed, if possible, such as the privatization of what even in free-market economics are 'natural monopolies', and those which should not. Would most of us seriously wish to return to the situation which kept modern technology out of British newspapers (and stopped the appearance of new ones), even as we grit our teeth at the thought that it was ended by the likes of Shah, Murdoch, and Thatcher? I think not.

However, the issue here is not so much whether there can or ought to be a blanket reversal of everything done since 1979, but a more profound one. Major change in the economy means major change. Too often, in the labour movement, it meant anything and everything except change in existing arrangements, especially the ones from which we benefited. If Labour wants to modernize Britain it will have to be as ready to disrupt old habits and practices as Gorbachev is in his effort to modernize the Soviet economy. And, in our own way, as ruthless as Thatcher in hers.

The second is that *modernization can be socially responsible.* There are plenty of examples of socially irresponsible development, such as in Brazil, where it has produced probably the highest degree of social and economic inequality in the world. (I do not include Thatcherism, for while it is spectacularly unfair and inegalitarian, it is *not* an effective recipe for modernization.) There are a number of European countries which prove that another way is possible, and which neo-liberal propaganda has therefore preferred to forget. They are the countries of the corporatist tradition in its successful, that is Social Democratic and labourist form: Sweden, Norway, Denmark, Finland and Austria. They are among the economic success stories because they have kept unemployment low – far lower than elsewhere in western Europe – and their welfare states in good order while navigating the storms of the years of global economic troubles, and adapting themselves to the inevitable structural changes in industry, the economy, and society.

They are not necessarily models for Britain – for one thing they have much smaller populations – but we can learn two things from them: that Thatcherism was not the only answer to the 1970s and that labourism can be one – but on one condition. These are regimes with, by and large, a wage policy co-ordinated between governments and unions. They do not have union movements which, as in Britain, still largely reject any interference in the individual union's right to ask for as much as it can get, and never mind the economy as a whole. This policy, effectively a form of free marketism which produces inegalitarianism and makes any kind of national economic planning impossible, socialist or otherwise, is still often supported by an unthinking left.

The third principle is that modernization requires *a combination of public control and planning with markets.* Using markets and private enterprise will not only be inevitable for any post-Thatcherite government, given the privatized economy in which it will have to begin operating. As the trend of reform in the socialist world also shows, socialist planning itself now feels the need of a market element. Actually, the main socialist discovery of the postwar era has been precisely that the social management of the economy can take other forms than total centralized planning under total public ownership. The socialist problem lies in finding the right combination to get economic and technical dynamism while maintaining equality and social justice.

There should be no need to argue this point any longer. On the other hand what needs to be said over and over again is that turning round a declining, obsolescent economy *cannot be done by following the free market*, and certainly not under British conditions. Nor has Thatcherism failed to halt the relative decline of Britain, in spite of the unnecessary mass murder of so much of British industry. Britain has not regained the comparative competitiveness – such as it was – which our industries had in 1978. We are still sinking. Italy has passed Britain in the league table of the major economies, or is on the verge of doing so. The reason is simple. Making money is the object of free enterprise, and in a declining country there are demonstrably better, and above all faster, ways of making a lot of money than in the long-term and expensive business of restoring the fortunes of Britain.

That is why practically all the major efforts at industrializing poor and backward countries, or transforming lagging and sluggish economies, have, in our century, been motivated by the non-market ideologies of socialism or economic nationalism, or a combination of both. Greed is not enough. Unlike Thatcherite neo-liberals, even serious non-socialist modernizers refuse to follow the free market where it conflicts with the interests of the country. This means that they have sought to transform their economies by means of deliberate and conscious state policy, state control, and planning, with or without a large public sector.

Leaving aside socialist regimes, a number of countries have set themselves this target since the Second World War, and several have been strikingly successful. None of them have been Thatcherite: Japan, France after 1945, Finland, Brazil and South Korea, to name some dramatic cases. Capitalist – yes. But it is bizarre to see Thatcherite economists claiming as triumphs of the 'free market', for example, the 'five year plans' of Korea since 1962, which have achieved probably the fastest industrialization in history, with their strict credit and exchange controls, their targeted 'development sectors' and export objectives, and a direction of the economy more centralized even than in Japan.

There is absolutely no reason to believe that a serious reconstruction of the British economy, and especially of our industries, will be possible without such development targeting, by government, without control, planning, incentives, and penalties. However, there are three additional reasons why the free market will not do for Britain.

First, there is the need to undo the damage of the rightwing Luddites – the destruction of the existing machinery for managing and regulating the economy, including the regulation of the market itself. Intelligent businessmen themselves admit that more regulation (including control of the irresponsible monopolies created – as Marxists could have told them – by deregulation and privatization) is necessary.

The second is the need to rebuild the country's infrastructure, which has not only been allowed to crumble but also contains much Victorian investment in, for example, public and private buildings, or drainage and water-supply systems, that is now reaching the end of its useful life. New York City (note: *not* the free market) is spending $15 billion in the 1980s on its transport system, and it is estimated that just to restore and rebuild the bridges of the USA would cost $50 billion. Apart from providing jobs, a systematic programme of this kind would be an essential investment for the country's future economy.

The third, and in some ways most vital, is the need for education. I know of no poor or backward country that has ever fully transformed itself into an advanced one without an educated labour force at all levels, and this is surely as true of turning round declining economies in the era of late twentieth-century hi-tech, as it was of Scandinavia. 'No amount of productivity', says an American banker, 'will survive competition with the Korean, Malaysian and Taiwanese standard of living. To create jobs and businesses that add high values to raw materials through skill and technology, we need an educated workforce. We are not creating one.'[2]

If this is true of the USA, which does not stint its spending on education, it is even more true of Britain, which provides vocational and technical education for only 6 per cent of its secondary pupils (the usual European figure is between 25 and 30 per cent); which sends a lower percentage of the relevant age group to higher education than any other country in western Europe, bar Portugal and Greece; and which has the almost unique record of letting the proportion of its GNP spent on education in the last ten years drop by something like 20 per cent.[3] Private enterprise has never done it, and will not do it now.

Here is the basis for a programme which can unite and increase the non-Thatcherite majority of the British peoples, for it opens a way to the necessary reconstruction of Britain. It is also the way forward for socialists, even though it does not guarantee a socialist future. For our main theoretical task is to demonstrate to people who see no reason to believe it, why public interest is better than private profit. It just will not do any more to issue statements to the faithful about 'developing a socialist economic policy, including the extension of common ownership into the financial and manufacturing sectors', for the non-faithful will inevitably ask 'what's in that policy?' and 'why more common ownership?'[4] Talking to the converted is unnecessary. It is the 70 per cent of others we should be bothered about. We have to show them *concretely* how and why public action, planning, and policy, including common ownership, is better: not only for the victims of society but for Britain as a whole; not only to share the national cake out fairly, but to make a bigger cake to distribute; not only in the abstract, but in the existing, hard, international competitive system. This is the way we can show them. What is more, someone has to show them, for in the circumstances of Britain, neo-liberalism, whether Thatcherite or dressed up as a 'social market economy', is not a way for reversing the secular decline of our country.

Notes

1. See above, pp. 63–76.
2. Felix Rohatyn, 'On the Brink', *New York Review of Books*, 11 June 1987, pp. 3–4.
3. As can be worked out from UNESCO *Statistical Yearbook*, 1986, Tables 3.2, 3.7, 4.1.
4. 'Labour, the Liberals and the unity of the Labour Left', *Tribune*, 21–28 August 1987, p. 5. The quotation is the *only* reference to the economy in this document.

Offering a Good Society (1987)

There are two reasons why the left should seriously rethink socialism. The first is that in countries such as ours the case of it seems less urgent than it used to be, whereas it is not. The paradox of global hunger amid butter mountains and wheat surpluses is as dramatic as it ever was, but while in the 1930s it automatically suggested the need for socialism, today it suggests to most people that they should give more to Oxfam or Bandaid. It doesn't seem to be *our* problem any longer.

The second is that most thinking and experience about socialist practice is out of date. Essentially the socialist ideas elaborated before the First World War (apart from various utopian community-builders) were critiques of capitalism rather than thoughts about socialism.

Until the Bolsheviks found themselves in power and Social Democrats in governments at the end of that war, there was unbelievably little thinking about how, concretely, socialism would or could work. For practical purposes *all* ideas and realizations in this field are the product of interwar experience and experiment, and bear its marks. This applies both to the Morrisonian 'nationalization' which became standard equipment in the Labour Party, and the centralized state planning for rapid industrialization in backward countries, which was evolved in Soviet Russia and subsequently, like the corresponding political system, transferred to other Communist regimes.

The crucial achievements of socialism, in both its Communist and non-Communist versions, date back to the period 1917–c.1950, which includes the great slump, the Second World War and postwar reconstruction, when British Labour also made its most lasting mark. But the situation has obviously been transformed since then. For one thing the interwar belief that a crisis-crippled capitalism would be economically inferior to planned socialism has gone. Producing wealth and a multiplicity of shopping choices is not the major problem of post-1930s capitalism, which does it better than socialism. What it can't do is to distribute it equitably.

For another, the Soviet-type economies are no longer emerging out of the medieval backwoods. The socialist models of the early industrial period, whatever their merits then, have shown severe defects under the conditions of the past 30 years. Hence the massive rethinking in those countries during that period. None of them any longer believe in the 100 per cent state-planned command economy with which ideologists (of both right and left) identify 'socialism'. The sluggishness of thinking on the sectarian Marxist and Labour left in Britain contrasts rather startlingly with the adventurousness of those who are actually in charge of socialist economies: Mikhail Gorbachev, to name but one.

However, rethinking is almost impossibly difficult when done in public by a leading political figure, who is constantly obliged to think about back-stabbers in his own party, about what bits of his text will be distributed to candidates by Tory Central Office, and whether they will put off the voters in Stevenage.

This is the handicap under which Roy Hattersley wrote *Choose Freedom*. No wonder its strongest parts – and they are very good – are the arguments against neo-liberalism on the right and the sectarianism of the extreme left. Neither Trotsky nor Friedrich Hayek carries many votes. Hattersley can allow himself to score freely and in fine style, and he has done so. He will, and ought to be, widely used in anti-Tory arguments.

On the other hand vague Thatcherite assumptions about freedom and state or bureaucratic tyranny are much more widely shared. Being far more defensive against the right than he need be against the ultra-left, Hattersley allows his argument to become skewed. And this leads him into a description of socialism which, though true, is vapid:

> It is a commitment to organise society in a way which ensures the greatest sum of freedom, the highest amount of real choice, and in consequence, the most human happiness. It is the understanding that the collective power should be used to enhance individual liberties.[1]

Except for anarchists of the right or the left, I doubt whether any practising politician of any party would refuse to subscribe to these sentiments, including those in Mrs Thatcher's cabinet, at least when speaking in public. Even if we add the Anthony Crosland phrase that socialism 'is about the pursuit of equality and the protection of freedom – in the knowledge that until we are truly equal we will not be truly free',[2] the description would still be acceptable to non-socialists left of High Toryism. In short, if we want to distinguish elephants from giraffes, it is not enough to explain that elephants are vegetarian mammals.

Such definitions are not only too vague, they also sidestep the central issues of what 'collective power' actually means and how it achieves equality and freedom. Traditionally for socialists it has meant 'that the ownership and control of the means of production should be held by the community as a whole and administered in the interests of all.' It is important to write freedom into the socialist script, since history has shown that socialism, like capitalism, can exist in notoriously unfree versions. But if we write common ownership out of it, what is the point of calling oneself socialist?

But what does 'common ownership and control' mean? Three things are at issue here. How much and what is to be owned or controlled and how? What are the objects for which control is mobilized? And how do we envisage the society which has achieved them?

Most socialists have undoubtedly modified a number of old beliefs about ownership and control since the 1930s, when John Strachey was exercised about the abolition of commodity production and money, and put a simple trust in 'the deliberate decisions of some central body as to what goods and how many of each shall be produced'.[3]

On the other hand there is nothing new in assuming that there are other forms of common ownership than state ownership in its various forms, that several such kinds of collective enterprise coexist with each other and with non-collective enterprises.

It has long been known that economies can be managed, controlled, and to some extent planned by other means than nationalization. Even socialists who disapproved of 'mixed economies' combining significant public and private sectors have accepted them in practice, at least since Lenin's NEP, and his early offers to foreign investors. For practical purposes it is inconceivable that such 'mixed economies' will not persist in presently non-socialist countries and quite possibly in some socialist ones. And, as experience in 'really existing' socialist countries has taught them, an entirely marketless socialism is a fantasy, an emergency, or a disaster. To this extent Hattersley is right to insist that socialism does not 'involve a directed economy governed by state monopolies through the bureaucratic allocation of resources.'[4] It is not new, but there is no harm in saying it again.

However, it will not do for socialists to be too defensive about the role of the state and the public sector. As against the Thatcherites we ought to say firmly that the public interest is better represented by public bodies of men and women who do not work for profit, rather than by private individuals or entities trying to make money. If Labour had always tried to conciliate what Hattersley calls 'the instinctive suspicion (in the public mind) that the state must be an instrument of authority rather than liberation', it would never have got anywhere. For this suspicion of interfering authorities has always existed. In any case, most Britons are perfectly ready to recognize state and public action which is liberating, such as instituting a National Health Service and social security – both condemned in their time as steps to slavery. They are even ready to accept sacrifices imposed by authority if they are plainly fair and in the interest of all.

What is more, the state cannot only represent the public interest, though it is obviously not doing so today. It is the only machine so far invented for changing the orientation of a national society within a fairly short timespan. Mrs Thatcher has used it, and dramatically reinforced its powers to interfere for the wrong purposes. Labour must equally use it, in a more democratically accountable and less centralized manner, for the right purposes.

Nor should we underestimate nationalization, state controls, and central planning or, like Roy Hattersley, appear to concentrate on defining the areas where it isn't necessary. This is to make unnecessary concessions to Thatcherism. For these things are not the exclusive property of socialists. No major modern war has been fought by any government, let alone British governments, on Thatcherite or Reaganite economic principles. It could not have been.

After 1945 most major efforts of postwar reconstruction set targets and planned them, even if the object of planning was to restore a private enterprise economy. 'National development plans' are not peculiar to socialist countries, as witness France and Brazil. And, as J.K. Galbraith has never stopped reminding us for the past twenty years, big business would not dream of relying on the spontaneous allocation of resources by the market. It plans, and has to. (Even the big speculators, as we now see, rely on rigged bets.) It seems faintly absurd that an author is more apologetic about planning when writing for voters than he would be were he to write exclusively for the shareholders and management of Shell or British Telecom; or that an American Democrat sounds more radical than a British socialist.

All this is important because what socialism is about is precisely taking the sort of decisions which cannot be taken if social resources are allocated by the market, that is, by a system whose basic mechanism is the reinforcement of inequality. For this, planning and public control, whatever they are called, are indispensable tools.

Socialism is about setting priorities and carrying out great public endeavours. And the first of these priorities for a Labour government will be precisely the ones which require a major planned effort: the massive reconstruction of an industrial economy which lies in ruins, the restoration of a social infrastructure dramatically dilapidated and eroded, and the reversal of Britain's decline or, if we prefer, the construction of a new role for the nation. It is senseless to think that this will not require at least as much national effort and state-led planning for revival as France and Japan undertook after 1945 (and Britain did not). Incidentally, there is no reason to believe that this would *not* have very wide political and public support.

The tasks of reviving Britain do not exhaust the question about the objects of 'common ownership'. They merely initiate them. What is more, its objects are not merely material and quantifiable, but moral and qualitative. A pragmatic case for them can be made. Greater equality can be argued to be good for the economy, though it seems accepted now in actually socialist societies that extreme egalitarianism can (as Marx foresaw for his 'first phase of socialism') slow down economic growth by diminishing economic incentives. Still, it is beyond dispute that the British social system which, as Hattersley says 'has simultaneously rejected mobility and equality' and entrenched a particularly counterproductive class system, has also been the worst brake on Britain's economic performance. But that is not the only reason why socialists want to change British society.

It is probable that pride and self-confidence, collective and individual, are economic assets for a nation. (They are not to be confused with over-compensating insecurity by jingo triumphs – real, if irrelevant, like the Falklands for Britain, or imaginary, like Grenada for the Americans.) But there are other and better reasons for deploring the hard-nosed disillusion, the shrugged shoulders, the privatized hopelessness, and the disbelief in Britain's future, which have crept across the country since the 1970s.

This is the decisive reason for rejecting Hattersley's description of socialist ends. For 'the most human happiness', however we define it, is *not* achieved only by 'the greatest amount of freedom' for individuals, and 'the highest amount of free choice': however desirable both are. It is achieved by people who live together as members of a social order with a sense of human community, in co-operation and what the old British socialists used to call 'fellowship'; by men and women who respect themselves and are respected whatever they are; who live lives that make sense to them, and offer hope to their children and future generations. The good society for which socialists strive should certainly contain 'the greatest sum of freedom', 'the highest amount of choice', and 'the most human happiness' achievable. But it cannot be *defined* by adding up individual freedoms, choices, and happinesses.

But what would such a society be like? Socialism is an instrument, not a programme, and all we can say about what the eventual future of socialism would be like is, like Karl Marx, that we do not know. Any attempt to construct the map of utopia along the lines of what we think desirable at the moment must fail (except perhaps in certain types of small and entirely self-sealing communities). There are certainly principles which, it can be argued, are fundamental to any good society, and justice, equality and freedom can be so defined as to be such foundations.

However, we cannot bind the future. The aim of socialism is to end a capitalist system whose results are profoundly unacceptable, and which destroys the bonds of human society and may destroy the world. We hope to establish a system which could one day give our successors the chance to contribute to society what they can and to get from it what they need and want, under institutions sufficiently flexible to allow adaptation to changing times. We believe that this requires 'common ownership and control' but this is in itself a means and not an end.

It is therefore idle to look for a time when we can declare socialism to be established, as national liberation movements can declare independence established. In any case, given the national and international political and economic constraints under which any single country operates, the question is academic. But this does not mean that socialists can or ought to give up the aim of a fundamental reconstruction of society, a human and moral order. Unlike Bernstein and his revisionists, we do not believe that 'the movement is everything, the final aim nothing'. Labour is not and cannot be just a party which offers the voters a better deal than the competition does on, say, pensions and bus services. It offers a good society. And today socialism is the only political force in civilized society, the only political force at all except those which, like religious fundamentalism, aim at a return to the dark ages, that recognizes the need for a society in which all men and women can live as human beings, and which is more than the sum of its individual members. It should once again recognize its mission, which is to offer this hope. To offer *any* collective hope. Hope is in desperately short supply in this country today.

Notes

1. Roy Hattersley, *Choose Freedom*, London 1987, p. 22.
2. Cited in ibid., p. xix.
3. J. Strachey, *The Theory and Practice of Socialism*, London 1936, pp. 29, 192.
4. Hattersley, p. 131.

18

No Sense of Mission (1988)

The other day, letting herself be interviewed on ITV, Mrs Thatcher took a small linguistic but a large political step to the right: she spoke, not of her government, but of her 'regime'. The word will not surprise readers of *Marxism Today*, which wrote, only a few months ago, that 'the Thatcher regime now has five more years to complete its reshaping of Britain and to make itself irreversible.' What is interesting is that today Mrs Thatcher feels confident enough to use such language herself.

For a 'regime' is no longer just a government. Its language is no longer that of traditional British politics, let alone of parliamentary democracy. (Mrs Thatcher makes no secret of the fact that she regards opposition as subversive.) It is the language of a 'New Order' that is being introduced by a revolution of the radical right, conducted by a platoon of fundamentalists who do not care what anybody thinks of their proposals, because they *know* they are right; and besides, who is to vote them down? It is the language of an authoritarian one-party government which is systematically setting about creating the conditions for staying that way.

For, as the years go by, it is increasingly clear that we were right from the start to see Thatcherism as something quite different from, and immeasurably more dangerous than, just another Tory government. It is an experimental model for post-democratic bourgeois society in the 1980s, as fascism (which was a very different species of political animal) was the model for bourgeois regimes in the 1930s which felt they could no longer afford democracy.

It is probably not easily exportable, if only because so far other conservative governments (for example, the West German) lack the lunatic ideological commitment to the abolition of all activities not performed for private profit, and especially of public welfare. Or else other conservative governments (Reagan's, for example) lack the uncontrollable centralized power which makes the Thatcher regime so dangerous. Nevertheless, Thatcherism has both and we are ruled by it. Consequently there is only one absolutely overriding political task before us in this country, namely to get rid of it. This is a task which will increasingly unite people in this country across the lines of class, gender, age, colour, and political parties, including the Conservative Party. There is no higher priority in British political life.

The first, and perhaps the only, question to ask about the present exercise in 'rethinking the Labour Party' is what bearing it has on this task. This exercise has already produced papers and pamphlets by David Blunkett and Bernard Crick ('The Labour Party's Aims and Values: An Unofficial Statement'), by Tony Benn ('An Agenda for Labour' and 'The Aims and Objectives of the Labour Party') and by Neil Kinnock and Roy Hattersley ('A Statement of Democratic Socialist Aims and Values').[1]

None of these would have been written but for the disasters which have hit the Labour Party and labour movement over the past ten years. All take it for granted, but none say, that a mere call to return to the pre-1979 status quo will get us nowhere (quite apart from being impracticable) and that the basic problem is how Labour can recover the lost supporters who still show no sign of returning, or acquire new ones. To this extent, rethinking does reflect the actual situation. As for the generalities of Labour's future policies, there isn't much real disagreement. Nor is there room for any since it is clear that a future Labour government will preside over a mixed economy, whether it wants to or not. There is actually no significant difference on the page between Kinnock and Hattersley's 'we are not, and have never been committed to any form of public ownership, but the objectives we seek clearly require a greater sector of the economy to be socially owned'; Benn's 'we must reject the old pattern of state corporations, and rethink our attitude to common ownership'; and Blunkett and Crick's slightly longer commentary on Clause 4. And, of course, all three documents insist that the Labour Party is a socialist party, though, paradoxically, the word is used less in Benn's papers than in either of the other two.

All this is welcome in so far as it suggests that there is a basis for consensus within the Labour Party, or at least that people are anxious to avoid the sort of public mayhem which looks better in kung fu movies than in political parties. But it is a weakness in 'operation rethink' that so much of it seems, in the first instance, addressed to an inner-party public rather than to the majority (including the majority of the working class) who are no longer or not yet with the party.

Of the three documents only Kinnock and Hattersley really seem to have the non-Labour voters in Thatcherite Britain in their sights. Who Tony Benn has in mind, other than his traditional supporters, is difficult to determine, for his documents are exceptionally unspecific (except on some odd matters like 'the upholding and enforcement of existing legislation relating to animal abuse, and efforts to secure the introduction of further legislation making all blood-sports illegal'). However, Benn has the merit of being the only one of the authors to deal seriously with international affairs and the question of war and peace, and he also recognizes the major significance of the issues raised by 'green politics', even though only in passing.

The Blunkett and Crick pamphlet is much the best and most convincing statement on the Labour Party's aims and values, in other words, on 'democratic socialism', among these documents. It can't help but win friends for Labour, though, alas, few people are prepared to read twenty-page pamphlets. However, what it will not and was not designed to do, is to convince those people who agree that Labour is a good and caring party whose heart and head is in the right place, to entrust Labour with the government of Britain again. It is an admirable statement, but it could have been written at any time since 1945.

As one might expect, the leader and deputy leader of the party, acting jointly, are rather more acutely aware of the political perspectives. However, their statement has the same weakness as Roy Hattersley's own earlier book, *Choose Freedom*: out of sheer defensiveness it gives the game away to the other side. Their statement begins with the proposition that 'the fundamental objective of government' in a socialist society 'is the protection and extension of individual liberty' and ends with the proposition that 'Socialism . . . is, above all else, committed to the protection and extension of individual freedom'.[2] Now while freedom, in the sense of free choice and a minimum of external restraint, is, or ought to be, a fundamental condition of any society for which socialists stand, it is simply not true that this is what socialism is essentially about, or that anybody really believes that it is, including Kinnock and Hattersley, most of whose document – for obvious reasons – explains why this doesn't mean that we are economic neo-liberals.

Four things are seriously wrong with this approach, quite apart from the fact that its definition of socialism is way off-beam. In the first place, it is very unlikely to carry conviction. To compete with Thatcherism in a race to show who best represents individualist freedom is to go in for the wrong contest. It is rather like trying to attract tourists from the Greek islands to the Alps on the grounds that you can get a suntan and swim in the mountains too. So you can, but that is not primarily why people who like mountains go there, summer or winter. It is better to sell one's own attractions rather than versions of someone else's.

Second, it suggests that Labour's main problem is how to convert or reconvert Thatcherites. But this is not the case. For every voter Labour lost to Thatcher – and even that doesn't mean exclusively enthusiasts for the 'enterprise culture' – at least another voter was lost to the centre on quite different grounds. Thirdly, it suggests that Labour's leader and deputy leader don't have much confidence in Labour's prospects, which is rather worrying, because if they don't seem to have it, then who else will? As the jargon has it, this is 'sending out the wrong signals'. And finally, the Kinnock and Hattersley document undoubtedly liquidates some of Labour's *old* thinking, as is indeed necessary, but it unfortunately neither contains nor implies any *new* thinking.

The problem here is not simply excessive defensiveness, though this is bad enough. It is a *lack of vision*: of the dangers of the present situation, of the nature of the British crisis which produced it, and which has not been solved; of the tasks of the future and of what non-Thatcherite or post-Thatcherite governments could actually do.

Thus there is not in this document – or in any of the others – any sense whatever that we are faced with a regime which is setting out to demolish what other brands of capitalism still accept, for example that the tendency to privatize *some* parts of economies previously belonging to the public sector, which is found all over the world today, is qualitatively *different* from the curious, but dangerous, Thatcherite combination of a rightwing stalinism (uncontrolled central state power) and the rightwing anarchism of ideologues who believe (to quote Charles Dickens's *Hard Times*) that 'what you couldn't state in figures and show to be purchaseable in the cheapest market and saleable in the dearest, was not, and never should be, world without end, Amen.'

The essential Thatcherite argument is that Britain's troubles are due to the fact that in the past it was never *really* a capitalist society in the way our more successful competititors were and are. To quote Prof. Norman Stone: 'It is a start towards that bourgeois revolution which, in my opinion, never really occurred in this country and (if this is so) Margaret Thatcher goes down in history as the natural complement to Oliver Cromwell.'[2] The argument has no good historical or comparative basis, although, for quite different ideological reasons, similar mistaken theses have long been put forward by a section of the Marxist left. But to accept the view that Thatcher is doing no more than any other business-minded government – say West Germany or Japan – is in effect to accept the Thatcherite analysis. It is to fall for the hype which is the essence of Thatcherite public relations.

Again, given the systematic undermining of civil liberties, of autonomous local government, of the freedom of speech and the press, and of democracy in general, it is quite extraordinary that these statements of 'democratic socialism' should pay so little attention to democracy, and the present dangers to it. Kinnock and Hattersley occasionally use the phrase 'democratic socialist' in place of Labour but, unless I am mistaken, the words 'democracy' or 'democratic' occur only *twice* in the fifteen typed pages of their statement, as distinct from the words 'freedom', 'free' and 'liberty' which occur forty-eight times. (For the record, words referring to 'equality' occur nineteen times, 'fraternity' zero times.) However, it must be said in fairness that the document specifically notes the threat to our civil and political rights and their erosion during the Thatcher years.

Tony Benn naturally pays more attention to democracy, but with the exception of a single, characteristically vague, phrase ('It is essential that we devote a great deal more work to the question of civil liberties which have been directly attacked in recent years'), his observations appear to have no specific relevance to the present situation. 'Democracy' is certainly the red thread that runs through Blunkett and Crick's document, and to this extent their pamphlet provides the best basis for a campaign to rally all defenders of democracy round the Labour Party. (Blunkett and Crick also make the only contribution to the debate which pays any attention to 'fraternity' or 'community', or for that matter which even mentions the famous old slogan 'liberty, equality, and fraternity' and recalls that while 'liberty' is good, *by itself* it is not uniquely socialist.) Nevertheless, one would not guess from Blunkett and Crick's text that British democracy today is under any special pressure.[3]

As for the nature of the British crisis which brought Thatcherism to power and has kept it there, none of the documents even hint at it. But this is to miss the point of operation rethink, which would not be taking place at all but for this crisis, and must address itself above all to people who are dissatisfied with the Labour Party as a result. It does no harm to offer a guide to healthy living to anyone at any time, but it does not satisfy people who are primarily worried *now* about, say, the health hazards arising out of Chernobyl. Besides, how can we work out a political vision and project for the post-Thatcherite future unless it is based on a proper analysis of the predicament of Britain, and the world, since the end of the great global boom in the early 1970s?

All this reflects two major weaknesses in Labour thinking. The first is provincialism: the world beyond the seas is more remote and unimportant in these documents than it is in real life. In Kinnock and Hattersley's document it appears only once, when the division between north and south is condemned, and help to the developing world through trade as well as aid is called for. There is nothing else. Blunkett and Crick are specifically worried about how to 'prevent international companies controlling national economies and dictating to elected governments', and are concerned about the north–south divide, and nuclear disarmament in which 'Labour believes . . . as a matter of principle, and in the need to put the principle into practice'. This is excellent, but hardly exhausts the problems of a Labour Britain in the international economy and power system. The Benn documents show the most careful political thought about international policy, though the combination of a non-aligned Britain and withdrawal from the European Community has its problems. However, like the others, he shows little sign of appreciating the nature and recent transformations of the world economy.

None of the documents give a mention to the experience of any other country, even when their situation might be thought directly relevant to Britain. Sweden, for instance, is just the sort of country which one might expect to have inspired anti-Thatcherite democratic socialists. It represents everything that Thatcherites blame for the failure of Britain in the dark pre-Maggie era: it has been run by labour, has one of the highest ratios of public expenditure to gross domestic product, high taxes, no fondness for the unrestricted free market, and plenty of controls. Yet Sweden, which must have one of the highest standards of living in the world, together with low unemployment, has had a much higher rate of growth than the USA, and remains at the forefront of technological progress. Why should British Labour not get a little mileage out of the achievements of its opposite number elsewhere? And why don't any of our statements? Probably because none of the authors thought about the Swedes.

The second weakness is intellectual. It may be illustrated by comparing the rethinking which has so far come out of Labour with a recent piece of rethinking by, of all people, a member of the (non-Owenite) Social Democrats: that of David Marquand in *The Unprincipled Society*.[4] Marquand's analysis, incidentally, demonstrates the considerable potential for a consensus on policy within a broad anti-Thatcherite coalition.

Marquand begins with the breakdown of the Keynesian Social-Democratic consensus which, in effect, dominated most developed countries for thirty years after the Second World War. It proved incapable of coping with British (and world) problems in the 1970s, but the two alternatives which have since emerged in Britain are equally incapable of coping with them. These are Thatcherite economic neo-liberalism and 'a more inchoate mixture of neo-marxism and the "fundamentalist" socialism of the 1920s and 1930s', which gained ground among the Labour rank-and-file.

Unlike Labour leaders, Marquand does not have to prove to anybody that he does not believe in all-purpose central planning, or to convince activists that markets are not pornographic. He can take it for granted that mixed economies are normal. He can therefore also take the weaknesses of 'state socialism' for granted – even though he points out that 'no better way has been found to mobilise society for war or for some great collective purpose'[5] – and can concentrate on the weaknesses of Thatcherite free markets. For that, after all, is what we are dealing with in Britain. Hence, paradoxically, Marquand's centrist analysis makes far fewer concessions to the marketeers than does, say, Hattersley.

The free market by itself, he argues, cannot solve the peculiar problem of Britain, which is how to adapt to the modern world, and to recover its economic impetus. This is because what makes a country tick, including economically, does not depend purely on economics. It depends on history, culture, politics, and a lot else. Neo-classical economics simply explains 'or purports to explain how resources are most efficiently allocated at a given level of adaptability',[6] but not how a country can be made more adaptable. 'Market-liberalism is a doctrine for those who are already well-equipped for the market. It is no friend to those who need to equip themselves.'[7]

Now, for historical reasons Britain, which was peculiarly suited to become the pioneer of capitalism in the nineteenth century, by the same token found it enormously hard to adapt to its economic and political decline in the twentieth. Her institutions and values gave her no help, even though they were well designed to ensure social and political stability. Thatcherism was quite right in seeing that a radical break was needed, but, according to Marquand, its diagnosis was and is the opposite of the truth. For what Britain lacked was not individualist values, ready to be released by the stimulus of profit. It had nothing but these. Britain, the original pioneer of industrialism, didn't need 'to evolve an entrepreneurial or developmental state'. Later capitalist economies had to and did, but:

> What is special about Britain ... is not that she abandoned market-led adjustment. It is that after abandoning it, she failed to become a developmental state on the pattern of her more successful competitors on the European mainland and in the Far East.[8]

But such a state – such a national effort – cannot be built without some sense of a *public purpose*, a public good. This, once again, can't be derived by adding up all the private purposes which all individuals pursue. This is why no definition of the aim of society purely in terms of the freedom of individual choice and action will do, whether it is capitalist or (like that of Kinnock and Hattersley) thinks it is socialist. Our problem is to recover the public purpose which is missing ('an intellectual and moral vacuum at the heart of the political economy').

I have cited this analysis at some length, not because I agree with it (which I only do in part), or because it has anything concrete to propose for the future (which it hasn't), but because, unlike most Labour rethinking so far, it is essentially a critique of Thatcherism and it is politically focused on the future. Let us imagine the typical non-Labour citizen who does not belong to the (not very large) ideological core of Thatcherites, and who, of course, is the man or woman who has to be won back to Labour or, more realistically, be won for a broad anti-Thatcherite coalition based on, and organized round, Labour.

Reading the Benn statements, which are essentially aimed at the faithful, he or she will conclude that nothing much has changed in the Labour Party, though honesty should compel even sceptical readers to recognise Benn's profound concern about democracy and *rights* (he is the only author who consistently uses the term), and to acknowledge that on east–west relations he talks sense.

Reading Kinnock and Hattersley's contribution, he or she will conclude that a future Labour government will not renationalize everything that has been privatized, and that it will in general recognize the role of the market more and planning less ('democratic socialists believe in market allocation . . . guided by agreement that the competitive system should pursue the objective of greater freedom, greater equality and greater choice'). In other words, that it will believe in something not very different from the 'social market' policies of 'market liberals with tender hearts' whose contradictions Marquand ruthlessly criticizes.[9] So what? Will readers regard this as an inspiring alternative to Thatcher, or merely as an indication that Labour leaders won't be bound by the old orthodoxies of their left? (When have they ever been?)

Reading Blunkett and Crick, he or she will be reminded once again how *good* and morally desirable the causes are that Labour represents and has always represented: liberty, equality, fraternity/community/solidarity; fairness and justice, altruism and tolerance, hostility to class snobbishness and, not least, self-organization and democracy. As an alternative set of values to the one represented by the world of the Tebbits and Parkinsons, it is convincing enough, but as a guide to the tasks of Britain and its governments in the late 1980s and 1990s? That is not so sure.

What we need are statements that are aimed not primarily at inner-party debate, but directly at all who are concerned about Britain's future. We need statements which are not trying to catch up with some free-market Joneses, so that we semi-apologize for what we believe in and hold to be essential to Britain's future, namely, social and public action, where necessary through the state. It is absurd that the most whole-hearted and self-confident critique of Thatcherite claims and of 'social market' ideologies, and the firmest call for a 'developmental state' should come from Marquand, an ex-Labour and now ex-Social Democratic member of the centre party.

What we need is not just a restatement of eternal and general aims and values, but an account of our aims and values *now*. This does not mean that general statements are bound to anticipate debates on the concrete programmes of a future anti-Thatcher and post-Thatcher government. However, it is perfectly reasonable to offer, within statements of aims and values, not just a general demand for 'the fullest access to education' for all, but a call for the urgent transformation of a notoriously undereducated people into an educated people and the reversal of the present educational counterrevolution of the inegalitarians.

We should offer more than generalities about 'changes in the economic and industrial basis of society' which should bring 'benefits which are available to everyone', as do Kinnock and Hattersley, but go on to include a specific consideration of what the modern micro-chip economy should mean for labour, leisure, life, and education. (None of the statements mention the current techno-scientific revolution, any more than they do the new international and transnational pattern of the world economy, though Blunkett and Crick hint at the latter.)

We should not just refer to 'stimulating the enterprise and innovation that creates the wealth upon which future generations will depend' (Kinnock and Hattersley again), but go on to set collective targets for reversing the decline of the British economy and discuss how to build the 'developmental state' which is needed for it. And not just talk generally about the need for environmental protection, or even say that 'only governments have the competence and authority' to do it, but make a statement that environmental ruin is perhaps a more immediate danger to the human race than even nuclear war, and that it can be dealt with *only* by governments which put the public and common interest before the market and private profit.

In short, these statements lack urgency, and a sense of national and social mission.

Again, what we need are statements with a sense of history. If Labour's rethinking does not include or hint at a diagnosis of what went wrong with Britain (and therefore what needs to be put right), we leave the field open for the diagnosis which lies behind, and gives force to, the Thatcherite project of forcing Britain into total privatization by total state power. Perhaps some of us are quietly tempted to accept that diagnosis of too much government and bureaucracy, overpriced workers, and the rest, ourselves. What is more, nobody will believe in a party which passes lightly over the question of what went wrong with Britain, especially if that party was itself involved in the going wrong. It will not do just to say that we are not like that any more.

Finally, we need to aim directly at our target audience, the potential voter for Labour as part of a broad anti-Thatcher alliance who is at present *not* voting Labour. We shall not convert the hard-core Thatcherites, middle or working class, whether they are 'I'm all right Jack' neo-liberals or those attracted by the chauvinism and racism which surrounds this regime. However, most polls show that these are a minority and not a growing one. We are concerned with the men and women who would prefer a non-Thatcherite government, many of whom are increasingly worried about the tendencies of this government, and even more of whom would be further worried if they stopped enjoying the economic benefits which, they are constantly told, are due to the economic policy of the past eight years.

I would guess that what troubles these people, irrespective of their age, gender or class, is whether they see a possibility of actually getting enough of the non-Thatcherite majority together to defeat this regime, whether they have enough confidence in the leadership of the Labour Party which will inevitably be the post-Thatcherite government, or the core of such a government, and whether such a government has any positive perspective, in addition to the negative advantage of stopping Thatcherism. They want to know: *what is Labour's project for the future?* Has it got the future in its bones, or is it still, as Marquand says of many of the left activists, 'more anxious to shelter from the changes of the last fifteen years than to adapt to them'? Will these statements satisfy our potential voters?

These are the people who will decide whether Labour's operation rethink is a success or not. The products of this operation so far are not encouraging. But it is early days yet. That is why it is important, and urgent, to help in getting the debate onto the right lines.

Notes

1. These documents were presented to a joint meeting of the Labour Party NEC and shadow cabinet on February 5. They provide the context for the more detailed policy review.

2. *The Sunday Times*, 6 March 1988.

3. Tony Benn stresses 'solidarity' which could mean much the same as 'fraternity', as Blunkett and Crick note; but it seems clear that what he has in mind is something much narrower, namely 'a moral responsibility to defend all those who are attacked for protecting their own democratically gained rights', and, concretely, trade union solidarity ('Aims and Objectives', pp. 3–4).

4. D. Marquand, *The Unprincipled Society*, London 1988.
5. Ibid., p. 6.
6. Ibid., p. 4.
7. Ibid., p. 5.
8. Ibid., p. 113.
9. Ibid., pp. 224–6.

19

The Signs of a Recovery (1988)

The first stage of the Labour Party's root-and-branch political review is now sufficiently advanced for a preliminary assessment. A considerable body of the party's leading figures have been involved in the policy review groups, including trade unionists but excluding – so far as one can see – Kinnock and John Smith on one side, Benn and the Old Believers on the other.

Seven overlapping documents have emerged from Walworth Road since April: 'A Productive and Competitive Economy', 'Democracy for the Individual and the Community', 'Physical and Social Environment', 'Britain in the World', 'Consumers and the Community', 'People at Work', and 'Economic Equality'. They may be supplemented by the set of speeches on industrial and economic policy which Bryan Gould has distributed under the uncollective title of 'The Gould Plan'. How is this corpus to be judged?

The party's policy review faced complicated problems of substance and diplomacy, since it had simultaneously to do three things which are as difficult to combine as it would be to write a single letter convincing one lover of undying devotion while assuring another that the writer's affections have not essentially altered. (Getting a committee on which all three parties are represented to draft such a letter would not make its composition any easier.)

First, the party had to rethink traditional Labour and socialist policies in the light of the 1980s in general, and almost ten years of Thatcherism in particular. This is essentially a matter of empirical enquiry and rational analysis.

Second, it had to devise an electable policy, that is, it had also to take account of the tastes of the voters irrespective of rationality. This is essentially a matter of market research. How much of perfectly sensible

233

policies (for example on nuclear disarmament) may have to be sacrificed for the sake of ending the Thatcher regime, is a matter of debate, which brings us to the third task of the review.

This was to produce drafts which could get through the Labour Party Conference, that is, which are acceptable to at least some of those in the party who do not really think a fundamental policy review is called for; and would prefer the minimum of concessions to an ideologically unsound electorate. In short, it has to establish that Labour actually wants to win, isolating those who do not think any alternative government short of the Levellers or Diggers is worth having. This requires a lot of political fudging.

Considering the problems of getting all this into the same documents, the party's review groups have done rather well. The party no longer seems to be merely reacting to Thatcher initatives, but is developing its own ideas. Most of the reports keep the main objective, devising policy perspectives for a post-Thatcherite Britain, firmly in their sights. Most of them start from a realistic base-line, both in considering the changes in Britain since 1979 and the attitude of the public. 'Consumers and the Community' (among whose authors are David Blunkett and Jack Straw) deserves special credit for plain speaking.

The rare relapses into ancient platform rhetoric stand out by their very untypicality ('only Labour offers a prospect of prosperity for all not just for a small and privileged minority'). The critique of Thatcherism is effective *because* the reviewers accept that real household disposable income has risen by a quarter while disparities have grown, and the increase 'in choice and access to material goods' has been striking. The problem of the left in developed countries is precisely that in these 'two-thirds societies' the bottom third alone cannot win.

Again, most of the reports take it for granted that their major task is to persuade potential voters rather than potential conference delegates. Many of these pages are expressed with clarity – always a sign of actual thought – and sound convincing. Such signs of thought are particularly obvious in 'Democracy for the Individual and the Community' (chaired by Hattersley and Jo Richardson), in 'Economic Equality' (John Evans, Robin Cook, Rodney Bickerstaffe, *et al.*), in 'Consumers and the Community', and in the section on trade union law in 'People at Work'. And while 'A Productive and Competitive Economy' sounds more muffled than is necessary, the policy it embodies, as expounded by its co-chairman Bryan Gould, is both clear and positive.

How bad things might have been is demonstrated by the one valueless policy report, that on 'Britain in the World Today'. No doubt the drafters had some excuse for evasiveness. Nevertheless, one might have expected reference to some actual problems of international policy, except in terms of pious generality, or even a mention of the words 'IMF', 'Palestinians', 'Gulf War', 'Ireland', or, for that matter, 'USA', and 'Japan'. Aids is referred to as often as nuclear arms (once). The only part of this vacuous document which approaches reality is that dealing with the EEC.

In spite of the generally positive impression, there are three reasons why this body of reports does not – or not yet – make as strong a case for Labour as it might do.

The first is a failure of central planning. Independently drafted by separate working parties with broad but imprecise terms of reference, the reports fail to provide *a general map of the terrain* on which post-Thatcherite governments will have to conduct their battles. Like Germany in 1945, Britain after Thatcher will be a scene of destruction. Those who will need to rebuild what has to be reconstructed – not necessarily in the same way as before – need a preliminary survey of the bomb-damage. What damage has been and is likely to be done to the country's material and institutional infrastructure – for instance to education and roads, to housing and science, transport and museums, health, radio/television, and the institutions of local government and social administration, not to mention political democracy, the Civil Service and civil liberties? Answers to particular questions are given by most reports, but nobody has sketched the general picture.

What is more, the lack of central planning has meant that the reports leave obvious gaps. In spite of being mentioned in several papers there is no specific treatment of education or health, housing or even local government and decentralization, though an (unavailable) 'consultation paper' on local government reform appears to exist. Perhaps the rethinkers felt that, being non-contentious matters within the party, these topics require neither rethinking nor special presentation to the outside world. If so, they are mistaken.

Secondly, there is the terrible *insularity* of these reports, singly and in combination. Why Labour should deprive itself of arguments in this way is hard to understand. On the one hand the Government's triumphalist economic hype rests largely on ignorance about the rest of the world. After three Thatcher elections, the only European countries with a lower GDP per head are Ireland, Spain, Portugal, Greece, and Turkey; in 1979 we were still ahead of Italy. On the other hand the left could point to plenty of examples of its own brand of prosperity, economic dynamism, and enterprise joined to a concern for social justice, the public good and culture.

Scandinavia and Austria are the usual examples – Sweden is actually mentioned a few times in the reports – but it is equally to the point that the most spectacular European examples of economic transformation by means of an enterprise culture are found in the 'red' regions of Italy, where local government and unions (stronger there than anywhere else) co-operate to see that small firms compete in product and process innovation rather than in wage and price cutting. And who would not rather live in Bologna than Basingstoke?

Moreover, insularity risks more than simply giving away arguments, for the actual policies of non-Thatcherite foreign countries – that is, all other developed countries – can provide useful pointers for British post-Thatcherism.

Thirdly, while the reports are not supposed to go into policy details, which will presumably come into subsequent stages of the policy review, some papers clearly already have a policy in mind, while others remain floating on the waves of generality and 'basic principles'. 'Democracy for the Individual and the Community', which already amounts to an outline programme for a post-Thatcherite Home Office, shows what can be done even now.

Nevertheless, these documents suggest that Labour has the makings of a coherent critique of Thatcherism and a coherent post-Thatcher strategy which could be acceptable, so far as it goes, to both non-socialist and socialist anti-Thatcherites. Of course, if Labour becomes the next government, alone or in alliance, it will not be because it is a socialist party, but because the British electorate, which has consistently refused in three elections to give Mrs Thatcher more than 43 per cent of its votes, considers Labour an electable party with a sensible programme, there being no practicable alternatives. The chances that it will do so are now improved.

However, in the face of impassioned cries from the direction of Chesterfield, it should be said that the policy rethink, at least as formulated in Gould's speech on social ownership, is not a sell-out of socialism, but a concise and well-argued case for the superiority of common ownership, as well as an exploration of the wide range of methods available to advance a mixed economy in the desired direction. It is a considerable advance on the era of incantation.

So far so good. The results to date are uneven, the gaps are substantial, and some reports are better at making the case against Thatcher's Britain than at proposing alternatives. And even so, the regime is still allowed to get away with far too much – for instance with the inconsistency between its free market utopia and its jingoism, which waves the union jack while the effective policy abolishes the British economy as a national entity, by transforming it into an off-shore base for the service operations of the transnational economy.

Still, these documents suggest that the time for Labour's breast-beating is over, though not yet, alas, the time of pre-Conference fudging.

The embarrassing exercises in restating 'socialist values' as consumer values may be allowed to fade out of sight. Labour once again is beginning to look like a party with a potential policy rather than a confession of faith.

And yet, two big questions remain. Does the policy review suggest the *urgency* of uniting all who dislike and fear the regime of know-nothing, rightwing radical ideologists which is transforming Britain today? The clear and present danger which it presents for the sort of country and people most of us took pride in belonging to? Does it suggest that, beyond salvaging what remains of the values of morality, society and civility, Labour has a positive project for the future – a mission for the nation, even in the vague sense in which Wilson's rhetoric of 'modernity' in the 1960s offered positive change?

The answers are not clear. There is a sense of real urgency and danger in the report on democracy, and there is a sense, real but perhaps not quite so sharp, of economic policy as the project of reversing the relative decline of Britain, and the impossibility of doing so 'as long as economic policy is dominated by those who hold assets rather than those who create wealth.' But it is not found everywhere. The best do not lack all conviction, but these documents do not show the passionate intensity which under Thatcher, has moved the worst. And yet, we find something that was long missing in Labour: a modest degree of self-confidence.

It may not yet be enough to lead the millions back to Neil Kinnock. But it may be just enough to make Labour once again credible as a potential government party, as it patently was not in 1983 and 1987. Anyway, oppositions rarely win: it is governments that lose. If sensible policy rethinking continues, a rather larger number of voters than before may be prepared to consider letting the government lose. Provided, of course, Labour can get over its ancient taste for public harakiri.

Postscript

Since the present collection of reprinted papers concludes, rather brusquely, with a provisional assessment of the Labour Party's then incomplete policy review, which was published in July 1988, it has been suggested to me that this piece should either be updated, or supplemented by a further postscript. I do not want to accept either of these suggestions. Articles can be up to date, but books, which are designed for a longer reading-life than twenty-four hours or even a week or two, cannot possibly keep up with the news for more than a very brief spell. It is pointless for them to try. After a short while they are read, if at all, for other reasons than weeklies.

However, it is possible to conclude this book by reminding readers of what will not become obsolete. Three things, on which I have insisted time and again in the course of the text, will not change between the date of publication and, at the earliest, the early 1990s. These things must determine our political actions. They are so fundamental that I do not apologize for repeating them. In this respect (but in no other) I follow the example of the Elder Cato, an ancient Roman politician who was so convinced of the overpowering need for Rome to eliminate its main rival, the city of Carthage, that he ended every speech in the Senate, whatever the subject, with the words: 'And furthermore, I vote that Carthage must be destroyed.' In the end the Romans did so.

My points are these.

First, the defeat and destruction of Thatcherism is the primary and essential task in British politics, not only for the British left, but for all people who care about the traditions and conventions of law and civility, of freedom and parliamentary government, of social responsibilities and values, which are now being gradually strangled. Alone among the states of Europe, none of whom, luckily, seem so far tempted by our example,

239

Britain in the 1980s has let itself fall into the hands of a government of the radical right. Our bad luck is threefold, for not only are we ruled by crusaders for the true faith (plus associated careerists), but we are saddled with an electoral system which can transform a permanent electoral minority into a permanent parliamentary majority, and, unlike most other constitutional countries, we lack any legal or constitutional safeguards against Downing Street excess – except, ironically, insofar as membership of the European Economic Community obliges the British Government to defer in some fields to the European courts of justice. Hence the curious reversal of political attitudes towards the EEC, which Mrs Thatcher now dislikes. Even this, however, would not prevent a British government quite legally perpetuating the current parliament for as long as it wanted, simply by passing an Act through the Commons.

We are living under a bad and a dangerous regime that must be ended. Democracy is today more acutely threatened in Britain than in any other country of parliamentary democracy.

Second, the Conservative government represents a *minority* of the British peoples, and the true believers of Thatcherism almost certainly represent only a modest proportion of the Tory vote. Ten years of Mrs Thatcher's governments, which have fundamentally altered the political and institutional scene, and ten years of intensive Thatcherite hype have not succeeded in winning additional hearts and minds. There has never been a Thatcherite, or even a Tory majority in the sense that there was a majority in favour of President Reagan, who could rely on something like 60 per cent of the votes of all white Americans except Jews, whichever way pollsters cut them. There is no Thatcherite 'consensus'. There is no reason to suppose that, under foreseeable circumstances, the 60 per cent of British electors who have voted against Conservative candidates will not still be there in 1992. Their numbers will probably have risen.

Third, it follows that Mrs Thatcher's electoral victories are, and will be, due entirely to the combination of two things: the existing electoral system and the fragmentation of the opposition. There is nothing that can be done about the electoral system without an Act of Parliament to change it, i.e., without the decision of Mrs Thatcher's government to commit suicide. This possibility may be excluded. The only other possibility is an electoral agreement between opposition parties, formal or informal, official or unofficial, with or without a name. There is really no way of avoiding this conclusion, unless we assume something like a total collapse *both* of the Conservative vote *and* of the centrist vote in the next general election, not to mention the Scots and Welsh nationalist votes. Who would bet on that? As a recent by-election has shown, it is quite possible for the Tories to lose one third of their support (dropping from 60 per cent to 40 per cent) and still win with a comfortable

POSTCRIPT241

majority when faced with three rival candidates, two of whom between them could have outpolled the Tories.

Readers of this book will know that I have made this elementary point on numerous occasions over the past five years. It remains unanswerable. It is not answered by psephological calculations, based on past elections or current polls, that electoral agreement would not have won in 1987 or 1988. These are not arguments against electoral unity but merely other ways of saying that some commentator believes Mrs T. to be unbeatable under current circumstances. If this regime is to be beaten (assuming it allows us to vote freely) it can, in the foreseeable future, be done only if the opposition, or a sufficiently strategic part of it, is not disunited. Even in party politics, logic cannot be kept at bay forever.

London
January 1989

Index

Abercrombie, Sir Patrick 149
Adams, Jack 36
Afghanistan 94
Albania 111
Allende, Salvador 115
Allgemeiner Deutscher Arbeiterverein 2
Amalgamated Carpenters and Joiners 149
Amalgamated Union of Engineering Workers 12
Anderson, Perry 120, 131
Alliance, SDP/Liberal
  and anti-Thatcherite coalition 65, 82, 181–5, 187, 201
  and consensus politics 44
  electoral performance of 64, 204
  and Labour 76
Argentina 51–2, 163
Arnot, R. Page 88, 98 n3
Arsenal 149
ASLEF 36
ASTMS 36
Attlee, Clement 70, 79
Attlee government (1945–51) 171–4, 179
Australia 124
Austria 150, 185, 210, 235
  and nationalism 121, 124, 138
  Popular Front in 104
Austrian Social Democratic Party 141 n14, 151
Azerbaijan 136

Baldwin, Stanley 88
Bangladesh 136
Basque separatism 137, 142 n25
Baxter, Dudley 10
Belgium 104, 111
Benjamin, Walter 132
Benn, Tony 97, 222–30, 233
  and Labour left 24, 25, 34

and Labour Party 38, 39, 81, 222, 223
  mentioned 65, 174, 208
Berlin 145, 150, 151
Berlinguer, Enrico 115
Bernstein, Eduard 220
Bevan, Aneurin 70, 171
Beveridge, W.H. 172
Bevin, Ernest 79, 173
Biafra 136, 141 n6
Bickerstaffe, Rodney 234
Blackburn, Robin 37
Blunkett, David 222–30 *passim*
Bolsheviks, and nationalism 141 n14
  see also under Lenin
Booth, Charles 152
bourgeois revolution, in England 131–2
Brazil 136, 150, 163, 211, 218
Brecht, Bertolt 95
Britain
  crisis of 131–7
  economic decline of 43–5, 48–9, 53–4, 174–5, 177–8, 197, 207, 234
  and Europe 196–200
  nationalist separatism in 121, 140
  relation to Falklands 51–2
British Road to Socialism, The 78, 98
broad alliance strategy 74–6, 78–9, 87–98, 108–9, 114–17
  see also Popular Front
Browder, Earl 98 n9
Brown, George 173
Bulgaria 111, 121
Burke, Edmund 45
Burns, John 152
Butler, R.A. 172

Callaghan, James 2, 97, 176
Callaghan government (1976–9) 37, 170, 177
Campbell, Bea 72

Canada 124
capital cities 147
capitalism, crisis of
  and Comintern policy 107, 113–14
  and labour movement 22, 30, 40,
    104–5, 160–61
  and Labour policy 225–6
  and socialist case 4–5
capitalism, structure of
  changes in 9, 14–15, 193
  and the nation-state 120, 122–4,
    128–9, 142 n19
Carron Company of Scotland 49
Carter, Pete 26
Catalan separatism 137, 142 n25
Cavour, Count Camillo 120
Chamberlain, Neville 91, 169
Chartism 58–9
Chile 114, 115, 116
China, People's Republic of 95, 105,
  125, 127, 162
Churchill, Winston 60, 70, 91, 109
city, and the labour movement
  143–57, 198–9
civil liberties 203
'class against class' line 91–2, 106
class consciousness
  and changes in the working class
    19–20, 190–92
  and the labour movement 161,
    164–5
  and locality 16
  and militancy 25
  and patriotism 60
  and stratification 12–13
'class politics' 91–2, 208
class solidarity 19, 21, 186, 190–92,
  194–5
coalition government 82–3
Cole, G.D.H. 173
Colombia 124
colonialism, and the Popular Front
  103, 104, 105
  see also decolonization;
    neo-colonialism
common ownership, definition of
  217–20
Communist International 4, 60, 91–2,
  107, 103–14
Communist Parties, European
  formation of 161–5

membership of 201
and Popular Front 106, 108,
  110–14
and US government 116–17
see also parties by name of country
Communist Party of Great Britain
  attitude to USSR 94
  and broad alliance strategy 87,
    97–8, 109, 111
  and 'class against class' line 106
  and Labour Party 77, 78, 81–2
  membership of 20, 25, 31,
    200–201
  and Scotland 135
communities, inner-city 148–50
Connolly, James 127, 128
Conservative Party 31, 169
  and Falklands War 52, 54, 56
  loss of support for 183, 185
consumer society 190–91, 193
conurbations, growth of 146
Cook, A.J. 70
Cook, Robin 234
Coote, Anna 81
coups, armed 49
craft unionism, and labour movement
  11–13
Craxi, Bettino 73, 206
Crick, Bernard 222–30 passim
Cripps, Stafford 176
Crosland, Anthony 176, 216
Crossman, Richard 175, 176
Cyprus 123
Czechs, and nationalism 121

Daily Express 46
Daily Mail 46
Daily Mirror 59
Daily Telegraph, The 46
debt crisis 189
decolonization, and the nation-state
  122, 141 n6
de-industrialization 43–4, 153,
  160–61, 198–9
democracy 220–21
Democratic Party (US) 155, 164
Denmark 136, 210
  and Popular Front 104, 111
de-selection 85
Devlin, Bernadette 27
Dickens, Charles, Hard Times 224

dictatorship of the proletariat 113, 114
Dimitrov, George 82, 92, 98 n7, 107, 108, 109, 113, 114
Disraeli, Benjamin 88
dock strike (1889) 12
Duffy, Terry 38
Dutt, Palme 93, 96
Dzerzhinsky, Felix 139

Eastern Europe, and the Popular Front 114
economic decline, *see under* Britain
economic policy
    and the Labour Party 171–8, 196, 209–13, 216–20, 225–6
    Thatcher government's 4–5, 177–8, 205–6
economism and militancy 21, 26–7
education 212
elections
    (1979) 23–4
    (1987) 203–5
    see also under Labour Party
electoral unity 3, 67, 203
    see also tactical voting
Engels, Friedrich 9, 15, 125, 127, 189
    on British working class 20, 21, 43
    Conditions of the Working Class 13–14
England
    bourgeois revolution in 131–2
    and nationalism 134–5, 140 n2, 142 n18
Eritrean movement 125
establishment, political
    under Thatcher 45–9, 90, 205–6
Ethiopia 125, 189
ETU 12
'Europe of Nations' 120
European Economic Community 197, 235
Europeanization 192–3
Evans, John 230

Falklands War 45, 51–7, 60–61, 62
family, changes in 193–4
fascism
    Comintern policy on 91–2, 107, 109–10, 116
    compared with Thatcherism 88–9, 165, 200

and economic crisis 189
feminism 81
Fenianism 127–8
Field, Frank 85
Financial Times 56
Fine, Ben 88
Finland 111, 210, 211
Finnish Social Democratic Party 162
First World War, political effects of 59
Fisher, Alan 38
Fitzgerald, Frances 190
Foot, Michael 35, 60, 70
football 144, 148
Foreign Office 57
foreign policy, and the Labour Party 174–5, 176, 226, 234–5
Forward March of Labour Halted?, The 29, 64
France 156, 211, 218
    and monopoly capitalism 109–10
    and nationalism 121, 142 n18
    Popular Front in 103, 111, 112, 116
    postwar reconstruction of 211, 218, 219
Franco, General Francisco 103, 111, 112
Franks Commission 52, 56
free market economy 48, 205–6, 211–13, 227
freedom, and socialism 216, 219, 223, 227
French Communist Party 38, 149, 163
    loss of support for 163, 164
French Socialist Party 38, 73, 163
Freud, Sigmund 43, 131
Friedman, Milton 159
fundamentalist left 4

Gaitskell, Hugh 79, 97
Galbraith, J.K. 218
Gallacher, Willie 97
Gamble, Andrew 68
general unionism 12
gentrification 154
geography of the working class 15–16, 17
German Communist Party 106, 107, 111, 201
German Democratic Republic 95
German Social Democratic Party 2,

144, 162, 163, 196
and coalitions 200
decline of 198, 199
Germany 200–201
cities in 150
and nationalism 121, 124, 130,
135, 137, 142 n10
see also West Germany
Gill, Ken 24, 38
Gladstone, W.E. 88
Glasgow 151, 152, 155
Glotz, Peter 2, 187–201
Gonzalez, Felipe 73
Gorbachev, Mikhail 210, 216
Gould, Bryan 234, 236
governments, socialist 75
Gramsci, Antonio 113
Greater London Council 87, 151, 157
Greece 111, 121, 189, 212, 235
Green Party (German) 194, 200
Guardian 56
Gutman, Herbert 144, 145

Hallam, Robert 95
Hardie, Keir 70, 149
Harris, Laurence 88
Harrison, Royden 24, 26, 27, 80
Hattersley, Roy 85, 222–30 passim,
234
Choose Freedom 216–20, 223–5
Hayek, Friedrich 193, 216
Healey, Denis 39, 65, 85
Heath, Edward 2, 88, 91, 197
Heath Government (1970–74) 24
Heffer, Eric 80
hegemony, battle for 60, 112–13
see also broad alliance stategy
history, consciousness of 196
Hitler, Adolf 48, 61, 62, 88, 91, 96,
103, 107, 108, 109, 111, 177, 198
Holland 111
Home, Sir Alec Douglas- 2
Horner, Arthur 70
House of Lords 90, 91, 96

Iceland 136
ideology, of Thatcherism 89–90
Independent Labour Party 77, 171
India 129
individualism 192–3, 194–5
industrial struggle 24–8, 31–3

industrial unionism 12
infrastructure, rebuilding of 212
inner cities 153–5
intellectuals, radicalization of 21, 35
international division of labour 193
international economy, and national
policy 122–4, 196, 226
Iranian revolution 163, 189
Ireland 163, 235
and nationalism 120, 127–8, 133,
137
Irish Labour Party 127
IRA 127
Irish working class 16, 185
Israel 125
Italian Christian Democratic Party 74
Italian Communist Party 74–5, 84,
195–6
and Popular Front 111, 116, 117
Italian Socialist Party 73
Italy 107, 117
economy of 211, 235, 236
and nationalism 121, 124, 136,
141 n3
and Popular Front 104, 111, 188

Jackson, Tom 38
Jacobin tradition 59
Japan 124, 141 n7, 211, 218
Jaruzelski, General 94
Jefferys, Stephen 25, 30, 31, 32, 36
Jenkins, Peter 184
Jenkins, Roy 38, 175, 183
jingoism 60, 61
Jones, Jack 30, 32, 33, 39–40, 176
Joseph, Sir Keith 25

Katanga 136, 141 n6
Kellner, Peter 184
Kennedy, John F. 175
Keynes, John Maynard 67–8, 171,
172
Kinnock, Neil 3n, 182, 183, 185, 186
and review of policy 222–30
passim, 233, 237
Kohl, Helmut 200
Kraus, Karl 131
Kun, Bela 112
Kurdistan 136

labour aristocracy 13–14, 17, 21

labour movement 9, 16–22, 24–8, 30, 161–5, 187, 197–8
  diversity within 38–40
  and individualism 194
  tradition of 188
  and urban areas 143–57, 190
Labour Party
  and development of policy 2, 209–13, 222–30, 233–7
  and electoral coalitions 181–6, 187
  and Europe 197
  and Falklands War 52
  growth of left in 33–4
  internal politics of 1, 24–5, 85, 177, 222
  and leadership of progressive movement 21, 49–50, 66–8, 76–81, 96–7, 206–9, 230
  level of electoral support for 20, 23–4, 25, 28, 30–31, 37–8, 40–41, 41 n1, 41 n2, 63–6, 164, 190, 203–5
  and nationalism 133, 134, 135
  nature and extent of popular support for 34–41, 68–76, 83–5, 194, 199, 207
  and public housing 152
  record of, in government 169–79
  relation of, to unions 32–3
  and urban areas 144, 150
labourism 77, 79
Lassalle, Ferdinand 2, 159
Lawther, Will 37
Lebanon 123
Le Cornu, Mike 27
Le Monde 48, 55
Lenin, V.I. 58, 84, 105
  on alliances 93–4, 97
  Leftwing Communism, an Infantile Disorder 79
  and nationalism 126–9, 139, 140, 141 n14
  mentioned 3, 4, 107, 125, 126, 131, 217
Leninist parties 106
liberal democracy 110
Liberal Party 71, 156
  and Falklands War 52
  and Labour Party 169, 170–71, 177
  and tactical voting 184

liberal-radicalism 35
lifestyle
  differentiation of 195
  emergence of working-class 14, 190–91
Livingstone, Ken 72, 87, 96
local government 187
London 143–51 passim, 156, 157, 199
London County Council 153, 191
Lozovsky, Aleksandr 112
Lukács, Georg 112
Luxemburg, Rosa 140, 141 n14

Macmillan, Harold 2, 88, 91
MacDonald, Ramsay 170, 171
McKenzie and Silver 34
manual workers, percentage of, in working class 10–14
Manuilsky, Dimitri 110
Marquand, David 230
  The Unprincipled Society 226–8, 229
Marx, Karl 26, 188, 215
  on British working class 9, 20, 21
  Communist Manifesto 120, 126
  on crises 185
  and nationalism 126, 127
  and popular fronts 93, 94
  mentioned 3, 4, 5, 13, 16, 22, 125, 131, 162, 193
Marxism and nationalism 125–40
Marxism Today, debates on Labour Party in 1, 2, 28, 29, 63, 81, 87, 88, 89, 91, 94, 96, 97, 181, 188, 207
mass media 207
mass production 14
material interests 195
Mayo, E. 88
Mazzini, Giuseppe 120
Meacher, Michael 85
Mexico 136
middle class
  identification with 13
  support for Labour in 39, 203–4
Miliband, Ralph 77, 78, 82–3
Militant Tendency 78, 97
military power 141 n7
miners' strike (1984–5) 88, 164, 188
Ministry of Defence 57

minorities, and political strategy 35, 155–6
Mitterrand, François 38, 73, 163
modernization of the economy 209–13
monopoly capitalism 14, 15, 18, 109–10
Morning Star 56, 95, 206
Morrison, Herbert 173
Murray, Roger 26
Mussolini, Benito 108

Nairn, Tom 125–40 *passim*
    The Break-up of Britain 119, 121
Naples 143, 157
National Front 135
National government 170
national liberation movements 127–8
National Union of Railwaymen 36
nationalism
    and the Falklands War 51–2
    and Marxism 125–40
nationality, and working-class division 16
nationalization 36–7, 172–3
    see also privatization
nation-state
    and capitalism 120, 122–4, 196
    history of 119–24, 142 n18
    and self-determination 129–30
navy, British 59
neo-colonialism 123–4, 128
    see also colonialism
neo-socialism 73–4
    see also socialist parties by country
new social movements 194
New York City 145, 146, 150, 151, 199
Newens, Stan 25
Nicaragua 124
North, Colonel Oliver 202
Northern Ireland 132, 139, 140, 142 n26
Norway 135, 136, 210
    and Popular Front 104, 111
nostalgia 46, 188
Nott, John 57

Observer, The 56
Occitanism 142 n25
Ordzhonikidze, Sergei 139
Oxford University 90

Owen, David 68, 183, 184

pacifist tradition 58, 59
Pakistan 136
Palestine 125
Palme, Olaf 74
Panorama 207
Paris 143, 146, 149
Parnell, Charles Stewart 137
Parti Ouvrier 144
Parvus 160
patriotism 52–3, 57–60, 196
peasantry 10, 193
People's Democracies 103, 114
Peron, Juan 51, 54
Plaid Cymru 58, 128, 135, 137
Poland 121, 163
'poor, the' 19, 155–7
Popular Fronts 4, 60, 81–2, 92–3, 103–17
    see also broad alliance strategies
Portugal 115, 212, 235
Portuguese Socialist Party 73
Powell, Enoch 27, 135
Priscott, David 89
privatization 89
professional employment, and support for Labour 13, 24
proletarianization 10
prosperity, political effects of 44, 46
public control and planning 210–13, 218–20
public housing 151–3, 170
public purposes, and socialism 227–8
public-sector employment 14–15

Quebec nationalism 141 n12

racism, working-class 16, 60, 156
Radek, Karl 106, 113
rank-and-file movement 25, 31
Reagan, Ronald 222
'red belts', urban 146–7, 149
regulation of economy 211
Renan, Ernst 125
rented housing 151
revolutions
    bourgeois 131–2
    and Comintern policy 105, 106 107–8
    in 1970s 189

Reynolds' News 59
Richardson, Jo 234
riots, inner-city 155
Rodinson, Maxime 140
Romania 121
Rothstein, Andrew 88, 98 n3
Rudé, George 155
Rule Britannia 61
Russia 121

Samuel, Raphael 11
Scargill, Arthur 38, 208
Scotland
    and bourgeois revolution 132
    and Marxism 125
    and nationalism 121, 130, 134,
        135, 136, 137, 140, 140 n2
Scottish Nationalist Party 128, 133, 135
Second Reform Act 10
sectionalism, in working class 16–19,
    27, 32
self-determination, right of 119, 127, 139
separatism 121, 129, 133–7, 141 n5
Shaw, G.B., *Pygmalion* 148
shop stewards movement 12
Sinn Fein 137
skill, transfers of, in production
    process 13
Slovaks 121
Slovenes 141 n8
Smith, Adam 4
Smith, John 233
Snowden, Philip 170
Soares, Mario 73
Social Contract 176
Social Democratic Federation 77
Social Democratic Parties 104–5, 108,
    161–5
    see also parties by name of country
Social Democratic Party (UK) 39, 45,
    65, 184, 204, 206
social security system 19, 175
socialism 4–5, 71, 132–3
    and broad alliance strategy 94–6
    and Labour Party 35, 78, 83, 170
    and mass parties 162, 163–4
    and nationalism 126, 134–5
    need for rethinking of 215–20, 223
socialist consciousness 20
socialist countries, as models 36, 95
Socialist International 58

Socialist Worker 80, 206
Socialist Workers' Party 77, 88
Sombart, Werner 161
South Korea 161, 211
South Wales Miners' Federation 135
Soviet Union 91, 95, 96
    attitude of Communist Parties to
        94, 106
    and Popular Front strategy 93,
        111–12
Sozialistischen Schülerbund 201
Spain 189, 235
    Popular Front in 103, 104, 111, 112
    separatism in 121, 137
Spanish Communist Party 111
Spanish Socialist Party 73, 163
Stalin, Josef 3, 93, 109, 139
standard of living, postwar rise in 15,
    191
state power
    and political support 115
    and the public interest 217–18
    and Thatcherism 46–7, 187, 205–6,
        219
Steel, David 183
Stone, Norman 224
Strachey, John 217
strikes, and sectionalism 18–19
students, radicalization of 21
suburbanization 153, 190
suburbs, absorption of 146–7
Sun, The 46, 56
Sweden 111, 136, 210, 224, 235
Swedish Social Democratic Party 85
Swedish Socialist Party 74
Switzerland 121, 124

tactical voting 184–6, 187–8, 204
Tawney, R.H. 27, 70, 175
Tebbit, Norman 65
technological development, and
    unions 11–12, 13, 14, 17
tenants' movements 151–2
Thatcher, Margaret
    and Conservative Party 205
    economic policy of 25, 177–8, 210,
        211
    and Falklands War 54–6, 60–61,
        62
    political strategy of 47, 164, 187,
        221

mentioned 69, 85, 88, 90, 159
Thatcherism
  electoral strength of 64, 203–4, 205
  and establishment politics 45–9, 90, 205–6
  nature of 2–3, 66, 88–90, 223–4
  opposition to 65–8, 82, 96–7, 181–6, 200, 206–7, 230
Thomas, J.H. 170
Thompson, Edward 155
Timor 123
Togliatti, Palmiro 107, 112
trade unionism 11–14, 19–20, 30
  and economism 21, 26–7
  and Popular Front 108
  and Thatcherism 88, 89
  and urbanization 154
  and Wilson government 176
  and working-class stratification 17–18
Trades Union Congress 24, 176
transition to socialism, and peoples' fronts 109–14
transport, as urban issue 150–51
Transport and General Workers Union 12, 151
Trotsky, Leon 114, 212
Turkey 121, 163, 235
'two-thirds society' 190, 191, 199
Tyrol, and nationalism 137, 138

unemployment 30, 62, 193, 196
United Front Policy 106
United Nations 122
United States 75, 159, 212
  and Communist Parties 116–17
  consumer society in 193, 194
  economy of 189, 196
  and nationalism 130, 133, 136, 138, 142 n18
  and neo-colonialism 124
  and socialism 159, 164
  and urban politics 156
unity, as core of popular front 108
urban development 154–5

Vienna 145, 146–7, 150, 151, 152

Vienna Union 105
Vietnam 127, 162

wage-payment, changes in 18
wage policy 210
Wainwright, Hilary 32, 33
Wales, and nationalism 133, 134, 135, 136, 137, 140, 141 n8
Wallerstein, Immanuel 120, 131
Webb, Sydney 171
Weir, A. 88
welfare state 89, 172
West Germany 136, 141 n5, 414 n7, 185, 190, 191–2, 196, 199–10
West Ham 149
Westergaard, John 34, 80, 84
'Wheatley Act' 170
white-collar workers
  and Labour support 35, 69, 208
  as percentage of workforce 11, 13, 192
  unionization of 13, 15, 21, 26
Williams, Raymond 31, 83, 84
Williams, Shirley 204
Wilson, Elizabeth 88
Wilson, Harold 2, 21, 97, 175, 176–7
  mentioned 76, 79, 170
Wilson government (1964–70) 37–8, 174–7, 179
women
  and socialist movement 15, 26, 81
  voting patterns of 203
Workers' Revolutionary Party 77
working class, British
  and broad alliance strategy 93
  changes in 9–21, 80–81, 192–3
  divisions within 16–18, 36, 190
  and minority interests 155
  and patriotism 57–60
  support of, for Labour 24, 34–6, 63–4, 68–73, 83–4, 93, 204–5
Wright, Thomas 58

youth culture 193
Yugoslavia 95
  and Popular Front 111, 114
  and nationalism 121, 124, 127

Zinoviev, Grigorii 140

Acknowledgements

Sources of chapters are as follows:

'Falklands Fallout', January 1983; 'Labour's Lost Millions', October 1983; 'Labour: Rump or Rebirth?', March 1984; 'The Retreat into Extremism', April 1985; 'Past Imperfect, Future Tense', October 1986; 'Snatching Victory from Defeat', May 1987; 'Out of the Wilderness', October 1987; 'No Sense of Mission', April 1988: all from *Marxism Today*. 'Socialism and Nationalism: Some Reflections on "The Break-up of Britain"', no. 105, 1977; 'Labour in the Great City', no. 166, 1988: from *New Left Review*. 'Looking Towards 2000: the Politics of Decline', *New Society*, 7 October 1982. 'Offering a Good Society', *New Statesman*, 6 March 1987. 'The Signs of Recovery', *Guardian*, 11 July 1988. 'Fifty Years of Peoples' Fronts', in Jim Fyrth, ed., *Britain, Fascism and the Popular Front*, Lawrence & Wishart 1985. 'The Emancipation of Mankind' from *Die Neue Gesellschaft*/Frankfurter Hefte, July 1987. 'The Forward March of Labour Halted?'; 'The Verdict of the 1979 Election'; 'The Debate on "The Forward March of Labour Halted?"': all from *The Forward March of Labour Halted?*, Verso 1981. 'Farewell to the Classic Labour Movement?', from Suzanne Miller & Malte Ristan, eds, *Gesellschaftlisher Wandel: Soziale Demokratie – 125 Jahre SPD*, Cologne 1988.